Psychologists with Lived Experience of Disability

A wealth of guidance is available on supporting clients with lived experience of disability – yet there is little available that focuses on understanding the first-hand experience of psychologists who themselves identify as having a disability. This book responds to this gap in literature by providing narratives of psychologists with disabilities and exploring how their disability interacts with their experience of working in clinical practice.

The accounts represented within this book are varied, reflecting the wide range of experiences and challenges that psychologists with disabilities may encounter during their practice. Reflecting on the contributing authors' lived experience, chapters provide guidance on a range of topics related to navigating disability in clinical practice. This includes, but is not limited to:

- Normalising mental health and disability
- Self-disclosure of disability, inside and out of the therapy room
- Late diagnosis of disability and adapting to shifts in identity
- Managing disability and unpredictability, including fluctuations in conditions
- Disability and intersectionality
- The role of autonomy

Providing a much-needed exploration of the experiences of psychologists who identify as having a disability, this will be an essential read for any mental health practitioner who resonates with this experience, or for any practitioner who wishes to better understand and support colleagues with disabilities.

Susan Jacques is an integrative counselling psychologist who has worked in the NHS for over 15 years. She now has her own private practice and works with both adults and young people specialising in the impact that disability and long-term health conditions can have on mental health. Susan identifies as having a disability and is passionate about giving voices to those with lived experience of disability.

Psychologists with Lived Experience of Disability

Navigating Clinical Practice

Edited by Susan Jacques

Routledge
Taylor & Francis Group
LONDON AND NEW YORK

Designed cover image: @ Delightful Disability

First published 2027
by Routledge
4 Park Square, Milton Park, Abingdon, Oxon OX14 4RN

and by Routledge
605 Third Avenue, New York, NY 10158

Routledge is an imprint of the Taylor & Francis Group, an informa business

British Library Cataloguing-in-Publication Data
A catalogue record for this book is available from the British Library

ISBN: 978-1-041-06555-5 (hbk)
ISBN: 978-1-041-06554-8 (pbk)
ISBN: 978-1-003-63601-4 (ebk)

DOI: 10.4324/9781003636014

Typeset in Times New Roman
by codeMantra

Contents

Contributors

Emma Bede, DClinPsy, BA, is a clinical psychologist who works with adults of all neurotypes as a therapist and supporting people through the process of formal assessment or self-identification as neurodivergent. She also supervises other clinicians and works in clinical research. Her main approaches are based on Acceptance and Commitment Therapy, attachment, and mindfulness. She is particularly interested in working with people who have had difficult life experiences, with issues around becoming a parent, and with chronic illness or life-changing diagnoses. She can be found at www.willowpsychology.co.uk.

Sam Fletcher is a consultant clinical psychologist working in the National Health Service in the UK. He has been qualified for 15 years and has worked in a range of clinical and academic settings. His predominant work has been in the field of Mental Health, Learning Disabilities, and Autism, and he has also worked in services researching and providing interventions for psychosis and bipolar disorder. His special interests include clinical neuropsychology and trauma, and his PhD in Cognitive Psychology investigated memory processes. He has a dissociative disorder.

Debra Ford PGDip (Neuropsychology), DClinPsy, MSc, BSc, is a clinical psychologist, qualified for over ten years, with extensive experience working in the field of neuropsychology. Debra currently works in an intermediate neurorehabilitation unit, supporting individuals recovering from brain injuries and neurological conditions. Debra has completed a postgraduate diploma in clinical neuropsychology and is working towards becoming a clinical neuropsychologist. Debra is a proud mother of two young children and enjoys interior design, gardening, and creative home projects.

Sophie Gwinnett is a clinical psychologist with over 20 years of experience working in the NHS and private practice in Wolverhampton, UK. She specialises in health anxiety and health trauma, drawing on both her clinical expertise and lived experience of type 1 diabetes and cancer. Sophie is the founder of Brightside Psychology, where she and her team deliver individual and group therapy, clinical supervision, and training to healthcare teams on psychological approaches to patient care.

Her approach is rooted in compassion, psychological formulation, and trauma-informed care. She is passionate about reframing health anxiety as an understandable trauma response, and she is actively building a model of care that honours both the science and the story.

Susan Jacques, CPsychol, DPsych, MSc, PGDip, BA, is a chartered (BPS) and registered counselling psychologist. Besides her doctoral training, she has completed several postgraduate courses with a psychodynamic framework and more recently in Transactional Analysis. She runs an independent psychology practice and has experience of working in a variety of specialist services in the NHS, including working in long-term pain clinics and obesity services. More recently, she has worked in the areas of cancer recovery and with those learning to manage the psychological and physical effects of Long COVID. Her specialist areas include working with disability, and she has an interest in the impact of long-term health problems on mental health. More recently, this interest has extended to locating her specialist area within a Transactional Analysis (TA) framework. She is the author of several published articles on disability and has published an article on women's health in The Transactional Analyst on behalf of the Diversity and Social Responsibility committee. In both her professional career as a psychologist and in her personal life she has been actively involved in putting disability on the map through her engagement with research and working for charity organisations. Identifying as disabled, she is particularly passionate about loudening the voices of people with epilepsy. She can be found at https://www.drsusanjacques.com.

Dawn Johnson works as a clinical psychologist in private practice, offering therapy, supervision, teaching, and training in contemporary third-wave contextual behavioural sciences. She has extensive experience of adapting ACT and other behavioural interventions to work with numerous populations and presentations. She also uses ACT systemically, including designing and delivering ACT-informed wellbeing workshops for organisations. Dawn is the President of the UK&ROI Chapter for the Association of Contextual Behavioural Sciences (ACBS) and an active member of strategic committees and special interest groups within the organisation. She is the co-author of *Acceptance and Commitment Therapy: Responses to Frequently Asked Questions*.

Stephanie Jones is a chartered clinical psychologist with over 15 years of experience working in the NHS, charity, and private sectors. She qualified in 2013 with a Professional Doctorate in Clinical Psychology from the University of East London, where she found fellowship and validation in the social constructionist ethos. Since then, she has specialised in supporting people adjusting to life-changing illnesses or injuries and experiencing PTSD in settings including care homes and hospices, Veterans' charities, and general hospitals. She has publications in the fields of psychology and medical education. Stephanie has been visually impaired her whole life but has only recently begun to identify as disabled.

Alice Kennedy is a clinical psychologist. Alice has spent many years working in the NHS, and training health professionals and psychologists, in university programmes, most recently leading placement provision for a Doctorate in Counselling Psychology. She has co-designed e-learning for the British Psychological Society and is currently part of a working groups writing the BPS guidance for ME/CFS. Alice runs an independent psychology practice in Yorkshire and online, providing therapy, clinical supervision, assessment, and expert witness services. She is Co-Founder and Clinical Director of Mind, Body and Spoons, a specialist service helping people navigate life with chronic illness.

Amy Millar (DClinPsy, MSc, PGDip, BSc) is a clinical psychologist working in an Occupational Health context for a large employer. Her role includes completing fitness for work assessments to advise organisations on workplace adjustments or accommodations for employees experiencing mental health problems, and offering psychological intervention and support for staff experiencing work-related psychological injury or difficulties. Amy has found Compassion Focussed Therapy a very applicable, well-accepted, and effective approach in this context.

After the privilege of good health for many years, Amy was diagnosed in 2023 with advanced-stage endometriosis which has required surgical and medical treatment. Learning to live and cope with the symptoms of this chronic, fluctuating condition both inside and outside of work has deepened her understanding of her clients' health experiences and of their challenges navigating and advocating for their needs within a workplace.

Helen Molden (C.Psychol) is a counselling psychologist and integrative psychotherapist (UKCP). She is an associate fellow of the British Psychological Society, registered with the Health and Care Professions Council. Helen is a clinician and researcher, offering consultations to children, young people, and adults, both online and based in Hampshire, UK. Helen is one of ten expert members of the Advisory Panel for Children's Viewing at the British Board of Film Classification, advocating for better online safety for children and informed choice for families' media content, wherever and however it is viewed. Helen is an associate member of the Chartered Institute of Ergonomics and Human Factors. Together with a team of scientists (chemists, toxicologist, and economists), she works on projects concerned with how our environment, and specifically air pollution, impacts mental and physical health. Helen has primary ciliary dyskinesia (PCD) together with situs inversus totalis (SIT).

Liza Morton, PhD, C. Psychol, HCPC Reg, is a chartered (BPS) and registered counselling psychologist and a senior lecturer in Applied Psychology at Glasgow Caledonian University. Liza is passionate about promoting a psychologically informed approach to healthcare to improve well-being and recovery and to mitigate medical trauma for people living with lifelong medical conditions. This approach is grounded in her research, practice, teaching, and healthcare activism, and she publishes and presents widely. Born with complete heart block and a hole in her heart, Liza was fitted with her first cardiac pacemaker at just 11 days old in 1978 and she has depended on pioneering medical treatment ever since. Liza co-authored the book *Healing Hearts and Minds: A Holistic Approach to Coping Well with Congenital Heart Disease* in 2023 and authored the book *Beyond the Medical Gaze: Practicing Psychologically Informed Healthcare* in 2025, both published by Oxford University Press.

Veronica Solaris, PsyD, brings extensive clinical pre- and postdoctoral expertise in cognitive behavioural therapy (CBT) and integrative, interdisciplinary approaches across a broad range of clinical and forensic populations. Her professional background spans training within a police department serving high-risk domestic violence populations, offender treatment programmes, community health initiatives, school-based campuses, correctional settings, workers' compensation programmes, adult rehabilitation settings, drug court programmes, interdisciplinary chronic pain programmes, and intensive inpatient and outpatient psychiatric hospital settings.

Grounded in both professional expertise and lived experience, Solaris draws upon her personal journey of overcoming disability to bring depth, compassion, and authenticity to her clinical practice. At the Halliday Center for Psychotherapy and Wellness, she specialises in supporting individuals and couples navigating post-traumatic stress disorder (PTSD), military-related trauma, complex trauma, unresolved grief, entry-to-prison preparation, and the relational impacts of trauma. Through evidence-based, strength-oriented interventions, she empowers clients to move beyond the disabling effects of emotional distress and reconnect with meaning, purpose, and resilience.

Acknowledgements

This book has by no means been an arduous task, but without the provision of support and guidance from a few key people in my life, I give my assurance that the path would have been a significantly more challenging one to navigate. Academically, I would like to thank my former personal tutor Susan Strauss whose guidance through my doctoral training at City University back in the day brought forth my inner strength and voice. From this chapter onwards, my life has been governed by self-determination and a desire to learn and create meaningful change as a psychologist. Postdoctoral training has guided me towards a rewarding trajectory that introduced me to Transactional Analysis (TA), a psychological framework that I can't quite seem to let go of and which inspired my own chapter on disability in this book. I would like to thank Suna Güvan, TA Counsellor, Psychotherapist, Supervisor, and Trainer for her encouragement and taking the time to engage with my work and equipping me with the confidence to bring this book to fruition.

To the contributors-a sincere thank you for taking the time to share their honest and truthful narratives which represent both insight and wisdom, and for which I have the honor to showcase here. Each chapter provides the reader with unique insight into the lives of psychologists with disabilities, accounts that typically may otherwise go unheard or remain undisclosed. Articulating their experience to a wider audience requires fortitude and courage and will be duly acknowledged.

I would also like to share my love and thanks to my husband Jean-François who was the one who encouraged me to write the book, and my dear son Célestin who took the time to design the front cover-thank you both immensely for being by my side on this journey.

Finally, a big thank you to my dearest friends-you know who you are, whose unwavering support, and motivation were the source of my resolve to keep going and edit a book on the pivotal areas of psychology and disability.

Introduction

Susan Jacques

A contextually informed understanding of disability as lived experience

In *Toward a Feminist Theory of Disability*, Susan Wendell (Wendell, 1989), a notable scholar who bridges her own experience of illness with feminist theory and disability literature, meaningfully notes that: 'If disabled bodies were truly heard, an explosion of knowledge of the human body and psyche would take place' (p. 120). This is a harsh but valuable reminder that disability has historically been misunderstood, unacknowledged, and arguably 'shut away' from the non-disabled world and deeply rooted in the practice of how disability has been conceptualised, which is typically within the context of 'diseases and disorders' (Wehmeyer, 2021), and ultimately, intrinsic pathology.

Since the dawn of history, the term disability has long been one of contention, and this is partly owing to the largely pejorative connotations it is often affiliated with. Countless attempts have been made to construct a universal definition that fits neatly into everyone's frame of reference, but this has been confounded by countless dilemmas. Why? Arguably because psychological insight into disability has rarely been accomplished with disabled people in mind. Further, disability is universally unique in that how I experience my disability and the lens through which I make sense of my experience are different from others. The civil rights advocate Kimberlé Crenshaw perfectly articulates the consequences of pairing homogeneity and disability by stating that 'treating different things the same can generate as much inequality as treating the same things differently' (1997, p. 279).

There has been remarkable interest in the topic of disability amongst a variety of scholars alongside some comprehensive literature from a broad range of perspectives and paradigms. Disability has invariably been framed through different conceptual models such as the medical model (Mackelprang & Salsgiver; 2009; Peterson & Aguiar, 2004); the social and critical psychology of disability (Goodley, 2024; Shakespeare, 2017); the Human Rights model (Degener, 2017); and the biopsychosocial model (Wade & Halligan, 2017). These models have unquestionably added conceptual and practical value to our understanding of disability, but they are heuristic tools rather than facts. What is evident is that whilst they offer a

DOI: 10.4324/9781003636014-1

framework for conceptualising disability, lived experience of disability is disproportionally integrated across the models; that is, it is either typically secondary to medical expertise, or first-person meaning is commonly underplayed. This is what ignited my interest in this book.

What do we understand by the term 'lived experience'? According to Sandhu (2017), lived experience denotes the unmediated effects of social issues on individuals. Shakespeare (2022) frames lived experience in terms of the knowledge that materialises from individual circumstances, thus making it inherently singular and unique in substance. In the context of disability, lived experience encompasses personal stories, diagnoses, and people's experience with services and systems (Clifton et al., 2025). Lived experience has the potential to reach both the traumatic and strengthening components of embodied life with disability and provides insight into how disabled people learn to navigate a world dominated by discriminatory behaviours and practices. Whilst attempts have been made to reflect the lived experience of disabled people in the field of psychology research and literature (Clifton et al., 2025; Malka, 2025; Gill, 1995), Hunt (2024) highlights a noticeable lack within psychology in terms of its ability to focus on this critical area. Lawthom and Goodley (2005) appositely suggest that if psychology is to be applicable to disabled people, then it needs to involve disabled people in the research process, 'working *with* disabled people, not *on* them' (p. 424).

It has been widely recognised that people with a disability have a deserved voice on matters related to healthcare, rehabilitation, policy, and research (Clifton et al., 2025), yet what these roles entail and how they sit within systems and power structures is unknown (McIntosh & Wright, 2019). Organisations are projected to consider the lived experience voice, but there is only vague knowledge on what this should resemble. As Clifton et al. (2025) point out, the disabled person's participation in clinical workforces and research which provide lived experience expertise is often conditional, ambiguous, and somewhat lonely.

As the chapters unfold in this book, there are ample examples of how psychologists with disabilities have been exposed to a range of life challenges. Understanding the social, political, and cultural context of disability is imperative if we are to identify the barriers imposed by society on disabled people, including the effects of discrimination, stigma, social exclusion, and exposure to inaccessible services. Each of the authors in this book has reflected on ways in which they have cultivated adaptive strategies in the face of imposed social barriers, and it is critical that these barriers are addressed if we are to begin to promote a more inclusive society.

A central tenet of this book is to promote understanding and the meaningful inclusion of disabled people through increased awareness of lived experience. To do this, I propose that we begin by tapping into the subjective, embodied experience of disability – that is, allowing the authors to be the experts on their own experience. This shared experience and knowledge are not anecdotal but authentic lived experience of disability that can be synthesised to create 'meaning over pathology', and move away from asking 'what's wrong?' to asking 'what does this experience mean to you?'

This book aims to capture a nuanced understanding of the authors' complex realities of living with a disability as the reader becomes acquainted with the heartfelt stories that arise from the inside, in place of those imposed from the outside. Returning to Wendell's (1989) abovementioned quote, I believe that it is a solemn prompt to begin listening to the rich and diverse lived accounts of disabled people as they are in the inimitable place to share their experiences.

This book unquestionably follows a different script to other psychology texts in that, unlike traditional psychology approaches that look outside the profession as a means of understanding human experience, this book purposefully looks within it. That is, the source of knowledge comes from the lived experience of a community of psychologists with disabilities. Furthermore, this book invites a different approach in that every psychologist is provided with the opportunity to conceptualise their lived experience of disability through a chosen therapeutic approach. As the editor, I believed that by doing this it offers psychologists the potential to construct their experience in more meaningful ways.

What we know is that disabled people continue to be under-represented in a wide array of domains, and this is shockingly discernible within the profession of psychology (Andrews et al., 2019). It is evident that the needs and authentic voices of psychologists with disabilities have undoubtedly been disregarded (Lund, 2018). Hackett et al. (2020) report that 21% of the total UK population identified themselves as disabled, but only 12% of psychologists have a declared form of disability (HCPC, 2020). This is rather disconcerting, as it serves to highlight the extent to which disabled psychologists are marginalised within the realm of psychology. This is particularly unfavourable given that psychology is a profession that prides itself on concepts such as equality, diversity, and inclusion.

As a psychologist with a disability, I have actively listened to fellow psychologists with disabilities share their lived experiences, and many have detailed the countless times they have been motivated by the pursuit of integration. This may result in placing others in a 'one-up' position whilst masking one's authentic self at the expense. This is often not a chosen pursuit, but one that is regularly imposed by the mainstream (Minikin, 2021). Many psychologists share how they fear upsetting the norm and have accordingly chosen to minimise their disability.

As the chapters unfold, the reader will learn of the many challenges experienced in the life of psychologists with a disability. This includes the felt need to develop protective coping strategies, learning to hold intersecting identities, and living with conditions that are grossly unrecognised. Navigating institutional and attitudinal barriers to disability poses many demands. As Turner (2021) fittingly points out: 'Difference is difficult. It is complicated. It is nuanced. This is why it is so important' (Turner, 2021, p. 21).

Significantly, the reader will tap into how we as disabled psychologists are keen to sidestep pathologising what are plausible responses to frequent systemic disadvantages. However, the reader will also learn of the valuable ways in which psychologists have learned to navigate their disability, of the positive interrelation between disability, decision-making, and agency, and how reflection on disability with their clients has positively enhanced the therapeutic relationship. In addition, by sharing our lived experiences of disability in this book, we as disabled psychologists are keen to promote the moving away from a corrective way of viewing disability that is enveloped by deficit and shame to a place where disability, in all its forms, is validated. Furthermore, the message is that the disability narrative is not simply one of suffering, but one of accomplishment and pride.

Disability discourse

As the authors in this book describe their experience of disability, they are active participants in the creation and reshaping of the disability discourse. Language has reflected acts of defiance whilst also serving to offer a clarified perspective. Significantly, language unveils signs of oppression and internalised shame. It informs us whether disability is grounded in an integrated self or consists of spilt-off parts that enable us to deal with threat (Hargaden & Sills, 2002), arguably from a society steeped in normative rules. Crucially, each author in this book uses the language that is meaningful to them. In Chapter 3, Fletcher meaningfully recounts her experience of living with complex dissociative disorders and illustrates the significance of finding the right language in inviting both ownership of her lived experience, whilst offering containment for something that once felt overwhelming and threatening. Fletcher's personal account suggests that language is not neutral and often reflects deeper personal identification.

The language we employ when referring to disability is a vital component in the shaping of our understanding of disability and impacts the value we assign to the notion of disability in the context of our different identities. Conventionally, when we ask the question 'what is disability?' the term is broadly associated with some form of difference, impairment or diminished way of functioning. Ordinarily, there is an association with a less than quality or the implication of some form of tragic aberration or defect. Typically, we visualise an image of a person in a weakened state, someone who may require some form of assistive technology (AT) or rely on the use of a wheelchair. Yet contrary to popular belief, there are also many non-apparent/invisible disabilities that can significantly impact a person's daily functioning. These include but are not exclusive to those who experience neurodivergence, mental health disorders, neurological disorders, and rare genetic conditions. When trying to understand disability, we therefore need to recognise more so than ever that whilst there are physical disabilities, not all disabilities are worn on the outside.

The term disability further conjures a sense of otherness, someone often seen not to fit in or exceed the parameters of our frame of reference. For Wendell (1989), 'when we make people 'other', we group them together as the objects of *our* experience instead of regarding them as fellow *subjects* of experience with whom we might identify' (p. 116). Historically, this sense of otherness has in turn resulted in the marginalisation of disabled people, or simply put, prompted a system of beliefs that is ableism (Bogart & Dunn, 2019). The development of disability language not unsurprisingly impacts both our relationship with it and how we choose to conceptualise it. To begin to question ableist discourse, we need to move away from the use of dehumanising language and begin to use language that reflects the choice of the people who experience a disability, a language which is anti-discriminatory and avoids deficit-based inferences.

According to the Equality Act 2010, disability is characterised as having a 'physical or mental impairment that has a 'substantial' and long-term negative effect on the ability to do normal daily activities'. The word impairment, whether it be physical or psychological, is essentially synonymised with disability. I would argue that they are essentially two different things. Shakespeare (2021) makes the distinction between the two terms stating that impairment focuses on physical restrictions, whilst disability is a result of a society that has placed the impaired body into a position characterised by systemic inequalities and discrimination. I concur with Yu's (2025) point that the word impairment, is often associated with 'diminishment' or a sense of weakening, so by synonymising disability with impairment, it not only infuses disability with negative connotations, but there is also the implication that one's disability is at the root of their negative life experiences.

This book highlights how disability can present itself in a variety of ways. The authors demonstrate how one's experience of disability can be influenced by prevailing discourse and structures (Voronka, 2016). Language needs to be negotiated, inclusive, respect difference, and acknowledge diversity. I believe that we have a right to accept or refuse certain disability narratives if we don't identify with them. Yu (2025) aptly voices how disability doesn't have to be a negative word; the '*dis*' in 'disability' no longer needs to represent disfunction but can signify discovery, distinctive and distinguished' (p. 13). This book affirms the significance of psychologists with disabilities using the language that offers meaning to their experience.

Culture and models of disability

Disability reflects the cultural assumptions of a given time. Emerging from each epoch are a set of belief systems, attitudes, and policies that are a driving force for how we experience this complex field of enquiry (Barton, 2022). The disquieted and compounded ways disabilities have been considered and received have metamorphised into several different models and frameworks. The models effectively impact how we make sense of disability today, and it is helpful to have a broad understanding of these as they serve to capture how disability has been conceptualised as a social, political and embodied experience. Here I will briefly consider the medical model, the social model and human rights disability model and how they diverge in terms of their theoretical underpinnings and where they focus their attention.

The dominant medical model is still pervasive in Western healthcare and clinical psychology and typically positions disability as problematic and dysfunctional (Martiny, 2015). In this model, lived experience is habitually minimised to diagnosis and treatment, stressing impairment, whilst postulating a need for repair. Debatably, the model has created a normative framework for viewing disability and has moulded our understanding of disability in a way that Loja et al. (2013) refer to as 'a physical, moral, emotional, mental and spiritual deficit' (p. 198).

Interestingly, Loja et al. (2013) found that people with disabilities repeatedly abide by ableist interjections, whilst Oates (2021) highlights how the all-too-frequent feeling of fear often serves to maintain conventions. The narratives in this book provide insight into the pressures that psychologists have faced to modify, minimise or deny their disability within their clinical practice, and the impact this has had on the quality of their life.

Marks (1999) has pointed out how the medical model has shaped modern society in innumerable ways. For psychologists working in the NHS, it is the model they are expected to work alongside given that it remains a dominant influence. In Chapter 4 on the 'embodied therapist', Molden adopts a critical stance towards the model. She valuably argues how, as a standalone model, its focus for understanding disability is conceivably too narrow. Moreover, Molden identifies how the model compartmentalises mental health and physical health, and, as the reader will learn, disability is, as she suggests, systemic and permeates the body's overall functioning.

Barton (2022) refers to a different dichotomy that exists in the medical model, one that serves to promote a binary us/them divide in which there exists projected fears and anxieties from the 'us people' onto 'them', or the 'others', those that we may class as the out group. I would go as far as to contend that the model promotes an OK/Not OK dichotomy in which the abled- bodied person is seen as normal and the disabled person as pathological or as the site of the problem. As a result, the disabled person is often exposed to a form of ableist judgement and invalidation.

In contrast to the medical model, Shakespeare (2021) addresses how the social model of disability challenges the over-medicalised and individualistic notion of disability and alternatively directs its attention to the disability movement and its focus on social oppression, cultural discourse, and the physical constraints of disability. Shakespeare notes how a significant component of the social model is its differentiation between the oppressed group – the disabled people- and the contributors to that oppression – the non-disabled people. The social model challenges the view that disability is a personal problem (Galvin, 2005) and posits disability as a political identity rather than residing in personal tragedy.

Whilst not denying the reality of the physical challenges, the social model proposes that it is not simply the disability itself that is at the root of our negative experience, but a society designed with non-disabled people in mind (Yu, 2025). Many disabled people have confronted attitudinal and systemic barriers which have undeniably bolstered feelings of helplessness and limit possibilities for disabled people to reach their potential.

Additionally, it recognises the demands of inaccessible environments, and the institutional and attitudinal barriers that disabled people routinely confront.

In Chapter 12, Millar contextualises the principles of barriers and constraints for disabled people by critically engaging with the role occupational health plays in protecting individuals' rights and protections in the workplace. Millar powerfully underscores the valuable function both self-advocacy and self-compassion perform in a society that typically lacks awareness and knowledge of lived experience.

Whilst the social model views disability as difference and not as a problem, Meekosha (1998) however points out a significant limitation, namely the idea of a 'taken for granted fixed corporeality' (p. 175), that is, the body somehow losing its place within the everyday experience. In this respect, the model can underemphasise challenges presented by the body or it has treated them as secondary. Many contributors in this book argue that bodily experiences remain highly significant, and internal variability poses as much of a daily struggle as do structural barriers. In Chapter 2, Kennedy addresses the issue of fluctuating conditions where there are no clear biomarkers and refers to how such conditions are often dismissed, stigmatised, and neglected. Whilst removing social and cultural barriers to understanding these conditions is favourable, Kennedy draws attention to the reality of the bodily discomfort resulting from these conditions and how they are routinely underappreciated.

Finally, the human rights disability model departs from the social model and the notion of uniformity, emphasising the individual's 'inherent right to dignity' (Degener, 2017). The model further favours the notions of social integration and the autonomy of the disabled person. In Chapter 5 I address my early script development through a Transactional Analysis (TA) framework, and I refer to moving from a dominant narrative of experiencing my disability as an obstacle and personal tragedy, towards an increased sense of ownership and autonomy. Ultimately, I learnt to recognise my own intrinsic worth. Whilst the human rights model is debatably a little abstract, it does encourage the eradication of prejudice and discrimination and recognises key barriers that pose challenges for disabled people.

The experience of disability is by no means simple. Researchers are increasingly recognising that the experience of being disabled needs to be understood as both a multifaceted and ever-changing phenomenon (Leonardi et al., 2006; Shakespeare, 2013). All models have analytic and contextual value and provide a lens through which disability can be understood. However, I posit that not only do they need to be held up against one another to achieve this value, but they also significantly need to be informed by lived experience. This book demonstrates how the models taken in isolation do not capture the meaning of the embodied, everyday reality of disabled people.

Disability, identity, and meaning-making

A fundamental component of the different interpretive frameworks through which disability is understood is the notion of identity. Forber-Pratt et al. (2017) report that 'disability identity can be considered on its own terms as a unique phenomenon that shapes a person's way of seeing themselves, their bodies, and their way of interacting with the world' (p. 15). Galvin (2005) identified that the most significant areas of identity to be affected by disability are related to work, independence, and appearance, all of which are gravely impacted by the negative perceptions of others.

Not unsurprisingly, there is little settlement amongst scholars on the exact definition of disability identity. Adler et al. (2019) pinpoint a common thread that disability identity principally contends with the issue of identity integration. From their study on identity integration in people with acquired disabilities, Adler et al. (2019) discovered there were participants who felt able to actively process their disability as part of their life and others who referred to their identity as being entirely remodelled by the experience of acquiring a disability.

For the vast majority of psychologists in this book, learning to navigate a life marked by change and disruption has feasibly demanded identity integration at some level. My experience as a psychologist has included working with spilt-off parts of myself, and learning to make sense of my disability, including in my professional practice with clients. In Chapter 5 I examine how I formerly concealed or minimised my disability through shame and fear of jeopardising the status quo. This desire to belong stemmed from a diminished sense of self and an inability to integrate disability as a meaningful part of my life. Yu (2025) accurately describes this shift in my script as a process of learning to 'not love every aspect of our [my] disability, body, mind, or experience, as 'it is nuanced and varied and means something different to each of us…' (p. 62).

A common theme in this book included questioning the validity of one's disabled identity. The notion of feeling like a fraud was particularly common amongst those with non-apparent disabilities, with some psychologists doubting if the title disability was a warranted title. Amongst some authors, a central theme included the acceptance that there is no cure for their disability. In Chapter 9, Johnson, in drawing from Acceptance and Commitment Therapy (ACT) demonstrates how *psychological flexibility* allows her to assume the role of a mindful observer of her disability. This over time has promoted both acceptance and empowerment. Johnson highlights how working alongside the constraints that accompany a disability and becoming familiar with its limitations and capacities, is more beneficial than making attempts to fight or cure it.

Understanding identity integration from a social psychological perspective, Dirth and Branscombe (2018) correlate a positive quality of life with the implementation of resourceful individual-level strategies which include 'integrating one's impairment/body into his or her personal self-concept' (p. 10). This may include moving one's narrative away from a deficit-orientated stance to an autonomous self-authored stance in which one's disability shifts from being framed as a problem to be corrected, to being framed as a condition to be lived with.

In Chapter 8, Solaris fluently demonstrates this shift using her own experience of how perceived restrictions of disability can be reconceptualised as both capabilities and constructive coping methods which can be used as valuable tools when working with clients. Solaris invites the reader to reflect on how a self-governed stance is highly consistent with concepts in cognitive behavioural therapy (CBT) such as cognitive flexibility and reframing underlying beliefs, and frames the psychologist not as a helpless practitioner, but one who brings resilience and adaptability to the therapeutic space.

In reflecting on the concepts of disability, identity, and integration, Bogart (2022) refers to 'disability self-concept'. This pertains to the degree to which disabled people accept their disability and feel confident to fully integrate it as part of their identity, and the level of assurance a person feels in addressing matters relating to their disability, or disability self-efficacy. This book demonstrates the many ways in which psychologists have learnt to incorporate their disability into their self-concept and, conjointly, how they have learnt to navigate the issues that stem from their experience of being disabled. Notably, every psychologist's relationship with their disability is different and will be set in the context of their culture and their personal experience of disability (Andrews et al., 2019).

Bogart (2022) draws our attention to how disability self-concept is impacted by the timing of the disability onset. All psychologists narrate their experience of living with a disability in the context of growth, adaptation, and acceptance, yet a common theme for those who have acquired a disability later in life – including those who received a late diagnosis – is a particular type of 'shift' in identity. This change in identity arguably rests with a type of adjustment that requires a different set of tools from those with a congenital disability who potentially experience what Bogart (2022) terms as 'cognitive flexibility'. Some psychologists with acquired disabilities refer to initially fighting their condition or working harder in the hope that their condition would improve, whilst others refer to the initial shock attached to their reality of being disabled. Such responses to a new disabled identity may be understood in the context of a loss of the self (Charmaz, 1995) or as a transition from 'one social world to another' (Denzin, 1992, p. 91).

The lived experiences of the authors in this book are unique but can be brought together by a synthesised perspective – we all situate ourselves within the context of disability. Sharing experience of a disability to a wide audience can be a complex decision for a psychologist to make, and a common thread running at different points in this book is the author's reflection on the potential challenges of disclosing their disability in the context of their clinical practice. This is a consideration for those experiencing both visible and non-visible disabilities. Psychologists generally agree that destigmatisation comes from open reflection on lived experience of disability (Victor et al., 2022), but fear that disclosure may lead to judgement continues to exist.

Research on disclosure points to fears linked to potentially jeopardising the client's welfare, or breaching boundaries, or even concerns over conflicts in roles (Barnett, 2011; Strasburger et al., 1992). Disclosure of a disability in and out of the therapy room undoubtedly remains a compelling topic, and more enhanced research does point to potential benefits of self-disclosure, specifically with those with lived experience (Conchar & Repper, 2014). Several authors in this book have noted how mindful disclosure of a disability has afforded both recognition and meaning for their clients, whilst permitting a more collaborative dynamic in the act of common humanity. In Chapter 6 Bede's experience of being an autistic psychologist illustrates how good disclosure practice involves making valuable clinical decisions based on the individual clients' needs. Bede also thoughtfully invites us to recognise that we as psychologists are not 'blank slates', in that our disability shapes the reflection that enters the room with the clients we work with. When this is in the form of professional allyship, for example with someone experiencing the same condition, this can foster mutual trust and compassion.

Intersecting disability and psychology

It is essential to note that as disabled psychologists we occupy an exclusive two-fold role in that we not only offer psychological knowledge as objects of inquiry, but we are also in the position to be active agents of change. Firstly, our lived experience has the potential to enhance clinical practice through experiential awareness. Secondly, our reflexive knowledge has the potential to inform, expand, and shape research and policy on disability within the discipline of psychology. This first-hand knowledge is particularly invaluable when addressing marginalised groups such as disabled people, as it frequently unmasks gaps or areas that remain unexplored (Bogart, 2024).

A central objective of this book is to advance our understanding of disability through psychologists lived experience, and a pivotal part of this process is to examine how disability is currently mapped within the foundations of our work as practitioner psychologists. Key reflections arising from psychologist's lived experience is how psychology can begin to think about promoting inclusive environments for disabled people. Without critically evaluating such areas, informative change may not exceed that of symbolic shift. To louden the voices of disabled people, we need to develop the capacity to use psychology as a reflective and empowering tool for debating and critiquing common (mis)understandings of disability (Marks, 1999) and begin to understand some of the wider barriers that continue to promote exclusion. As psychologists with disabilities, we should intrinsically be leading the way forward.

Historically, the relationship between psychology and disability has been fractious, and this can invariably be linked to the pathologising of disability within the domain (Hunt, 2024). Typically, how psychology has positioned disability has largely been functionalist in its approach; that is, disability has been seen as the consequence of somatic or cognitive shortfalls (Lawthom & Goodley, 2005). Considerable weight has been placed on the notion that an individual with a disability is required to adjust to their condition, and this has been a recognisable focus in both psychology training and literature, something that disability studies have heavily criticised (Reeve, 2006). In representing disability in a way that stresses a model of correction, there is huge room for error. The consequence is the failure to perceive people with disabilities as possessing accomplishments and strengths (Wehmeyer, 2021). In Chapter 1, Morton clearly exemplifies ways in which she has employed her disability – a lifelong heart condition, to inform advocacy, research, and practice in psychology. Morton considers the valuable role that dual expertise can play in informing psychological inquiry, and in expanding our understanding and inclusion of disability. In the chapter, Morton purposefully frames disability in a way that offers both the potential for meaning and positive change.

The notion of *physis* in TA represents the idea that as humans we possess the motivation to achieve positive change, to evolve, and to advance our potential (Piccinino, 2018). Erskine (2013) fittingly expressed how 'physis is the source of our internal thrust to challenge acquiescence, to explore different ways of doing and being…' (p. 6). As a disabled psychologist, this suggests the notion of self-determination, agency, and autonomy, not incapacity and ineptitude. Achieving autonomy and modifying approaches to living is however not without challenges, as Ford in Chapter 10 describes when addressing the task of navigating the shame arising from her experience of dyslexia. In this chapter, Ford demonstrates the value of cultivating self-compassion in promoting a reassuring self that feels equipped to undertake tasks with greater ease. The chapter conveys the benefits of a compassion-focused approach in transitioning from a need to conceal a disability to integrating it as a key component of the self.

It is vitally important that disability is not positioned as a problem to manage in psychology, but one that prioritises meaning-making over pathology, alongside the integration of disability into identity. Psychology arguably has a responsibility to make the public aware of positive psychological thinking around disability. Steps forward have been made in shifting the disability research and practice attention to well-being and autonomy, yet obstacles in the form of attitudes to disability remain intact (Wehmeyer, 2021).

Pathologising disability further overlooks both structural and interpersonal disablism and vitally disregards potential barriers to areas such as training and services (Hunt, 2024). Significant hurdles may include inaccessible training environments, such as overlooking the learning needs of psychologists or an environment in which there is a lack of wheelchair access. Barriers may take the form of experiences with disability bias in the psychologist's professional work with clients, including feeling the obligation to disclose their disability (Taube & Olkin, 2011). Many authors in this book share how both an increase in their professional experience and shifts in their relationship with their disability have streamlined challenges relating to self-disclosure of their disability. The principal assertion is that it is vitally important for the discipline of psychology to understand some of the wider contextual issues that psychologists with a disability are confronted with, both in training and in their professional activity.

Psychologists in this book openly describe some of the specific physical barriers to work they have encountered, alongside numerous obstacles to training and a lack of suitable services. As the chapters progress, we learn of the unfortunate but common occurrence of an absence in understanding of their disability, of high institutional expectations, and a lack of reasonable adjustments to name but a few. Professionals taking the time to understand the lived experience of a disabled person allows us to move beyond labels and to depart from unconscious bias. Gwinnett, in Chapter 7, points out the value of psychologically informed care in aiding normalisation and validation of long-term conditions. She draws our attention to the complexities of health anxiety rooted in her experience of type 1 diabetes and highlights how psychologically informed practice and curiosity about disabling conditions foster both relational safety and trust. Gwinnett effectively addresses the dual role of lived experience of disability and being a professional in healthcare practice.

In UK law under the Equality Act (2010), reasonable adjustments are a legal requirement and are a law that is in place to remove significant disadvantage for disabled employees. However, even when told as disabled people that we are experts on our own experience, we can often be disregarded by fellow healthcare professionals (Wilkinson & Wisdom, 2022). Psychology professions are however starting to appreciate the value of disabled employees, and this, in part, is due to our capacity to present alternative, overall perspectives (Wilkinson & Wisdom, 2022). Furthermore, our lived experience delivers effective results as regards to building strong therapeutic relationships with our clients – a vital component to consider when recruiting disabled employees.

In this book, psychologists voice the need for employers and supervisors to consider adaptations to entitle them to equal treatment to their non-disabled peers. This includes, for example, flexible working arrangements, such as a reduction in hours and workload. Others bring attention to the need for robust policies that guarantee awareness of potential individual and institutional bias as a means of working towards anti-ableist practice.

In Chapter 11, Jones discusses being visually impaired and applies a social constructionist perspective to examine how disability is mutually shaped with societal expectations and the environmental context. The chapter considers how a social constructionist approach empowers individuals to oppose internalised ableism and question assumptions, thus promoting greater inclusivity within psychology practice. A central challenge for many disabled people rests with the expectation that adjustment lies with them, and Jones draws our attention to disability being seen not as personal limitation, but as grounded in societal expectations.

Supple (2005) identified how psychology research has been responsible for branding disabled people into a homogenous group, with assumed shared characteristics and experiences – arguably informed by the social model of disability. However, as demonstrated by the psychologists' experience of disability, more consideration needs to be given to the rich and diverse disabled community that exists. By categorising people into distinct groups, it not only overlooks the notion of individuality but further runs the risk of preserving ableism and marginalisation in psychology research, practice and training (Cieza et al., 2018).

In a recent exhibition I attended on 'Design and Disability' at the Victoria and Albert Museum, Macdonald (2025), the exhibition manager, made the moving statement that 'disability should never be seen as a monolith', signifying that the world of every disabled person is their own and they have varying needs and preferences. In essence, the path disabled people choose to take with their disability is unique, and they are to be regarded as the specialists on their own bodies, minds, and needs. Psychology research that fails to accommodate this diversity may neglect significant nuances in the lived experience of people with disabilities.

As a psychologist, I fully endorse the message that 'psychologists are well placed to address the complexity of the position of disabled people in society by studying and talking about the behaviour of the oppressors as well as the victims' (Frankish, 2005, p. 416). I would go one step further by saying that as disabled psychologists, we not only have professional competency within applied practice, but also direct lived experience.

Knowledge and insight into the experience of disability is equally, if not more, valuable when sought from the inside, that is, by gaining access to first-person accounts of psychologists with a disability. What does this allow for? Significantly, it puts the person with a disability at the centre, thus parting from traditional hierarchies in psychology where the clinicians are viewed as being the experts. Secondly, it provides insight into how disability is felt and experienced, thus avoiding perceived, projected interpretations of disability. A central challenge of psychology is to guarantee that it works both for and alongside disabled people to ensure the promotion of disabled people's rights whilst valuing difference (Lawthom & Goodley, 2005), and one positive way of doing this is by focusing on their lived experience.

References

Adler, J.M., Lakmazaheri., A., O'Brien, E., Palmer, A., Reid, M., & Tawes, E. (2019). Identity integration in people with acquired disabilities: A qualitative study. *Journal of Personality*, 89, 84–112. https://doi.org/10.1111/jopy.12533

Andrews, E., Forber-Pratt, A.J., Mona, L.R., Lund, E.M., Pilarski, C.R., & Balter, R. (2019). #SaytheWord: A disability culture commentary on the erasure of "disability." *Rehabilitation Psychology*, 64(2), 111–118. https://doi.org/10.1037/rep0000258

Barnett, J.E. (2011). Psychotherapist self-disclosure: Ethical and clinical considerations. *Psychotherapy*, 48(4), 315–321. https://doi.org/10.1037/a0026056

Barton, J. (2022). Disability-who and what is disabled? *The Psychologist*. https://www.bps.org.uk/psychologist/disability-who-and-what-disabled

Bogart, K.R. (2022). Disability as social identity: It's time for therapy to affirm it. *Developmental Medicine & Child Neurology*, 65: 300. https://doi.org/10.1111/dmcn.15412

Bogart, K.R. (2024). Increasing disability inclusion through self-relevant research. *Community Psychology*, 2(9). https://doi.org/10.1038/s44271-024-00056-x

Bogart, K.R., & Dunn, DS. (2019). Ableism special issue introduction. *Journal of Social Issues*, 75, 650–664. https://doi.org/10.1111/josi.12354

Charmaz, K. (1995). The body, identity, and self: Adapting to impairment. *The Sociological Quarterly*, 36(4), 657–680.

Cieza, A., Sabariego, C., Bickenbach, J., & Chatterji, S. (2018). Rethinking disability. *BMC Medicine*, 16, 1–5.

Clifton, S., Cooper, E., Bourke, J., Connor, S., Denton, S., Dominish, B., Gibellini, C., Gilroy, J., Hallahan, L., Jessep, S., Katterl, S., Mellifont, D., O'Brien, B., Farrant, F. Q., Watharow, A., & Wynn, R. (2025). Disability lived experience and expertise: recognising the expert contributions of people with disability. *Evidence & Policy*, 21(4), 578–595.

Conchar, C., & Repper, J. (2014). "Walking wounded or wounded healer?" Does personal experience of mental health problems help or hinder mental health practice? A review of the literature. *Mental Health and Social Inclusion*, 18(1), 35–44. https://doi.org/10.1108/MHSI-02-2014-0003

Crenshaw, K.W. (1997). Intersectionality and identity politics: Learning from violence against women of color. In M. A. Fineman & R. Mykitiuk (Eds.), *The Public Nature of Private Violence* (pp. 93–118). New York: Routledge.

Degener, T. (2017). A new human rights model of disability. In V. Della Fina, R. Cera, & G. Palmisano (Eds.), *The United Nations Convention on the Rights of Persons with Disabilities: A Commentary* (pp. 41–59). Cham: Springer.

Denzin, N. (1992). *Symbolic Interaction and Cultural Studies*. Oxford: Blackwell.

Dirth, T.P., & Branscombe, N.R. (2018). The social identity approach to disability: Bridging disability studies and psychological science. *Psychological Bulletin*, 144, 1300–1324. https://doi.org/10.1037/bul00 00156

Equality Act (2010). https://www.legislation.gov.uk

Erskine, R. (2013). Vulnerability, authenticity, and inter-subjective contact: Philosophical principles of integrative psychotherapy. *International Journal of Integrative Psychotherapy*, 4(2), 1–9.

Forber-Pratt, A., Lyew, D., Mueller, C., & Samples, L. (2017). Disability identity development: A systematic review of the literature. *Rehabilitation Psychology*, 62, 198–207. https://doi.org/10.1037/rep0000134

Frankish, P. (2005). Disability. *The Psychologist*, 18(7), 416–417.

Galvin, R.D. (2005). Researching the disabled identity: Contextualising the identity of transformations which accompany the onset of impairments. *Sociology of Health & Illness*, 27(3), 393–413.

Gill, C.J. (1995). *A Psychological View of Disability and Culture*. Internet Publication. https://www.independentliving.org/docs3/gill1995.html

Goodley, D. (2024). *Disability Studies: An Interdisciplinary Introduction*. London: Sage Publications.

Hackett, R.A., Steptoe, A., Lang, R.P., & Jackson, S.E. (2020). Disability discrimination and wellbeing in the United Kingdom: A prospective cohort study. *BMJ Open*, 10(3), e035714. https://doi.org/10.1136/bmjopen-2019-035714

Hargaden, H., & Sills, C. (2002). *Transactional Analysis—A Relational Perspective*. Hove: Routledge.

Health and Care Professions Council (2020). *Equality, diversity and inclusion data report 2020*. London: Health and Care Professions Council. Available at: https://www.hcpc-uk.org/resources/reports/2020/edi-data-2020-report/ (Accessed: 3 July 2026).

Hunt, J. (2024). Will psychology ever 'join hands' with disability studies? Opportunities and challenges in working towards structurally competent and disability-affirmative psychotherapy for energy limiting conditions. *Medical Humanities*, 50, 728–739.

Lawthom, R., & Goodley, D. (2005). Community psychology-towards an empowering vision of disability. *The Psychologist*, 18(7), 423–425.

Leonardi, M., Bickenbach, J., Bedirhan Ustun, T., Kostanjsek, N., & Chatterji, S. (2006). The definition of disability: What is in a name? *Lancet*, 368, 1219–1221.

Loja, E., Costa, M.E., Hughes, B., & Menezes, I. (2013). Disability, embodiment and ableism: Stories of resistance. *Disability and Society*, 28(2), 190–203.

Lund, E.M. (2018) Disability as diversity in professional psychology: A continued call for research and action. *Training and Education in Professional Psychology*, 12(4), 295–296. https://doi.org/10.1037/tep0000218

Macdonald, C. (2025). Exhibition Manager, *Design and Disability, Victoria & Albert Museum*, London

Mackelprang, R.W., & Salsgiver, R.O. (2009). *Disability: A Diversity Model Approach in Human Service Practice*. Chicago, IL: Lyceum Books.
Malka, M. (2025). Disability as a transitional state in the lives experience of undergraduate students navigating disabilities in academic arenas. *Disability and Society*, 40(11). https://doi.org/10.1080/09687599.2025.2458687
Marks, D. (1999). *Disability-Controversial Debates and Psychosocial Perspectives*. London: Routledge.
Martiny, K.M. (2015). How to develop a phenomenological model of disability. *Medicine, Health Care and Philosophy*, 18, 553–565. https://doi.org/10.1007/s11019-015-9625-x
McIntosh, I., & Wright, S. (2019). Exploring what the notion of 'Lived Experience' offers for social policy analysis. *Journal of Social Policy*, 48(3), 449–467, https://doi.org/10.1017/s0047279418000570
Meekosha, H. (1998). Body battles: Bodies, gender and disability. In T. Shakespeare (Ed.), *The Disability Reader: Social Science Perspectives* (pp. 163–180). London: Continuum.
Minikin, K. (2021). Relative privilege and the seduction of normativity. *Transactional Analysis Journal*, 51(1), 35–48. https://doi.org/10.1080/03621537.2020.1853349
Oates, S. (2021). What if my 'I'm ok, you're ok is different from yours? Could the inherent optimism in transactional analysis be a form of compulsory ableism? *Transactional Journal*, 51(1), 63–76.
Peterson, D.B., & Aguiar, L. (2004). History and systems: United States. In T.F. Rigger & D.R. Maki (Eds.), *Handbook of Rehabilitation Counseling* (pp. 50–75). New York: Springer Publishing Company.
Piccinino, G. (2018). Reflections on physis, happiness, and human motivation. *Transactional Analysis Journal*, 48(3), 272–285. https://doi.org/10.1080/03621537.2018.1471293
Reeve, D. (2006). Towards a psychology of disability: The emotional effects of living in a disabling society. In D. Goodley & R. Lawthom (Eds.), *Disability and Psychology: Critical Introductions and Reflections* (pp. 94–107). London: Palgrave.
Sandhu, B. (2017). The value of lived experience in social change: the need for leadership and organisational development in the social sector. https://thelivedexperience.org/
Shakespeare, T. (2013). *Disability Rights and Wrongs Revisited* (2nd ed.). Routledge. https://doi.org/10.4324/9781315887456
Shakespeare, T. (2017). *Disability: The Basics*. London: Taylor & Francis Ltd.
Shakespeare, T. (2021). *The Social Model of Disability in the Disabilities Studies Reader* (6th ed.). L.J. Davis & R. Sanchez (Ed.). New York: Routledge.
Shakespeare, T. (2022). Recognising lived experience is essential to empowering disabled patients. *BMJ*, 378, o2359. https://doi.org/10.1136/bmj.o2359
Strasburger, L.H., Jorgenson, L., & Sutherland, P. (1992). The prevention of psychotherapist sexual misconduct: Avoiding the slippery slope. *American Journal of Psychotherapy*, 46(4), 544–555. https:// doi.org/10.1176/appi.psychotherapy.1992.46.4.544
Supple, S. (2005). Getting our house in order. *The Psychologist*, 18(7), 418–420.
Taube, D, & Olkin, R. (2011). When is differential treatment discriminatory? Leal. Legal, ethical, professional considerations for psychology trainees with disabilities. *Rehabilitation Psychology*, 56, 329–339. https:// doi.org/10.1037/a0025449 [PubMed: 219289201].
Turner, D. (2021). *Intersections of Privilege and Otherness in Counselling and Psychotherapy*. London: Routledge.

Victor, S.E., Devendorf, A.R., Lewis, S.P., Rottenberg, J., Muehlenkamp, J.J., Stage, D.L., & Miller, R.H. (2022). Only human: Mental-health difficulties among clinical, counseling, and school psychology faculty and trainees. *Perspectives on Psychological Science*, 17(6), 1576–1590. https:// doi.org/10.1177/17456916211071079

Voronka, J. (2016). The politics of people with lived experience of experiential authority and the risks of strategic essentialism. *Philosophy, Psychiatry, & Psychology*, 23(3–4), 189–201. https://doi.org/10.1353/ppp.2016.0017

Wade, D.T., & Halligan, P.W. (2017). The biopsychosocial model of illness: A model whose time has come. *Clinical Rehabilitation*, 31(8), 995–1004. https://doi.org/10.1177/0269215517709890

Wehmeyer, M.L. (2021). The future of positive psychology and disability. *Frontiers and Psychology*, 12. https://doi.org/10.3389/fpsyg.2021.790506

Wendell, S. (1989). Toward a feminist theory of disability. *Hypatia*, 4(2), 104–124. Available at: https://doi.org/10.1111/j.1527-2001.1989.tb00576.x (Accessed: 3 July 2026).

Wilkinson, L., & Wisdom, C. (July 2022). It's as if it's seen as an unfair advantage rather than an attempt to level the playing field. *The Psychologist*. https://www.bps.org.uk/psychologist/its-if-its-seen-unfair-advantage-rather-attempt-level-playing-field

Yu, T. (2025). *The Anti-Ableist Manifesto—How to Build a Disability Inclusive World*. London: Souvenir Press.

Chapter 1

From the heart

Using my lifelong heart condition to inform advocacy, research, and practice in Counselling Psychology

Liza Morton

As a child, I enjoyed playing at being a school teacher or a nurse, although, in reality, we didn't know if I would survive until adulthood, let alone be able to work. Born in the late 1970s, with a heart condition, I spent a lot of my childhood in the National Children's Hospital. As a 'guinea pig', dependent on cutting-edge developments in the nascent field of paediatric cardiology, my care was survival-focused. Back then, little attention was given to the psychological and emotional impact of growing up with a serious health condition. Besides my own experiences, I witnessed the suffering of other children, some of whom didn't have the opportunity to live beyond the confines of our children's heart ward. As a child, my condition restricted my physical activity which meant that learning, reading, drawing, and writing became valued pursuits offering not only enjoyment but a sense of escape, connection, and purpose. These unique circumstances have left a lasting impact deeply shaping my identity. As a teenager, I searched in vain for books on the psychological impact of growing up with a serious health condition. This void became a key motivation for my eventual career as a psychologist, researcher, advocate, and author. While I feel deeply grateful to have reached this point navigating the educational system and employment has been far from easy.

Chronic health conditions (CHCs) are persistent, incurable, and often impose a significant 'patient burden', demanding self-management, adherence to treatment regimens, and the endurance of symptoms like pain and fatigue. Affecting approximately one-third of the global population (Hacker, 2024; World Health Organisation [WHO], 2023), CHCs can impact on daily functioning, personal relationships, self-esteem, body image, parenting, and life choices increasing vulnerability to mental health conditions, including depression, anxiety, and post-traumatic stress (Sloan et al, 2023; Hinz et al, 2019; Vilchinsky et al, 2017; Parker et al, 2015). These multifaceted challenges can significantly affect educational achievement, career development, and financial stability. For individuals with CHCs, employment and professional training may be affected by the need to manage symptoms, take medical leave, and navigate energy limitations (Morton, 2020). CHCs are more prevalent among lower socioeconomic and other marginalized groups (Barnett et al, 2012).

DOI: 10.4324/9781003636014-2

Despite the growing emphasis on diversity and inclusion in the field of psychology, individuals living with CHCs remain significantly underrepresented in both academic and applied psychology professions. Here, I share my journey, with the aim of highlighting both the barriers and enablers I have encountered, in my pursuit of a career in psychology by considering how my healthcare experiences inform my advocacy, research, teaching, and practice, with a focus on trauma theories, medical trauma, compassion focused, and polyvagal theory (PVT).

As normal a life as possible: chronic childhood illness

Over the past half-century, medical advances have significantly improved survival rates for children with health conditions. Today, one in four children lives with CHCs such as asthma, gastrointestinal disorders, diabetes, juvenile arthritis, cancer, or epilepsy (Cortes et al, 2020). Survival into adulthood for infants born with congenital heart disease (CHD), the most common birth defect affecting nearly 1% of newborns, has improved by 75% over the last five decades. CHD comprises a heterogenous range of heart conditions, present from birth, which vary widely in terms of complexity. An estimated 12 million people worldwide now live with CHD, around a quarter of whom require cardiac surgery within their first year of life (Gong et al, 2020). While these medical advances have saved countless lives, they have also given rise to a growing population living with the complex physical, emotional, and psychological realities of lifelong health conditions. Despite an evolving understanding of early trauma, the psychological impact of recurrent, early medical interventions remains under-recognized, and access to mental health support is often poor (Morton, 2020).

At birth, my health deteriorated rapidly, and because my heart rate was too slow to sustain life, at 11 days old, I was fitted with an implantable pacemaker. I was diagnosed with complete heart block; a condition where the electrical signals within the heart are blocked, causing a very slow heartbeat. I have been dependent on a pacemaker, for every heartbeat, since. While I owe my life to the NHS and innovative cardiac care, living with a congenital heart condition has been deeply challenging. By the age of seven, I had undergone five thoracotomies for pacemaker implantation; open-heart procedures that required breaking my ribs. These early pacemakers were bulky and had limited battery life and fragile leads. They propelled my heart to beat at the same rate, regardless of what I was doing. For much of my childhood, my heart was fixed at 70 beats per minute which was a compromise that allowed both gentle activity and rest. Confusingly, despite being advised I should be able to function relatively normally, I often felt nauseous and dizzy and my lips and fingers turned blue when cold. Looking back, it is apparent that I was physically limited by a body that could not adjust to the hemodynamic demands of normal life.

I underwent countless, often painful, diagnostic and surgical procedures all while trying to remain still and composed. One vivid memory is of lying motionless while a professor of physics taught the cardiology team to test my pacemaker, adjusting its rate using a large external magnet, leaving me dizzy and breathless. At 13 years of age, I underwent open-heart surgery to repair a hole in my heart. Afterwards, I clearly remember waking up in intensive care panicking because I was still attached to a ventilator and couldn't breathe. Around this time, I was fitted with my first rate-responsive pacemaker. This more modern device automatically adjusts the heart's pacing rate to better meet metabolic demands by detecting physiological signals like body movement or breathing. This development improved my quality of life but introduced further complications. Soon after, a faulty lead meant that the new device had to be replaced. Now placed beneath my collarbone, it broke through my skin on several occasions, leading to multiple return surgeries during a crucial time in my education, meanwhile I underwent surgery to remove the old device involving yet another thoracotomy. During adolescence, I acquired a growing, unwelcome collection of scars.

While pacing technology has improved significantly since those early days, adulthood brought new challenges. Accessing appropriate specialist care became more difficult, compounding the physical and emotional toll. At times, I have been dismissed, my concerns ignored, even in life-threatening situations. The Adult Congenital Heart Association (ACHA) estimates that fewer than 10% of adults with CHD remain in specialist care, despite lifelong monitoring being essential. Continually having to advocate for the care I need has significantly added to the burden of living with this condition. As a result of my medical history, I require specialist and complex pacing care. Each time I require a new device, a multidisciplinary team have to carefully plan the next intervention which can lead to a tenuous wait for complex surgery and a sustained absence from study or work. To illustrate, I received my 11th pacemaker a few years ago, after another lead malfunction. I waited for two months for a surgical slot at a specialist centre, spending one month in hospital away from my young family.

Stuck in survival mode

On reflection, it is evident that my health challenges profoundly shaped my development. I spent the first six weeks of life in paediatric intensive care. By the time I got home, I had undergone two heart surgeries and a stroke. A 'clingy' baby, during my formative years I was very shy. I recall feeling self-conscious and wanting to make myself invisible. I was late to walk and talk, milestones shaped by early trauma. Children with complex conditions often face medical barriers to basic developmental needs for affectionate touch, secure attachment, and play (Narvaez, 2018). Recurrent medical trauma can impact on emotional development, impairing the development of self-soothing, feelings of psychological safety, and emotional regulation (Christian-Brandt et al, 2019). Psychological difficulties are commonly associated with childhood chronic diseases, such as epilepsy and cystic fibrosis (Secinti et al, 2017). In total, 18.2% of children with CHD experience anxiety or depression, compared with 5.2% of their heart-healthy peers (Gonzalez et al, 2021). One-third of children undergoing surgery for CHD develop PTSD

(Meentken et al, 2017), while post-traumatic stress is commonly experienced in adolescent childhood cancer survivors (Abbey et al, 2015). It is important to note that, understandably, parental mental health is also at risk when caring for a child with a serious health condition which may further impact on family dynamics (Helfricht et al, 2008).

Despite the hurdles, I attended mainstream school performing well academically. While I always had friends, I was reserved. My condition placed countless restrictions on daily life. I had to avoid physical activities and miss school for medical appointments and surgeries. Additional academic support was not provided, and I was left to catch up on my own. Primary school felt more manageable, perhaps because I stayed in a single classroom providing the opportunity to build a trusting relationship with one teacher and class of children. In contrast, high school posed new challenges. At this point, we moved house meaning I had to make new friends. Meanwhile, high school was a larger, more impersonal environment with long walks between classes, and a constant rotation of teachers, some overly anxious about my condition, others outright dismissive because I 'looked fine'. I vividly remember sitting exams while discreetly wearing a heart monitor. The pressure to fit in, for social inclusion, increased during my teenage years. Children with CHCs, on average, perform worse in school, in part, due to more frequent school absences as a result of hospitalizations, healthcare appointments, symptoms, and recovery needs which can hinder academic progress and isolate young people from their peers (McKinley Yorder and Cantrell, 2019). However, school absence does not solely account for this attainment gap, and policies that solely focus on reducing absence can have adverse consequences. Interventions to improve educational outcomes require a more flexible and holistic approach that enables children to stay engaged with education both in and out of school which is more feasible nowadays given the development of hybrid and online educational platforms (Jay et al, 2023). Raising awareness and training educational staff are essential to fostering inclusion, understanding, compassion, and feelings of psychological safety.

Growing up, friends' parents and extended family members were often afraid to include me in outings or have me for a sleep over. Many normalcies of childhood, such as active play, dancing, and horse-riding lessons were simply out of reach. During gym class, I found myself sitting on a wooden bench at the side of the hall, watching my classmates climb the monkey bars, leap over the pommel horse, and skip. On sports day, I cheered them on from the sidelines, seated on the grass, while at high school I was allowed to escape to the library during physical education class. Such exclusion from physical education and play is not uncommon for children living with CHCs (Smith et al, 2021).

While I was generally content, teachers noted in my school reports that I could be a quiet, withdrawn and 'serious child'. Back then, I didn't have the words to describe my healthcare experiences and on the odd occasion when I tried I risked being met with enacted stigma through pity, mockery (for example, being called a bionic girl, a cyborg, or fragile), disgust, or anger for 'being weird' and 'bringing the mood down'. While people were generally supportive and trying their best, at times, I met with invalidation through 'toxic positivity' with comments such as 'God gives His hardest battles to His strongest soldiers', or 'What doesn't kill you, makes you stronger'. Perhaps because my condition is hidden and I looked young and healthy, some other children (and adults) questioned why I was getting 'special treatment' for example, by 'getting out of' gym class, time off school or a new toy following surgery. At times, they made unsolicited comments invalidating my fatigue, accusing me of being lazy, malingering, or attention seeking. This seemed unfair and left me feeling down and annoyed. The fact that healthcare professionals considered some of my symptoms, such as the debilitating fatigue, as 'unexplained' consolidated these opinions. I internalized this stigma becoming self-critical often pushing myself beyond my limits.

People with serious health conditions have experienced stigma, social exclusion, and segregation throughout history (Bogart, 2014). Belanger and Laube (1979) described that historically, people with a disability have been viewed as sub-human, objects of pity or ridicule, and holy innocents. Such marginalization, exposed during the COVID-19 pandemic in media messaging about 'herd immunity' and 'survival of the fittest' (Morton et al, 2022), can lead to diminished self-worth and internalized stigma. As inherently social beings, exclusion from our social group can activate the brain's threat system, leading to emotional responses such as panic, anger, and shame. Research shows that the relational threat of social exclusion activates the same neural pathways as physical pain (Eisenberger, 2012), and if shame is experienced repeatedly, it can contribute to an overactive threat system, increasing susceptibility to hopelessness, disconnection, anxiety, depression, self-criticism, and a desire to withdraw as a form of self-protection (Gilbert, 2014). Shame can lead to rejection of parts of our identity, including the condition itself. In response, we may overcompensate by holding ourselves to unrealistic standards and engage in self-punitive behaviours such as perfectionism, disordered eating, substance misuse, risk-taking, or neglecting our health. Accessing meaningful support can be further challenged because few people truly understand the impact of living with a serious health condition, especially during childhood and young adulthood. Yet, social support is one of the most important protective factors for mental health. Usually, we turn to others at times of adversity by communicating psychological safety with each other through compassion, building trust, and shared experience (Porges, 2022). While medical interventions were a regular part of my life, nobody else I knew needed them, isolating me from my peers and limiting social support and understanding.

Anticipated stigma, the expectation of being rejected or treated unfairly, led me to 'downplay' my symptoms, suppress concerns, and overcompensate (Quinn and Chaudoir, 2009). Being pitied, mocked, or left out made me feel self-conscious and ashamed. I had to be strong, lest I be labelled the vulnerable girl with the weak heart. I didn't want my condition to become my identity or to stop people from seeing me. I learned young that the cost of being accepted was to minimize part of myself, suppress my feelings, and present myself as a 'good patient' and 'brave heart warrior'. My stoicism was also rooted in my gratitude for being gifted life, an attempt to protect my caregivers and healthcare providers from further concern and because I routinely had to keep still and quiet during healthcare procedures, even when they were uncomfortable and painful, for survival. From infancy, I was rewarded for being a 'good patient' with 'bravery stickers'.

It is also true that when I miraculously survived yet another surgery, I wanted to fully embrace life. As soon as we left the hospital, I didn't want to talk what had happened there. Like many people who face adversity from infancy, I honed determination, grit, and humour for survival 'getting on with it' because there was no other choice. Experiencing pain and suffering made me more appreciative of periods of better health, while growing up with an awareness of the fragility of life provided me with clarity and focus from a young age. My health condition also strengthened my relationships with those who stood by me while managing chronic symptoms taught me how to efficiently use my energy and time. I was humbled by periods of serious illness which left me dependent on others and by witnessing other children in hospital who had it far worse than I did; honing empathy and compassion. The obstacles that I face mean that I've had to think independently and find my own path. Research has recognized positive change following adversity, which encompasses five areas including increased personal strength, changed priorities, more meaningful relationships, changed philosophies, and spiritual development, termed post-traumatic growth (Tedeschi et al, 2018).

For many years, I faced the world as this 'strong and stoic' version of myself. Yet, while outwardly I seemed to be coping by my mid-teens, I developed chronic fatigue which became so debilitating that I missed most of my senior year at high school. Privately, I felt anxious and low, overwhelmed by fears about completing my education, finding work, and one day managing life independently. I also experienced brain fog and frequent nightmares about being in hospital while cues such as the smell of toast (the first meal I was allowed after surgery) or disinfectant triggered flashbacks about my hospital experiences. Yet, I stubbornly resisted any form of 'special treatment', determined to prove myself in environments where needing help was stigmatized and rarely provided. I navigated school, higher education, and a career, often without sufficient understanding or support, while facing not only chronic symptoms but also periodic medical crises that required life-threatening surgeries, lengthy recoveries, and caused major disruptions to my education and career. I compared myself to heart-healthy peers without recognizing the additional barriers I faced, resulting in harsh self-criticism. To cope, I became a 'perfectionist' putting pressure on myself to achieve academically because this was an area where I knew I could succeed. While this facilitated social acceptance, it also denied me the full support I needed and the opportunity to be myself, often leaving me feeling like an imposter pretending to be a well person. Overcompensating, in this way, prevented me from listening to my body and managing my health as well as I could leading to a 'boom and bust' cycle. I often felt tense, prepared for the next medical emergency, or exhausted from navigating my condition while trying to live as normal a life as possible. Looking back, my body was stuck in survival mode, oscillating between hyper-arousal and hypo-arousal, with little capacity for feeling safe, calm, and connected; a common response to repeated trauma (van der Kolk, 2014; Porges, 2022).

Facing my shadows: personal and professional development in Counselling Psychology

Despite the challenges, determined to understand and create meaning from my experiences, I pursued psychology gaining a place at a university close to home to accommodate my need for daytime naps. I worked hard gaining a First-Class Honours degree. However, traditional clinical psychology training proved inaccessible, due to the full-time schedule. I pursued a PhD with the hope that academia would offer more flexibility. After completion, I was awarded a post-doctoral fellowship during which another health crises derailed my trajectory and led to me reconsidering my career options. By then, it was clear that the unforgiving demands of academia, such as an expectation to work full time, to travel regularly for international conferences, move where the job takes you, and the constant pressure to acquire funding and publish regularly, were incompatible with managing my health condition. As such, I was delighted to discover the British Psychological Society's Independent Route in Counselling Psychology; the profession's commitment to social justice, relational depth, and valuing lived experience aligned deeply with my values (Cooper and McLeod, 2007) and finally provided me with an accessible route to becoming a Chartered Psychologist.

Professional and personal development is a dual process in Counselling Psychology where practitioners expand their therapeutic skills while engaging in personal growth through therapy, supervision, reflection, and awareness. This is essential to manage personal triggers and prevent them from negatively impacting on client work (McLeod and McLeod, 2014). To this end, during my training in Counselling Psychology, in addition to mandatory therapy, I underwent a further two years of body psychotherapy.

During therapy, my therapist asked me how I was coping to which I replied that I was 'fine' and 'I just get on with it because there's no other choice'. Then they asked me to imagine putting my head on the adjacent chair and tell them how my body was feeling. Unexpectedly, I got upset saying that my body was exhausted. I wanted to be left alone. I felt horrified at the thought of needing more things done to it and an urge to protect myself. Instinctively, I drew my left arm up protectively placing my hand on my chest. I have since realized that I often make this gesture subconsciously; an embodied defense that I developed as a child when my ribcage or chest bone and scars were healing from heart surgery. Trauma can leave a sensory imprint rather than a story, especially if the trauma occurs when you are preverbal. When we experience trauma, the limbic system takes over which can result in speechless terror, whereby the parts of the brain responsible for language and memory are affected by the traumatic experience leaving us unable to find the words to share our experience (Herman, 1998; Ogden, 2015; Rothschild, 2000; van der Kolk, 2014).

Paying attention to my body in this way was the start of my long journey towards recognizing and healing from extensive medical trauma. This therapeutic work was my first experience of being validated about the embodied impact of my healthcare experiences without feeling that I needed to be brave, protect others, or be 'normal'. I had to deal with countless invasive medical procedures and cardiac surgeries which left me attached to an array of medical equipment and feeling very unwell. After each surgery, I had to endure excruciatingly painful broken bones and a scar held by dozens of stitches. Unless you have experienced it personally, I don't think you can understand how unwell and how much pain it is possible to feel. Feeling disempowered increases risk of developing post-traumatic stress following adversity, and I was routinely disempowered by healthcare practices in the 'patient role' (van der Kolk, 2014). The human mind is incredibly powerful, and it can protect us at times of extreme adversity. To cope, I learned to focus my mind and somehow float outside my body. From a young age, I learned to 'live in my head' by suppressing my feelings and symptoms and using cognitive defense strategies such as such as intellectualization, humour, perfectionism, and dissociation (Herman, 1998; Ogden, 2015; Rothschild, 2000; van der Kolk, 2014).

When I was a child, we were told by my healthcare team that the heart was a simple pump and, even though my childhood pacemakers meant my heart was set at a fixed rate, if the pacemaker was working, I should be able to function relatively normally. While my healthcare providers were doing their best with the knowledge they had their medical textbooks and this biomedical approach to healthcare simply did not account for my lived experience. I often felt tired, dizzy, and agitated. I was easily startled and physically sick on exertion or when I got excited or nervous. We kept asking the doctors why I was sick every birthday and Christmas, to be told it was simply a coincidence. I dehydrated easily, lacked temperature control, had a poor appetite, and restless legs when I tried to sleep. I caught every cold or virus on offer with a persistent cough. I watched other children in awe at their boundless energy, wondering why I could not keep up, at times berating myself for being lazy. Life felt like a relentless struggle through a fog of tiredness, yet everyone else seemed to manage. 'Absentminded' I was often caught up in my own thoughts losing or forgetting things. As a child, my cheeks betrayed the characteristic ruddy appearance of a heart condition, and I was small for my age. The incongruence between my embodied experience and what I was told I should be feeling made it even hard for me to trust my body fuelling self-criticism and leaving me feeling confused, silenced, disempowered and in a constant battle with myself. I felt chronically unsafe in my body.

PVT offered a holistic framework to understand my embodied experience accounting for both the impact of traumatic life events and the physical limitations of my condition. Grounded in neurophysiology, psychology, and evolutionary theory, PVT describes how the autonomic nervous system (ANS) subconsciously and continually assesses situations for safety or threat, termed neuroception. PVT states that our ANS is both expressive and receptive; not only do we constantly assess threats and safety in our environment, but we also communicate this with each other. To this end, we are adept at reading social cues via facial expression, eye movement, vocalizations, prosody, and body language. As social beings perceived threat is often interpersonal, while safety with other people is communicated using compassion. Feeling safe is recognized as a distinct state important for rest, restoration, and social bonding (Porges, 2022). In situations detected via neuroception as psychologically safe, our bodies operate in the ventral vagal system of the parasympathetic nervous system, which activates physiological, affective, and cognitive processes that optimize social engagement. In this 'social engagement system' mode, we feel calm, relaxed, and psychologically safe while our bodies are optimized for healing, learning, and social connection. We want to be in this system most of the time for general wellbeing. PVT proposes that homeostatic variability of the ANS is shaped during our early years (Porges, 2022). An adverse history, such as medical barriers to the soothing presence of early attachment figures and traumatic medical experiences, may narrow the window for feeling safe and contribute us responding to past threats as if they are current. Looking back, my window for feeling psychologically safe was likely narrowed by both traumatic healthcare experiences and relational trauma from social stigma contributing to me being very shy and reserved. I only felt safe enough for social connection, play, and humour with close and trusted family and friends. I felt safer with animals, especially my dogs. Growing up, I was 'very sensitive' to any perceived criticism which left me feeling deep shame and led me to withdraw from others. Even with loved ones, I avoided being emotionally vulnerable for self-protection, leading to perfectionist traits and presenting a strong and stoic face to the world through fear of stigma and rejection. However, this coping strategy prevented me from being able to share and process my feelings in a safe space, from asserting my needs, and reaching out for support.

When we detect threat, via neuroception, our bodies shift into self-defence mode, most commonly via activation of the sympathetic system, which leads to fight or flight behaviours that are supported by increases in heart rate, shortened breathing, and increased muscle tension. Whereas, when we perceive a threat to life, our most primitive threat response is activated via the dorsal vagal pathway, and our bodies experience hypoarousal, often reported as feeling numb or dissociated. From infancy, I have felt tense, nauseous, and anxious when attending a hospital appointment because my body is preparing to act to fight or flee the perceived danger. As described, during painful and distressing medical procedures, where there is no escape, to cope I focus my mind and dissociate from my body. One of the hardest things for me about living with a lifelong medical condition is that I need to go through the same traumatic experiences throughout my life, from cradle to grave. Even now, as an adult, each time I go to get my pacemaker checked, or for an appointment with a cardiologist or when I need to go back to theatre, I can momentarily flit back to feeling as I did as a child. In those moments, my body detects threat, and I feel butterflies in my stomach, catch my breath, and my body tenses. Yet I am regularly told by healthcare professionals, family, and friends that I 'must be used to it'.

A fourth response, the fawn response, has recently been described in situations where we neurocept danger and both the fight/flight and immobilization responses are activated simultaneously. Known as appeasement, during this response, it is proposed that the sympathetic system provides the fuel for movements to meet the needs of others, while the dorsal vagus circuit enables dissociation and disconnection to protect ourselves. This enables us to pacify interpersonal threats and is associated with 'people pleasing' whereby we aim to regulate the other's nervous system to protect ourselves (Schwartz, 2016, 2020). As a child, I appeared to happily comply with painful medical treatments going along with narratives to be brave, strong, and a good patient, while feeling distressed or dissociating, because I wanted to keep the adults around them happy, and I did not feel safe enough to share my feelings or vulnerability. Besides, I grew up with the understanding that I had to be polite and well-behaved during healthcare encounters. I knew that I depended on healthcare professionals to keep me alive. I still find it challenging to assert myself during healthcare encounters.

PVT seems to have important implications not only in terms of exposure to adversity but also regarding the physical limitations of my condition. Specifically, if my heart, central to my ANS, can't adaptively respond to my body's needs, then homeostatic control of my ANS in response to the environment may be compromised (Porges, 2022). This framework validated my embodied experience, particularly as a child when my heart was limited to a fixed rate, accounting for many of my 'unexplained' symptoms such as being easily startled and being physically sick on exertion or when I got excited or nervous. My window of tolerance for feeling psychologically safe may have been further narrowed by having a fixed heart rate that was unable to adapt to the physiological demands of my nervous system. Even modern pacemakers are not truly physiologically responsive, and I have wondered if this contributes to the chronic fatigue I still experience daily. I have had the opportunity to share these reflections with Stephen Porges, who has been very supportive, working with him to develop my understanding of these unique experiences (Morton, 2018).

Together, therapy and these psychological insights have helped me to heal emotionally and better manage my health condition (Herman, 1998; Ogden, 2015; Porges, 2022; Rothschild, 2000; van der Kolk, 2014). It has been a long and ongoing journey, but through this process I've learned that, paradoxically, by suppressing my hurts, shame, and trauma, they leak out in other ways contributing to fatigue, nightmares, and by impacting on my mood. While dissociation and cognitive defense strategies have been a necessary part of my survival response, and at times my only choice, longer-term, they can lead to significant physical and mental health costs, especially when my nervous system is unnecessarily triggered into states of hyperarousal or hypoarousal. Overreliance on cognitive defense strategies, while completely understandable, also presents a barrier to sharing, understanding, and processing difficult feelings. Rather than helping me get on with life, longer term, this approach hinders me from making the most of it. To liberate myself, I had to face my shadows and learn to live beyond survival mode.

Working with and becoming more aware of my body has been challenging, but I have endeavoured to befriend it by listening to, respecting, and working with it while appreciating the adversities I've survived. I challenge myself to become more embodied through movement and holistic body treatments such as reiki, massage, Mindfulness, and EFT (emotional freedom technique) tapping. I am better at pacing myself and challenging old habits of pushing through. I try to attend to somatic markers to avoid a boom-and-bust cycle, self-criticism, disconnection, and low mood. Through enhanced self-compassion, I can better address unrelenting high standards and perfectionist tendencies. Through PVT, improved understanding of my nervous system and emotional responses helps me self-regulate, especially during periods of poor health or hospital encounters. By paying attention to my autonomic state, I can compassionately identify my triggers (cues of threat) and glimmers (cues of safety and connection) and proactively work to expand my window of tolerance for feeling psychologically safe and connected (Dana, 2018). This allows me to be more present with my family, friends, colleagues, and students.

In therapy, I also found a safe space to grieve the loss of a normal childhood, express anger at the unfairness of living with a heart condition from birth, and give 'little me' a voice. Over time, rather than considering myself fundamentally 'different' from others, I began to view myself as a normal person who happened to be born with a heart condition. I am just someone that's found myself in the unusual position of having to live on the edge of medical science from 'cradle to grave'. Liberated from shame, I found my voice, going from hiding my condition and its emotional impact to 'coming out' and being more open about my healthcare experiences and needs with family, friends, and healthcare professionals, and more assertive in the face of attitudinal barriers and stigma. I've also set firmer boundaries and stopped unfairly comparing myself with heart-healthy peers while recognizing the limitations that I face. I still have regular nightmares where I am back in hospital, often as a child, attached to medical equipment and surrounded by doctors discussing what to do with me as I await surgery. I can be triggered by smells and sounds; I get a fright easily and automatically flinch if someone throws something my way. But now I can make sense of these experiences and manage my body's response compassionately, as part of my condition, and look after little me.

Bessel van der Kolk (2014) proposes that overcoming trauma involves (re)establishing community. As such, an important part of my healing has been finding my community to enhance feelings of social connection, shared understanding and support. For example, I started to reach out to condition-specific third sector organizations. In this way, I made other friends with congenital heart disease, and I ended up co-writing 'Healing hearts and minds: A holistic Approach to Coping Well with Congenital Heart Disease' with another mental health professional and 'first generation' survivor living with CHD from the USA. This was the book we had both being looking for but couldn't find (Livecchi and Morton, 2023), and it has been incredibly emotional and fulfilling to find and work with someone who shares my unique experiences on a project to improve things for other people like us coming up.

I am also better at recognizing ableism, instead of internalizing stigma. For example, when I return to work after a health crisis, while it feels like a relief and a privilege, I often feel disconnected from my peers, who seldom understood what I had just experienced or the reality that another health crisis could de-rail my life at any time. I feel like I live in a no man's land between health and illness somehow having to travel from being very unwell in hospital to navigating the world as a healthy person with no bridge in between. As someone who cannot sustain full-time hours, at times, I've struggled to find a suitable part-time role, while this significantly impacts my pension and finances. My condition also limits travel, essential for networking and conferences, which can lead to exclusion from professional opportunities. On some occasions, I have had to resign from roles due to management changes resulting in revoked accommodations. I am far from alone in these experiences, for example, Gong et al (2020) report that compared to healthy adults, even among the healthiest adults with congenital heart conditions, there are significant decrements in employment and lifetime earnings. These insights have made me more assertive about advocating for myself, communicating my needs and asking for reasonable adjustments in the workplace.

Of course, it is crucial that I continually critically reflect on and recognize my professional limitations. My personal experiences have deeply influenced the development of my professional identity as a counselling psychologist, prompting me to continually engage in critical self-reflection regarding my use of self in therapy, research, and teaching. Although I conduct research and publish on psychologically informed healthcare, ableism and medical trauma, I remain mindful of potential transference and boundary issues in clinical practice and my positionality in research. Consequently, I conduct careful assessments of prospective clients, openly discuss concerns during clinical supervision, and make referrals when I judge that I cannot fully meet a client's needs or risk burnout. For example, one limitation of my practice is that I don't work with clients presenting with medical trauma. As a reflective practitioner, it is essential that I prioritize self-care and carefully manage the physical, psychological, and emotional aspects of my health condition to maintain fitness to practice (Health and Care Professions Council [HCPC], 2024; British Psychological Society [BPS], 2021).

Effective action

In his seminal book, *The Body Keeps the Score*, Bessel van der Kolk (2014) proposes that feelings of helplessness and powerlessness during adverse experiences contribute to the development of trauma disorders. In turn, healing from trauma involves being able to take effective action. As such, like many 'wounded healers' drawn to helping professions my experience as a 'dual expert', both a mental health professional and someone living with a CHC, continues to motivate and shape my career, driving my commitment to improve psychological support and social inclusion for people living with CHCs (Bager-Charleson et al, 2010). I've become a vocal advocate, for example, by successfully campaigning the Scottish Government for national healthcare standards for Congenital Heart Disease in Scotland (Healthcare Improvement Scotland Blog, 2024; Alliance, 2024). Further, when I began my psychology training, I found little recognition of what it means to live with a serious health condition. While the tide is turning, we are far from adequately addressing the psychological and emotional impact of living with a CHC, while medical trauma has been neglected in psychology research, training and practice. This has influenced my research interests which focus on addressing disempowering healthcare experiences (such as backless hospital gowns and epistemic injustice in healthcare) to reduce medical trauma, improve wellbeing and promote psychologically informed healthcare (Cogan et al, 2024a, 2024b; Morton et al, 2022, Morton, 2020; Roche et al, 2025), for example, by developing a measure of psychological safety to track progress in psychological therapy (Morton et al, 2023; Cogan et al, 2024a, 2024b, 2025).

As a Senior Lecturer in Applied Psychology, I have the opportunity to introduce innovative teaching on Anti-discriminatory Practice and Ableism, Medical Trauma, and Psychologically Informed Healthcare to the curricula. This Anti-discriminatory Practice and Ableism teaching aims to explore the socio-cultural-political context affecting people with CHCs, emphasizing the importance of acknowledging intergenerational and social determinants of physical and mental health, structural inequalities, systems of oppression, and power-oppression dynamics within therapy (Khan, 2023). People living with a CHC often share disadvantages with other minority groups including disparities in civil rights, discrimination, income, education, employment, social representation, self-efficacy, and underrepresentation (or misrepresentation) in the media and politics (Bogart, 2014). Conversely, those experiencing discrimination are more vulnerable to developing CHCs or worsening symptoms. I encourage trainees to critically foster cultural humility and challenge unconscious bias, for example, about disability and serious health conditions, value difference, recognize ableism and health privilege, appreciate clients' strengths, and apply these principles to their own practice.

Further, I have developed and deliver specialized training on Medical Trauma and Psychologically Informed Healthcare drawing from my personal experience, research, advocacy and practice (Morton, 2025a, 2025b). This teaching aims to provide an evidence-based approach that integrates mind-body connections and proactively promotes protective factors while mitigating psychological risks during healthcare experiences and beyond. Drawing on contemporary theories such as PVT, attachment theory, compassion-based, and trauma-informed approaches I have developed a framework grounded in the core principles of R.E.S.P.E.C.T. to provide a lens to consider healthcare from a *Psychologically Informed* approach, as briefly outlined below.

- Relational safety through compassionate healthcare delivery, leadership, and teamwork;
- Empowerment by supporting self-management, health literacy, and challenging disempowering healthcare practices;

- Soothing presence of caregivers throughout the healthcare journey;
- Psychological safety (informed by PVT) by normalizing responses to adversity, integrating coping strategies into care, and supporting staff wellbeing;
- Environments conducive to healing, recovery, rest, and wellbeing;
- Culturally sensitive care that addresses ableism, health inequalities, and intersectionality; and
- Trauma-informed practice and environments.

For example, during this teaching Polyvagal informed therapy is explored as a way of working with clients with a CHC to help them become more aware of and work with their body to improve regulation of their ANS and emotions. By applying the principles of PVT, through safe therapeutic presence, containment and recognition of client's non-verbal safety signalling, therapists can better attune to their client's emotional and physiological state. Via co-regulation, therapists can provide signals of safety through intonation of voice, body language and compassion. This entrainment can help the client develop skills to self-regulate emotional and physiological states of defense and safety in a safe and supportive space. Further, sensitively working with clients towards better understanding their ANS and emotional responses can help them self-regulate beyond the therapy room. This can be facilitated by paying attention to their autonomic state and helping them map their nervous system (Dana, 2018). Psychoeducation about self-containment techniques, such as breathing exercises, self-soothing touch, loving-kindness meditation and self-compassion, can help them to calm the nervous system and enhance feelings of psychological safety (Neff and Germer, 2017). I hope to share this work more widely, for example with healthcare professionals and policy makers, to influence psychologically informed healthcare motivating the publication of my book 'Beyond the Medical Gaze: Practicing Psychologically Informed Healthcare' (Morton, 2025a, 2025b).

Going forward, it is vital that practitioner and academic psychology lead by example by welcoming diversity in educational, professional training and career pathways to improve representation of the growing number of people living with a CHC to challenge cultural norms, ableism and promote inclusion. It is important to review whether educational programmes and workplaces proactively embrace inclusive practice, provide opportunities for part-time and flexible work arrangements, have robust policies and training to ensure staff and managers are aware of their own health privilege, biases and promote inclusive practice. Further, by enhancing curricula, policy, and practice for psychology and healthcare professionals we can better meet the needs of the growing number of people living with a CHC in therapeutic practice and public health.

Despite the hardships, I am proud of the life I have built and deeply appreciative of the privileges that being a psychologist brings. I continue to advocate for better awareness, inclusive practices, and greater psychological support for those of us living with CHCs. Our experiences matter, not only as statistics but as deeply human stories that inform compassionate systems of care, education, and employment. There are a growing number of us living with complex health conditions, and we have much to contribute given the chance.

My key tips for navigating a career in psychology with a chronic health condition

- Be self-compassionate, recognize that you probably face additional barriers, on a daily basis, and try to not compare yourself with healthy colleagues or peers.
- Recognize that challenging life events and medical trauma, especially during childhood, can narrow your nervous system's window for feeling safe, yet psychological safety is central to mental health and well-being.
- You can proactively enhance feelings of psychological safety. Different strategies work for different people such as practicing mindfulness, meditation, grounding, yoga, relaxation exercises, breathing techniques, spending time out of doors, coping statements, self-compassion, reassuring touch, soothing sounds, patting a pet and switching off from things that challenge feelings of psychological safety (e.g. news or social media).
- Surround yourself with supportive allies and keep firm boundaries with anyone who brings you down.
- Know your rights in terms of education and employment.
- Advocate for yourself and communicate your needs calmly but assertively. Many people do not know what it means to live with a long-term condition and everyone is affected differently. It is worth trying to explain your situation to people who are in a position to support you.
- If required you are legally entitled to reasonable adjustments to your workload (Equality Act 2010) ensure you discuss this with your academic tutors, occupational health and/or your line manager.
- Employees have the right to request flexible working (Employment Relations (Flexible Working) Act 2023, c. 33). In reality, some employers are more inclusive. Try to find an employer who embraces flexible working with a supportive organizational culture.
- Allow yourself time to acknowledge and process the challenges and losses, then re-consider and set your goals.
- Be creative and flexible about your career pathway, you may need to take the road less travelled, but it might just be more interesting that way.
- If you feel able to and have done the work to process your own healthcare experiences consider using your dual-expertise to inform psychology practice, policy, education and broader social awareness and inclusion. This can help to create meaning from challenging experiences and inform positive change for those coming up.
- Ensure that as a reflective practitioner you prioritize self-care and carefully manage the physical, psychological, and emotional dimensions of your health condition.

References

Abbey, G., Thompson, S.B., Hickish, T., & Heathcote, D. (2015). A meta-analysis of prevalence rates and moderating factors for cancer-related post-traumatic stress disorder. *Psychooncology*, 24, 371–381. https://doi.org/10.1002/pon.3654. PMID: 25146298; PMCID: PMC4409098.

Bager-Charleson, S., & Chatterjee, S.G., Critchley, P., Lauchlan, S., McGrath, S., & Thorpe, F. (Collaborators). (2010). *Why therapists choose to become therapists: A practice-based inquiry.* Karnac Books.

Barnett, K., Mercer, S.W., Norbury, M., Watt, G., Wyke, S., & Guthrie, B. (2012 Jul 7). Epidemiology of multimorbidity and implications for health care, research, and medical education: A cross-sectional study. *Lancet,* 380(9836), 37–43. https://doi.org/10.1016/S0140-6736(12)60240-2. Epub 2012 May 10. PMID: 22579043.

Belanger, E., & Laube, J. (1979). Discounting the disabled. *Transactional Analysis Bulletin,* 9(1), 47–50. https://doi.org/10.1177/036215377900900111

Bogart, K. R. (2014). The role of disability self-concept in adaptation to congenital or acquired disability. *Rehabilitation Psychology*, 59(1) (February), 107–115. PMID: 24611927. https://doi.org/10.1037/a0035800.

British Psychological Society (BPS). (2021). *Code of ethics and conduct.* British Psychological Society.

Christian-Brandt, A.S., Santacrose, D.E., Farnsworth, H.R., & MacDougall, K.A. (2019 Dec). When treatment is traumatic: An empirical review of interventions for pediatric medical traumatic stress. *American Journal of Community Psychology*, 64(3–4), 389–404. https://doi.org/10.1002/ajcp.12392. Epub 2019 Oct 16. PMID: 31617588.

Cogan, N., Campbell, J., Morton, L., Young, D., & Porges, S. (2024a). Validation of the neuroception of psychological safety scale (NPSS) among health and social care workers in the UK. *International Journal of Environmental Research and Public Health*, 21(12), 1551. https://doi.org/10.3390/ijerph21121551

Cogan, N., Morton, L., Campbell, J., Irvine Fitzpatrick, L., Lamb, D., De Kock, J.,…, & Porges, S. (2025). Neuroception of psychological safety scale (NPSS): Validation with a UK based adult community sample. *European Journal of Psychotraumatology*, 16(1). https://doi.org/10.1080/20008066.2025.2490329

Cogan, N., Morton, L., Georgiadis, E., Butler, S. H., Fleck, V. J., & Johnstone, J. (2024). Exploring the perspectives of healthcare professionals concerning the use and utility of the hospital gown to develop theoretically informed behaviour change interventions. *Public Health Open Access*, 8(1). https://doi.org/10.23880/phoa-16000265

Cooper, M., & McLeod, J. (2007). A pluralistic framework for counselling and psychotherapy: Implications for research. *Counselling and Psychotherapy Research*, 7(3), 135–143. https://doi.org/10.1080/14733140701566282

Cortes, J.B., Fernández, C.S., De Oliveira, M.B., Lagos, C.M., Martínez, M.T.B., Hernández, C.L., & Del Cura González, I. (Engl. ed.). (2020). Chronic diseases in the paediatric population: Comorbidities and use of primary care services. *Anales de Pediatría*, 93, 183–193. https://doi.org/10.1016/j.anpede.2019.12.006

Dana, D. (2018). *The polyvagal theory in therapy: Engaging the rhythm of regulation.* W. W. Norton & Company.

Eisenberger, N.I. (2012 Feb–Mar). The neural bases of social pain: Evidence for shared representations with physical pain. *Psychosomatic Medicine*, 74(2), 126–135. https://doi.org/10.1097/PSY.0b013e3182464dd1

Employment Relations (Flexible Working) Act. (2023). c. 33 (UK).
Equality Act. (2010). s. 20.
Gilbert, P. (2014). The origins and nature of compassion focused therapy. *British Journal of Clinical Psychology*, 53(1), 6–41.
Gong, C.L., Zhao, H., Wei, Y., et al. (2020). Lifetime burden of adult congenital heart disease in the USA using a microsimulation model. *Pediatr Cardiol.* https://doi.org/10.1007/s00246-020-02409-9
Gonzalez, V.J., Kimbro, R.T., Cutitta, K.E., Shabosky, J.C., Bilal, M.F., Penny, D.J., & Lopez, K.N. (2021). Mental health disorders in children with congenital heart disease. *Pediatrics*, 147, e20201693. https://doi.org/10.1542/peds.2020-1693
Hacker, K. (2024). The burden of chronic disease. *Mayo Clinic Proceedings: Innovations, Quality & Outcomes*, 8, 112–119. https://doi.org/10.1016/j.mayocpiqo.2023.08.005
Health & Care Professions Council (HCPC). (2023). *Standards of proficiency for practitioner psychologists.* https://www.hcpc-uk.org/globalassets/resources/standards/standards-of-proficiency---practitioner-psychologists.pdf
Healthcare Improvement Scotland Blog. (2024). *Congenital heart disease standards – Bridging the gap between physical and mental health*, 14th Feb, 2024.
Helfricht, S., Latel, B., & Fisher, J.E. (2008). Surgery related post traumatic stress disorder in parents of children undergoing cardiopulmonary bypass surgery: A prospective cohort study. *Pediatric Critical Care Medicine*, 9(2), 217–223.
Herman, J.L. (1998). Recovery from psychological trauma. *Psychiatry and Clinical Neurosciences*, 52, S98–S103. https://doi.org/10.1046/j.1440-1819.1998.0520s5S145.x
Hinz, A., Herzberg, P.Y., Lordick, F., Weis, J., Faller, H., Brähler, E., Härter, M., Wegscheider, K., Geue, K., & Mehnert, A. (2019 Sep). Age and gender differences in anxiety and depression in cancer patients compared with the general population. *European Journal of Cancer Care (Engl)*, 28(5), e13129. https://doi.org/10.1111/ecc.13129. Epub 2019 Jul 9. PMID: 31290218.
Jay, M.A., Sanders-Ellis, D., Blackburn, R., Deighton, J., & Gilbert, R. (2023 Jun 9). Umbrella systematic review finds limited evidence that school absence explains the association between chronic health conditions and lower academic attainment. *Front Public Health*, 11, 1122769. https://doi.org/10.3389/fpubh.2023.1122769. PMID: 37361156; PMCID: PMC10288991.
Khan, M. (2023). *Working within diversity: A reflective guide to anti-oppressive practice in counselling and psychotherapy*. Jessica Kingsley.
Livecchi, T., & Morton, L. (2023). *Healing hearts and minds: A holistic approach to coping well with congenital heart disease*. Oxford University Press.
McKinley Yorder, C.L., & Cantrell, M.N. (2019). Childhood disability and educational outcomes: A systematic review. *Journal of Pediatric Nursing*, 45, 37–50. ISSN 0882-5963. https://doi.org/10.1016/j.pedn.2019.01.003
McLeod, J., & McLeod, J. (2014). *Personal and professional development for counsellors, psychotherapists and mental health practitioners*. Open University Press.
Meentken, M.G., van Beynum, I.M., Legerstee, J.S., Helbing, W.A., & Utens, E.M. (2017 Feb 13). Medically related post-traumatic stress in children and adolescents with congenital heart defects. *Frontiers in Pediatrics*, 5, 20. https://doi.org/10.3389/fped.2017.00020
Morton, L. (2018). Born with a heart condition: The clinical implications of the Polyvagal theory. In Porges, S. & Dana, D. (eds.), *Clinical application of the Polyvagal theory.* Norton Professional Books, 397–417.
Morton, L. (2025a). *Beyond the medical gaze: Psychologically informed healthcare*. Oxford University Press.

Morton, L. (2025b). *Beyond the medical gaze: Practicing psychologically informed healthcare. The Psychologist*. British Psychological Society. https://www.bps.org.uk/psychologist/beyond-medical-gaze-practicing-psychologically-informed-healthcare

Morton, L., Calderwood, C., Cogan, N., Murphy, C., Nix, E., & Kolacz, J. (2022). An exploration of psychological trauma and positive adaptation in adults with congenital heart disease during the COVID-19 pandemic. *Patient Experience Journal*, 9(1), 82–94. https://doi.org/10.35680/2372-0247.1638

Morton, L., Cogan, N., Kolacz, J., Calderwood, C., Nikolic, M., Bacon, T., Pathe, E., Williams, D., & Porges, S.W. (2023). A new measure of feeling safe: Developing psychometric properties of the neuroception of psychological safety scale (NPSS). *Psychological Trauma: Theory, Research, Practice, and Policy*, 16(4), 701–708. https://doi.org/10.1037/tra0001313

Morton, L., Cogan, N., Kornfält, S., Porter, Z., & Georgiadis, E. (2020). Baring all: The impact of the hospital gown on patient wellbeing. *British Journal of Health Psychology*, 25, 3.

Narvaez, D. (2018). Basic needs and fulfilling human potential. In Narvaez, D. (ed.). *Basic needs, wellbeing and morality*. Palgrave Pivot. https://doi.org/10.1007/978-3-319-97734-8_5

Neff, K. D., & Germer, C. K. (2017). Self-compassion and psychological well-being. In Seppälä, E. M., Simon-Thomas, E., Brown, S. L., Worline, M. C., Cameron, C. D., & Doty, J. R. (eds.), *The Oxford handbook of compassion science*. Oxford University Press, 371–386.

Ogden, P. (2015). *Trauma and the body: A sensorimotor approach to psychotherapy and sensorimotor psychotherapy: Interventions for trauma and attachment*. W. W. Norton.

Parker, A.M., Sricharoenchai, T., Raparla, S., Schneck, K.W., Bienvenu, O.J., & Needham, D.M. (2015). Posttraumatic stress disorder in critical illness survivors: A metaanalysis. *Critical Care Medicine*, 43(5), 1121–1129. https://doi.org/10.1097/CCM.0000000000000882. PMID: 25654178.

Porges, S.W. (2022). Polyvagal theory: A science of safety. *Frontiers in Integrative Neuroscience*, 10(16), 871227. https://doi.org/10.3389/fnint.2022.871227. PMID: 35645742; PMCID: PMC9131189.

Quinn, D.M., & Chaudoir, S.R. (2009). Living with a concealable stigmatized identity: The impact of anticipated stigma, centrality, salience, and cultural stigma on psychological distress and health. *Journal of Personality and Social Psychology*, 97(4), 634–651.

Roche, H., Morton, L., & Cogan, N. (2025). Barriers and facilitators to psychological safety during medical procedures among individuals diagnosed with chronic illness in childhood. *Healthcare*, 13(8), 914. https://doi.org/10.3390/healthcare13080914

Rothschild, B. (2000). *The body remembers: The psychophysiology of trauma and trauma treatment*. W. W. Norton & Compa.

Schwartz, A. (2020). *A practical guide to complex PTSD: Compassionate strategies for childhood trauma*. Callisto.

Secinti, E., Thompson, E.J., Richards, M., & Gaysina, D. (2017). Research review: Childhood chronic physical illness and adult emotional health—A systematic review and meta-analysis. *Journal of Child Psychology and Psychiatry and Allied Disciplines*, 58, 753–769. https://doi.org/10.1111/jcpp.12727

Sloan, M., et al. (2023 Jul 26). Prevalence and identification of neuropsychiatric symptoms in systemic autoimmune rheumatic diseases: An international mixed methods study. *Rheumatology*, 63(5), 1259–1272. https://doi.org/10.1093/rheumatology/kead369

Smith, B., Mallick, K., Monforte, J., & Foster, C. (2021). Disability, the communication of physical activity and sedentary behaviour, and ableism: A call for inclusive messages. *British Journal of Sports Medicine*, 55(20), 1121–1122. https://doi.org/10.1136/bjsports-2020-103780

Tedeschi, R.G., Shakespear-Finch, J., Taku, J., & Calhoun, L.G. (2018). *Posttraumatic growth: Theory, research, and applications*. Routledge.

Van der Kolk, B.A. (2014). *The body keeps the score: Brain, mind, and body in the healing of trauma*. Viking.

Vilchinsky, N., Ginzburg, K., Fait, K., & Foa, E.B. (2017 Jul). Cardiac-disease-induced PTSD (CDI-PTSD): A systematic review. *Clinical Psychology Review*, 55, 92–106. https://doi.org/10.1016/j.cpr.2017.04.009. Epub 2017 Apr 25. PMID: 28575815.

World Health Organisation (WHO). (2023). *Noncommunicable diseases*. Available online: https://www.who.int/news-room/fact-sheets/detail/noncommunicable-diseases

Chapter 2

Psychologists' management of fluctuating conditions without clear biomarkers

Alice Kennedy

Introduction

Fluctuating Illness without a clear biomarker has long been a subject of debate where patients have faced dismissal, stigma, and systematic neglect. Such illnesses include myalgic encephalomyelitis/chronic fatigue syndrome (ME/CFS), fibromyalgia, chronic migraines, functional neurological disease, and more recently, long Covid. There are many umbrella terms used to describe these illnesses, such as contested illnesses, medically unexplained symptoms, and persistent physical problems. It is important to note, however, that just because there is not currently a clear and accessible diagnostic biomarker for these illnesses, they are not mysterious.

We have decades of patient reports, and the term myalgic encephalomyelitis (ME) was first coined in the Lancet in 1956 (cited in The Medical Staff of the Royal Free Hospital, 1957), and numerous studies exploring potential biomarkers for ME have sought to differentiate people with ME from healthy control subjects (Maksoud et al., 2023). The ongoing Decode Study has just released a preprint of its initial findings at the time of writing and has identified eight genetic "signals" for ME (Boutin et al., 2025). It is possible that in the future, with adequate research funding, we will learn much more about these illnesses.

However, research funding into these illnesses continues to be inadequate, with campaigns for one such illness, ME, only gaining an estimated £10m investment in the preceding 12 years leading up to 2025 (Westminster Hall Debate Tessa Mund MP, 2025). This equates to only £0.60 pence per person living with ME. A 2016 report found that funding for ME research constituted approximately 0.02% of all active awards by mainstream funding agencies. By comparison, at the time, 250,000 people were estimated to have ME in the UK (but received 20 times less funding than MS which affected 100,000 people) (Radford & Chowdhury, 2016).

Given this lack of funding, perhaps these illnesses are not medical mysteries at all, but might better be termed "under-funded illnesses", which reflects the low levels of funding into causes and effective treatments compared to the disease burden they bring.

DOI: 10.4324/9781003636014-3

First experiences of Illness

My own experience of such illness began when I was diagnosed with ME, before being fortunate enough to improve, and then experiencing Long Covid several years later. Despite working in healthcare, I previously held onto the general story that if I became ill, it was a temporary state, one of suffering but one that would pass. My "job" when ill was to follow any medical advice, rest, recover, rehabilitate, and then return to my normal life. At some level, I still subscribed to a "just world" fallacy and expected that if I did the "right things" and just worked harder, then I could be well again. Chronic illness, however, ripped through my life as a huge, never-ending "reality slap" (Harris, 2012). It created a "biographical disruption" (Bury, 1982) that led me to reconsider how I view myself and my place within the world, how I find meaning and value, and ultimately whether a chronically ill life feels worth living. Acceptance and Commitment Therapy (ACT) became an essential tool for adapting to my new life.

ME arrived seemingly out of nowhere, when one day I awoke to find I was unable to get out of bed. Although, upon reflection, it most likely started earlier. I remember leaving work only to fall asleep in the work car park or falling onto my bed as soon as I arrived home, waking only when the morning alarm sounded. I was, however, disconnected from my body and failed to recognise the warning signals, and instead handled it the only way I knew, by continuing to push through. This is a common theme for many of the clients I encounter with such illnesses.

Perhaps inevitably, this led to a crunch point where I could no longer get out of bed. After that first day being unable to move, my memories of these early months are largely absent, as my days consisted of crushing fatigue, all-over bone-deep aching, and an inability to think clearly. My experience in psychology misled me initially, and I assumed I must be experiencing depression, but as time passed, I noticed my mood was fine, but my body was most definitely not, and it showed no signs of improving. My GP referred me to the local ME/CFS service where I was formally diagnosed.

Losing my job in the NHS was the hardest professional moment, and I had no idea whether I would ever be able to return to the career I had fought so hard to establish. Over the preceding years, my world had narrowed as I had focussed on my career, and my identity had become wrapped up in my job and my ability to be productive. As any psychologist, and probably many who are not psychologists will attest, this leaves a person mentally vulnerable. Not only was my ability to earn a living under threat, but also my purpose and identity.

Aspiring to be a Clinical Psychologist had involved leaving behind my first career and taking a significant pay cut with consequent financial stresses and strains, studying for a degree whilst working, completing a postgraduate qualification, further years of experience, and then a Doctorate in Clinical Psychology. Ironically, by the very nature of the career path, it led to little time for finding meaning or purpose outside of work.

Coping with negative self-thoughts

Any chronic illness can present a threat to sense of self, as activities and achievements by which a person previously understood themselves are taken away. Over the following months, I accepted that I could no longer care for myself and was fortunate to be able to move in with family. With my basic needs now met, I could focus what little energy I had on reconsidering my life.

When well enough to think, I found my mind drifting to all that I had hoped to do with my life, and the very real possibility that my health would not significantly improve. In crept many doubts and self-critical thoughts, such as "I am useless" and "I am a failure", in essence perhaps without productivity, I was nothing. In CBT (CBT), one might challenge these thoughts, attempting to gather and weigh up evidence both in support of and against these thoughts. Whilst this is a useful technique, when largely bed bound by illness my mind was only too quick to conclude that I am indeed useless, as I had achieved little of external significance in the day. Instead, ACT teaches the concept of self-as-context or observing self where there is a perspective from which a person observes their own thoughts, feelings, and experiences without judgement. In the words of Russ Harris, it is "the locus/space from where noticing happens" (2019, p. 174). It is possible to take a metaphorical step back and observe what arises, noting them without judgement. Instead of using my limited energy to struggle between negative and positive thoughts, I could choose instead to "drop the struggle". Using the ACT metaphor of "tug of war" (Hayes, Strosahl & Wilson, 1999). I pictured my difficult thoughts and experiences as a big, ugly monster with endless energy pulling on the other end of a rope that I was holding. I could not defeat this monster with its endless energy, and I felt exhausted trying to fight it. Instead, I chose to lay down the rope, to drop the struggle, and to allow these critical thoughts and disliked physical symptoms to be present.

Following ACT principles, I tried to observe my thoughts or feelings without judgement, make space for all experiences, and allow thoughts and feelings to be present without them dominating my sense of self or choices. As Harris (2021) states, acceptance means willingness to make room for unwanted cognitions, memories, urges, and sensations. This is not always as easy as it seems, and practical strategies and exercises can help in engendering this new way of reacting. In a common ACT exercise, a person is asked to picture a stream with leaves falling from a nearby tree. They are then asked to observe their unwanted thoughts, feelings, or sensations and to imagine placing each one on a leaf and watching it be carried gently away by the stream. Whilst some will return, they can once again be placed on another leaf and watched as they drift away. Through this, a person learns to notice but not overly engage with what arises. As often used in ACT, I found mindfulness a useful tool for learning to watch my own thoughts and feelings without buying into them. I might think I am useless, and this might be accompanied by feelings of shame, but I could watch these thoughts float by, in the same way as many other thoughts drifted in and out of my mind, without attaching particular significance to them.

Values

Illness also led me to grieve for my lost relationships and friendships, the community I had left behind in the town I had made my home, and the aspirations that now felt impossible. When I could no longer fulfil my goals, I used ACT to explore what aspects of life carried the most meaning and importance. Understanding your own values in a core component in ACT and values can provide a direction for life, even when goals are unachievable or do not offer lasting satisfaction or happiness. As Russ Harris states, goals are things that we are trying to achieve, or complete or have, but a value is something different and speaks to how we wish to treat ourselves, others, and the world (Harris, 2025).

As I examined my wish list for life, I noticed that there were values that underlay each goal I had previously held. Motivating my goal as a Clinical Psychologist were values including connection, caring, contribution, encouragement, and skilfulness. This recognition allowed me to take committed action, choosing behaviours that were consistent with my values (Hayes, Strosahl & Wilson, 2016).

ACT invites us to question the meaning we build our life upon, asking what values do we want our lives to be about. Perhaps there was a me, an "observing self", that was distinct from my "conceptualised self" that was defined by career achievements or professional titles. Whist I couldn't yet work again, I could be flexible about how I moved in the direction of values such as giving to others. Taking committed action involved accepting obstacles whether it was being too fatigued to buy, write, and post a birthday card or accepting the difficult emotions that arose when I realised I could not be physically present for a special occasion. Despite this, I could still use my limited energy to act in accordance with my values, with small steps such as sending a thoughtful text to a friend going through a hard time. I still felt bleak about ever being able to visit the places I had dreamed of seeing, but I could connect with the values of growing an open mind and of exploration and adventure. I used my moments of energy to hear tales of others' life stories, about their travels, and enjoy the photographs and stories.

A particularly useful ACT exercise is to imagine that someone is giving a eulogy at your funeral (Hayes, Strosahl & Wilson, 1999) and what you would want the speaker to say about you. When asked this question, few people instinctively want their CV read out. Rather than listing accomplishments, most people want to be remembered for the values they held and the people they helped. A eulogy might reference a person's working life but usually in the context of who they helped and what drove them to do their meaningful work. When walking through a graveyard looking at headstones, most speak of relationships and the impact on others, rather than sounding like a LinkedIn post, boasting of "deliverables" or material success. In the cold light of death, our most important values become visible. I realised that I could still be of value in the world and connect with others, whether or not I healed enough to work again.

During these dark months spent largely in bed, I also found it helpful to relive old memories of good times, marinading in the mixture of gratitude and pleasure for having experienced such wonderful moments. Reminiscence has been shown to have positive effects on wellbeing (Pinquart & Forstmeier, 2012). It felt very different to rumination, as I was no longer dwelling on negative emotions or thoughts but instead valuing and enjoying what I had already experienced. Over time, it became easier to access these memories and to enjoy every gift they brought. It also provided an opportunity to feel gratitude. Where I had once taken my health for granted, I was now grateful for those times when I had been healthy. There are so many people with these illnesses who never had the chance to be a healthy teenager or adult. Naturally, there were days when I knew I should connect to my values or practice gratitude and yet it was inaccessible. At these times, it was also important to allow myself to feel the hurt and to be compassionate to myself.

Recovery and growth

I was extremely fortunate, and over the years that followed my ME improved, and I returned to work and many of life's activities. The idea of post-traumatic growth (Tedeschi & Calhoun, 1996) has been applied to the experiences of people with chronic illness. There is a recognition that the adjustment of a person's previous concept of themselves and of the world is challenged (Murphy & Harris, 2025) and specifically in ME (Arroll & Howard, 2013).

I found post-traumatic growth a useful concept to apply to my own situation. I do not claim to have been through a trauma that would meet criterion A of the DSM-5, but the idea of growing and changing as a result of the experience resonated. I had a newfound appreciation for life, health, and their temporary nature. I was given a second chance to rectify some of those regrets, albeit with modifications and plenty of pacing.

These areas of growth occurred in my life in a myriad of ways. My improvement following ME felt like a second chance at life, one taken up in the full knowledge that it could be fleeting. This led to a deep and great appreciation for the experience of life and a desire to live fully. For instance, I took opportunities to travel, and on a particularly beautiful day, I sat gazing across to the Acropolis. That day health prevented me from making the climb up the hill to the Acropolis. Yet I believe that my joy in simply regarding it from a distance was beyond anything I would have felt had I never experienced ME and had easily made my way up the hillside. I had learnt to savour, defined as "the capacity to attend to, appreciate and enhance positive experiences in one's life" (Bryant & Veroff, 2017, p. xi).

Instead of living in the past, ruminating about not being able to walk up the hill or living in the future, hoping one day to be able to do this, I could instead choose to engage with the present moment and practice gratitude (Lavin, 2015). This meant savouring the sights, sounds, smells, and tastes as I sipped my frappe and looked across to the famous sight. This had been a skill I'd learnt when stuck in bed, only able to savour and revel in the softness of the duvet or the pleasure of a cold drink. I have sought to hold onto this, appreciating the small moments.

Whilst enjoying such moments, I also try to remember that I was extremely fortunate as there are many people who remain severely ill with ME. Those with "Severe ME" are unable to do any activity for themselves or can only carry out minimal daily tasks such as cleaning their teeth, whilst those with "Very Severe ME" spend all day in bed and are dependent on care (National Institute for Health and Care Excellence [NICE], 2021). They may need tube-feeding (Baxter, Speight & Weir, 2021) and be hypersensitive to sensory input (NICE, 2021).

Long Covid

In 2020, my world changed yet again as I became ill with Long Covid after contracting the virus in the first wave. The initial illness itself was hard, but as time passed, it seemed as though I had recovered, albeit still feeling tired and struggling to think clearly. At this point, the world was also rapidly changing, and I was busy trying to support clients who were navigating a pandemic at a scale and speed not seen on these shores in our lifetimes.

I brushed aside my own lingering symptoms and pushed on, repeating the mistakes of my early days with ME. Sadly, we would later learn that not resting at the time of the initial illness is a risk factor in the development of Long Covid (Greenhalgh, Sivan, Perlowski & Nikolich, 2024). Over time my symptoms worsened. Breathing became more difficult, I experienced sporadic chest pains, I was dizzy, and I struggled to stand or walk.

As my health worsened, I noticed familiar stories popping up in my mind. Taking the "observer self" stance advocated by ACT (Harris, 2021), I noticed these stories and named them. In order to create "cognitive defusion" from these thoughts, I adopted the stance of a curious observer noticing the myriads of thoughts my mind generated and named the stories that occurred. There was a story of "this is unfair" as I watched neighbours depart for their daily hour of exercise and social media posts about life making banana bread during lockdowns, yet I was struggling to walk for a few minutes at a time. This was swiftly followed by a barrage of shaming thoughts, telling me I was a bad person for envying others' activities. Challenging these thoughts often led me to become more entwined in them, whereas adopting "cognitive defusion" approach created space between a thought occurring and believing it was true.

My health deteriorated, as my ability to move reduced to walking along the street, to the end of my driveway, and finally even standing became too much. I was later given an additional diagnosis of POTS and dysautonomia which is common in Long Covid (Fedorowski & Sutton, 2023). The fatigue was crushing and gradually robbed me of my ability to sit up for extended periods of time, and once again, my world drastically contracted. After research and talking with a GP, tests were ordered, and yet no relief was found. By this time, my mind was constantly supplying me with thoughts that formed the "I will always be ill" story. I could choose to either buy into this story whole heartedly or to notice it and let it come and go without latching on to it. At a time when so little was known about the long-term outcomes for Long Covid, I could acknowledge the thoughts that I would always be ill were unhelpful and not based on facts. Instead, I unhooked from this story my mind had created by allowing space between my thought and whether or not it was true. I said "thank you" to my mind for reminding me of my desire to recover and resume activities.

Cognitive symptoms

A symptom that greatly affected my sense of self was "brain fog". Many of the illnesses without a clear biomarker include the colloquially termed "brain fog" which includes problems with attention, memory (Denno, Zhao, Husain & Hampshire, 2025) that relates to cognitive difficulties such as word finding difficulties, impairment in working memory, and problems in executive functioning. In the case of ME, this can include slowed thought and concentration including a sense of confusion, disorientation, and difficulty with decision making, alongside short-term memory loss which can include difficulty retrieving words or information, and poor working memory (Carruthers et al., 2011). Similar cognitive impairments are seen in Long Covid (Asadi-Pooya et al., 2022).

These cognitive symptoms presented difficulties in many areas of my life. In the domain of language, it was difficult to retrieve words or name objects. I can find myself stuck, unable to recall a simple word that I have known and used for decades. I know there is a specific word I want to use, and yet my brain just cannot retrieve it, however hard I strain. Sometimes this can be comical, as I search for another word to substitute or find a roundabout way to describe something.

My memory has also been affected, particularly free recall. To combat this, I often need a cue to remember a piece of information. This can be any kind of prompt of information stored with the original information. There are many strategies I use to help me with this, when recalling information about a client, I practice cues which will later bring the memories of our work together flooding back.

When overly fatigued, it is not just one word that is lost but trying to find any words at all feels like wading through a sea of treacle, trying and failing to link basic ideas. Relationships flounder as it becomes difficult to remember what a friend is saying or to find the words to respond. Those close to me recognise the change as it occurs partway through an event or conversation, as I start to feel my cognitive capabilities seeping away. I have learnt how to notice these signs and leave a gathering whilst I still have time to navigate my way home, and by offering myself compassion for these struggles. Whilst my mind wants to tell me a story that this means I am a terrible friend or an uncaring person, I instead take a moment to take a mindful breath and then tell myself that I am trying and that is ok that it is difficult.

Sleep

With Long Covid, I was fatigued beyond anything I can describe, and yet often unable to sleep during the day, and sleep at night was broken, as I was unable to rest properly due to restless legs, pain, enforced inactivity during the day, or a combination of all these symptoms.

I was no stranger to broken nights and had previously drawn on CBT strategies such as good sleep hygiene, challenging negative assumptions about not getting enough sleep, relaxation techniques, associating bed with sleep rather than activities such as watching TV or doomscrolling, and restricting time in bed. Whilst these remained important, several of them became more difficult with a chronic illness. When managing the illness requires extended periods of laying down during the day, unless one has multiple areas in the house, it is not possible to restrict time in bed solely to sleep.

Drawing on ACT principles became a useful addition. This included not fighting insomnia but instead increasing my own willingness to accept the short-term discomfort. There was a primary suffering that comes with not being able to sleep, but there is a secondary suffering, driven by the interpretation we make of it. In ACT, these are sometimes known as the "clean" discomfort in this case of being tired the next day, and "dirty" discomfort (Hayes, Strosahl & Wilson, 1999) which was additional discomfort resulting from trying to wrangle with and force sleep. As I became a curious observer of my thoughts, I noticed that my secondary or "dirty" suffering was driven by fears that a lack of sleep would lead to post-exertional malaise (PEM) in the following days or that it could lead to a much longer-term worsening of the illness or prevent recovery.

Hayes, Strosahl and Wilson (1999) gave a metaphor of two dials, which has been applied to insomnia (Dalrymple, Fiorentino, Politi & Posner, 2010). The metaphor describes two scales, each with a dial, one for discomfort and the other for willingness. I wanted to dial down the discomfort of not sleeping and the feared consequences but instead needed to dial up my willingness to accept my wakefulness. By accepting, I save myself the extra energy expenditure of trying to force sleep or raging against the insomnia. Once again, the principle of "cognitive defusion" in ACT became a cornerstone of coping. I learnt not to judge how long I was awake or to berate myself for my inability to drift off, but instead adopted the perspective of an observer, noticing these thoughts come and go. Instead, I had to speak kindly and gently to myself, offering myself compassion for my primary suffering, but reassuring myself that sleep would eventually come.

Pacing

One of the most important principles for managing an energy-limiting condition is to pace activity, and this includes both physical and mental exertion. PEM is a core symptom of ME and for at least a subset of people with Long Covid. It describes a worsening of symptoms that can follow minimal cognitive, physical, emotional, or social activity (NICE, 2021). If I was over-exerted in any of these domains, I experienced a resurgence of symptoms, including crushing fatigue. This over exertion might stem from seemingly simple tasks such as having a shower or speaking on the telephone. I have heard many describe it as feeling like having flu and that is a good way for me to describe my own reaction to overexertion as it feels as if the original illness has returned.

The primary way of managing PEM is through pacing. It is a strategy for noticing and responding to the warning signs of over-exertion and adjusting physical and mental activity to avoid or limit symptoms (Goudsmit, Nijs, Jason & Wallman, 2012). This involves working out what your current baseline for activity is and then attempting to stay under this baseline, also known as staying within the "energy envelope" (Jason et al., 1999). Another analogy often used is of a bank account. Just as with a bank account, going overdrawn comes with penalties and often awful interest rates. In other words, if you use more energy than your allowance, then you will pay it back, in the form of increased symptoms and rest needed, at what feels like an extortionate rate of interest.

Sticking within an energy budget in some ways sounds simple, but in reality, it is much more difficult to manage. It doesn't help that the baseline keeps moving, what you can do one day is not necessarily replicable. Instead, it becomes a process of trial and error, of trying to guess in advance what energy you have for that day and weigh it against the most necessary activities. Naturally, there is always more that needs to be done than the amount of energy left in the envelope. For those who are parents or carers, this is even more complicated as small children or loved ones needing care cannot often wait while the person rests and paces. It may feel impossible for some parents with Long Covid to both care for their children and keep within their energy envelope.

Navigating the healthcare system

Navigating the healthcare system with a fluctuating illness without a clear biomarker is inherently difficult, but an area where I could use several privileges to my advantage. Having worked for years on both the clinical and non-clinical sides of several NHS Trusts, I knew broadly how the system worked, and as a white person with a professional background, I was more likely to be listened to (Smyth et al., 2024). I was fortunate to see GPs open to exploring my symptoms. The onus, however, remained on me to research as best I could this new emerging illness and to request investigations. When ill, this was a significant burden, and often my only energy for the day was spent researching my symptoms and possible tests or treatments, fearful that a crucial window for recovery might be missed. As a clinical psychologist, I am used to searching the evidence base, and yet the studies I could find were sometimes in biological detail that they were beyond my areas of expertise. As Long Covid was a new phenomenon, in the early days, there was little reliable information available. Alternatively, I needed to navigate anecdotal reports and then try to weigh up their utility, scope for causing harm, and seek out research from similar conditions. I worked in partnership with a GP, presenting her with information and asking her to apply her knowledge of medicine and the body to evaluate its usefulness. She was also constrained by what was possible by guidelines and responses to referrals from specialists. For instance, my first referral to cardiology was refused, and it was another year until the same cardiology service accepted the referral, diagnosed Postural Orthostatic Tachycardia Syndrome (POTS), and prescribed medication. Navigating a complex NHS has increased by appreciation of what so many of my client's experience and the emotions of frustration and despair that often accompany this.

Long Covid Clinics

I was also referred to a Long Covid Clinic. My initial intervention was to join a group class, but in the first session, an NHS staff member leading the group suggested that we try graded exercise therapy (GET), albeit using different language. I was there as a patient, but I was also a health professional who knew this was not recommended in the current guidance (NICE, 2021) and may cause harm in those with ME (Maes & Twisk, 2010) and by extension, potentially those with Long Covid where PEM is a key component. I experienced a tension between the two roles of being a patient and a healthcare professional. I felt I could not sit passively as a patient whilst witnessing potential harm to others. I chose to speak up both in the group session and later to the service. In time, I had other assistance from the Long Covid Clinic centred on pacing and breathing exercises. What was striking was other people's reactions to the Long Covid Clinics. When I mentioned to people that I was attending such a service, they often assumed this meant I was now receiving curative treatment. This seemed to be an opinion echoed more widely in society. A politician would appear on the news to declare that new Long Covid Clinics were being opened, and no follow-up questions were asked. Yet the Long Covid Clinic had very limited access to medical staff. At times, it felt like I had been assigned the label Long Covid, and any curiosity or further investigation stopped there.

Resting

Consequently, I sought any actions I could take at home. I looked for ways to calm my nervous system and engage my parasynthetic nervous system (Porges, 1999). My local Long Covid Clinic also emphasised the need to retrain breathing, and there are some small-scale studies showing the benefits of mindfulness for people with Long Covid (Vandenbogaart et al., 2025).

It wasn't always easy to calm my mind. As many others do, I experience a busy mind, and the idea of a mind that is at rest and thinking about "nothing" is alien. Instead of trying to will this into existence, I found it helpful to occupy my mind with calming and lower-level stimulation. I chose body scans or yoga nidra guided exercises over meditations with long gaps between instructions. Another option was to listen to an audiobook that I already knew well, giving my mind just enough to satisfy it whilst also being able to lie down and block out all light with an eye mask and use breathing exercises.

Another invaluable resource was the referral from the Long Covid Clinic to the English National Opera Breathe programme (Philip et al., 2022). People, at all stages of Long Covid, gather online for a programme of weekly singing exercise led by professional opera singers. Alongside learning ways to push breath through my chest, there were moments of beauty of being sung lullabies by a fantastic singer. Also, importantly, amid the loneliness and separation from community that can occur as life constricts owing to illness, I found in these sessions understanding and connection. Finding social connection has long been recognised as an important factor for mental and physical health (Holt-Lunstad, 2024). I still attend drop-in sessions and value the support we offer one another. Whilst many services are being reduced or cut altogether, I remain hopeful that this programme can and will continue for as long as it is needed by the Long Covid community.

Disbelief and stigma

People with illnesses without a clear biomarker have not only to manage their symptoms, but all too often must contend with disbelief and stigma (Asbring & Narvanen, 2002; Goudsmit, Brostoff & Challacombe, 2002). These chronic illnesses are not mysterious. Many have been researched, and distinct differences have been found between healthy controls and those with these illnesses. This has not, however, yet translated into a readily available test and instead doctors are often reliant on patient history to make a diagnosis. Sadly, this has led some to question the validity of patients' symptoms, either claiming that these illnesses are "all in the head" or even that some people might fabricate symptoms in order to access secondary gains.

It is impossible to ignore the long history of psychologising illnesses without a clear biomarker and the role of psychology in perpetuating this. Without a definitive biomarker, ME has often been framed within psychological or psychosomatic models which may be harmful (Geraghty & Blease, 2018), and yet there is growing evidence of the role of genetics (Boutin et al., 2025), abnormalities in the immune system, vascular system, and energy metabolism (Thoma et al., 2024).

I was fearful of such stigma, and worried about returning to the Health Psychology Department I had worked in to attend appointments for ME. I wondered what school of thought my colleagues believed. I, like many others, have been deeply hurt by suggestions by some health professionals that those of us experiencing these illnesses have particular personalities, talk of secondary gains or even accusations of "malingering" (Horton-Salway, 2007). Later, with Long Covid, I encountered a variety of reactions in my professional life. Thankfully, many were understanding, although some are perplexed that it is still ongoing, five years later. It does not help that Long Covid has not been given prominence in national discussions of the impact of Covid, and sadly, research funds remain paltry when compared to the disease burden. A few people have actively sought to deny my experience of Long Covid, and I have wondered whether cognitive dissonance (Festinger & Carlsmith, 1959) plays a role in this; people want to believe that Covid no longer poses any threat, and yet the existence of people with Long Covid is a constant reminder that this narrative does not tell the full story. Others with Long Covid have found that they are dismissed by those who refuse to believe in the existence of Covid (Eberhardt et al., 2024).

Some people manage the idea of Long Covid being a possibility by reassuring themselves that people who get it are different and therefore they are safe. Those of us who get Long Covid are othered, and our acquisition of the illness is ascribed to an attribute we hold. As a middle-aged, larger woman, some might comfort themselves by thinking that they, as a person who is young, slim, fit, and otherwise healthy, are immune to potentially lasting effects from Covid. Whilst a healthy lifestyle has been found to reduce the risk of acquiring Long Covid by up to half, it does not eliminate it (Wang et al., 2023). There remains an ongoing risk of developing Long Covid, albeit a thankfully lower one following vaccination (Notarte et al., 2022).

Conversely, there have also been wonderful moments of sharing experiences of Long Covid with other psychologists. For several years, I have been part of an online group with other psychologists with Long Covid. While much of the time, we discuss possible interventions, trials, and latest research findings, we also offer each other understanding and emotional support, moments of connection, and a place to explore our identities as psychologists who also have Long Covid.

Psychology professionals

As psychologists, we understand the fundamental need of humans to be understood by others, to connect, and to live in community and yet being diagnosed with an under-researched illness threatened my role in my professional community. The psychologisation of ME can be traced back to the 1980s and 1990s, when proponents of a psychological paradigm argued that unhelpful thoughts and avoidance behaviours maintained symptoms (Wessely, David, Bulter & Chalder, 1989).

This assumed that a person either had recovered from an acute illness but was misattributing symptoms to the original illness and so avoided activity. A person was therefore encouraged to begin GET to recondition. CBT was also recommended to help people challenge illness beliefs. The idea being that thinking they needed to rest was faulty thinking that could be challenged and changed. These approaches were endorsed by key institutions, including NICE, and promoted in NHS settings for many years.

The revised 2021 NICE guidelines marked a turning point, removing recommendations for GET and emphasising the need for a more patient-centred and biomedical understanding of ME (NICE, 2021). As psychologists, we still have much to offer. We are trained to attend to meaning, context, and the lived experience of distress. Yet this history forces us to ask difficult questions. How often have we, perhaps inadvertently, privileged psychological explanations, and thereby reinforced stigma?

As psychologists, we need to be mindful of the previous stigma and disbelief a person with an illness without a clear biomarker might have faced before their first appointment with us. The offer of psychological support to someone with a physical illness does not mean that the illness is "all in their head" and as psychologists, we need to be careful that our services are not positioned as direct treatment for physical symptoms.

Some psychologists may disagree and argue for the importance of offering clients hope that psychological intervention will improve or even cure their symptoms. But I would argue that we owe our clients accurate, evidence-based information about what we offer and what we can achieve. To offer false promises not only undermines any sense of informed consent but also adds to the narrative that the client is perhaps not doing enough or is somehow psychologically blocking an improvement, either consciously or unconsciously.

It is uncomfortable and confronting to meet the edges of what our profession can offer, but we have a duty to act within our scope of practice (Health Care and Professions Council [HCPC], 2024). It can seem difficult to say "I'm sorry, we can't offer anymore" or "I don't know". Instead, we may seek other explanations. Perhaps it is easier to wonder aloud if a patient really wants to get better, or to float the idea of secondary gains as a possibility.

The notion of secondary gains is that someone may be benefitting in some way from being in the sick role. This might be financially through access to benefits, or other assisted support. Perhaps a person's world has needed to adapt to their symptoms with loved ones taking up caring roles, the loss of work, and being tied into a benefits system that is not built to cater to fluctuating illnesses. If someone makes enough of an improvement to return to work, will they be able to access benefits again if their health worsens? In addition, what if the next benefits assessor is unsympathetic to fluctuating illnesses without a clear biomarker? All of which can hamper physical and mental recovery or return to employment.

Employment

I remember the dilemma I faced when an improvement in health during ME meant I was ready to undertake some paid work. I started with just a few hours a week, and my employer offered me more working hours as the year progressed, and gradually, I was able to increase my work and become financially independent without the need for benefits.

This was made possible by my earning ability. With a long work history, qualifications, and skills that were in demand, I could earn significantly above minimum wage, allowing me to return to part-time work. This is not possible for many people. For example, those who were unlucky enough to become ill earlier in life may never have had opportunities to build a work history. I also had a safety net in the form of a supportive partner and family, none of whom would see me living on the streets. Many have no-one to turn to, especially as their social circles shrunk as their illness left them unable to socialise. I could also work whilst sitting down. However, this may not be so straight-forward for someone who's job is more physically demanding. In many jobs, physical fatigue might put theirs or others' lives at risk. Add to this the numerous ways in which others are marginalised, whether that be through racism, sexism, ableism, classism, transphobia, homophobia, weight stigma, height stigma, ageism, or other barriers to the workplace, such as caring responsibilities, poor transport links, or a difficult economic outlook.

This is why a dismissive remark such as "no-one wants to work" as an explanation for symptoms could be misplaced and harmful. Instead of assuming that a person may be unwilling to notice symptom improvement, I find it helpful instead to explore with the person their experiences, what this means for their life and potential fears. The fluctuating nature of these illnesses means an improvement may only be temporary, and it takes time to trust that it might become stable.

Self-disclosure

When I sit with clients experiencing not only the devastating effects of their physical symptoms on their lives, but also disbelief and rejection from those around them, I find that I can offer greater validation. I have grappled with whether to be open about my experiences of Long Covid with clients. My training and early clinical experience led me to guard against self-disclosure, fearing it would lead the focus to fall on me rather than as it should, on the client. As I have become a more experienced psychologist, I have been less fearful of this. Research has suggested that self-disclosure has potential benefits (Henretty & Levitt, 2010). I have noticed clients searching for recognition of their experience or outright asking if I too have experienced something similar.

After careful consideration and discussion in supervision, I made the choice to disclose that I have Long Covid by adding it to my website. This chapter marks another step along this journey as I share my experience in more depth. For me, crucial factors in choosing this self-disclosure are that it is contained and must not divert the attention of clinical sessions away from the client.

As attitudes to self-disclosure within psychological professions evolve, it will be interesting to see what else we can offer our clients. Whilst my own experience will never be representative of others' experiences, I hope to draw on the understanding I have gained to offer something meaningful to clients.

References

Arroll, M. A., & Howard, A. (2013). The letting go, the building up, [and] the gradual process of rebuilding': identity change and post-traumatic growth in myalgic encephalomyelitis/chronic fatigue syndrome. *Psychology & Health*, 28(3), 302–318. Epub 2012 Sep 11. PMID: 22963543.

Asadi-Pooya, A. A., Akbari, A., Emami, A., Lotfi, M., Rostamihosseinkhani, M., Nemati, H.,…, & Shahisavandi, M. (2022). Long COVID syndrome-associated brain fog. *Journal of Medical Virology*, 94(3), 979–984.

Asbring, P., & Narvanen, A. (2002). Women's experiences of stigma in relation to chronic fatigue syndrome and fibromyalgia. *Qualitative Health Research*, 12(2), 148–160.

Baxter, H., Speight, N., & Weir, W. (April 2021). Life-threatening malnutrition in very severe ME/CFS. *Healthcare*, 9(4), 459. MDPI.

Boutin, T., Bretherick, A. D., Dibble, J. J., Ewaoluwagbemiga, E., Northwood, E.,…, & Ponting, C. P. (2025). Initial findings from the DecodeME genome-wide association study of myalgic encephalomyelitis/chronic fatigue syndrome. *medRxiv*. https://www.medrxiv.org/content/10.1101/2025.08.06.25333109v1

Bryant, F. B., & Veroff, J. (2017). *Savoring: a new model of positive experience*. Psychology Press.

Bury, M. (1982). Chronic illness as biographical disruption. *Sociology of Health and Illness*, 4, 167–182.

Carruthers, B. M., et al. (2011). Myalgic encephalomyelitis: international consensus criteria. *Journal of Internal Medicine*, 270(4), 327–338.

Dalrymple, K. L., Fiorentino, L., Politi, M. C., & Posner, D. (2010). Incorporating principles from acceptance and commitment therapy into cognitive-behavioral therapy for insomnia: a case example. *Journal of Contemporary Psychotherapy*, 40(4), 209–217.

Denno, P., Zhao, S., Husain, M., & Hampshire, A. (2025). Defining brain fog across medical conditions. *Trends in Neurosciences*, 48(5), 330–348.

Eberhardt, J., Gibson, B., Portman, R. M., Carthy, N., Rowlands, S., Batchelor, R.,…, & Kılınç, S. (2024). Psychosocial aspects of the lived experience of long COVID: a systematic review and thematic synthesis of qualitative studies. *Health Expectations*, 27(5), e70071.

Fedorowski, A., & Sutton, R. (2023). Autonomic dysfunction and postural orthostatic tachycardia syndrome in post-acute COVID-19 syndrome. *Nature Reviews Cardiology*, 20(5), 281–282.

Festinger, L., & Carlsmith, J. M. (1959). Cognitive consequences of forced compliance. *Journal of Abnormal and Social Psychology*, 58(2), 203–210.

Geraghty, K. J., & Blease, C. (2018). Cognitive behavioural therapy in the treatment of chronic fatigue syndrome: A narrative review on efficacy and informed consent. *Journal of Health Psychology*, 23(1), 127–138.

Goudsmit, E. M., Brostoff, J., & Challacombe, S. J. (2002). The psychologisation of illness. In J. Brostoff and S. J. Challacombe (Eds.), *Food allergy and intolerance* (pp. 685–693). WB Saunders.

Goudsmit, E. M., Nijs, J., Jason, L. A., & Wallman, K. E. (2012). Pacing as a strategy to improve energy management in myalgic encephalomyelitis/chronic fatigue syndrome: a consensus document. *Disability and Rehabilitation*, 34(13), 1140–1147.

Greenhalgh, T., Sivan, M., Perlowski, A., & Nikolich, J. Ž. (2024). Long COVID: a clinical update. *The Lancet*, 404(10453), 707–724.

Harris, R. (2012). *The reality slap: finding peace and fulfilment when life hurts*. New Harbinger Publications.

Harris, R. (2019). *ACT made simple: an easy-to-read primer on acceptance and commitment therapy*. New Harbinger Publications.

Harris, R. (2021). *Trauma-focused ACT: a practitioner's guide to working with mind, body, and emotion using acceptance and commitment therapy*. New Harbinger Publications.

Harris, R. (2025). Psychwire course. https://psychwire.com/free-resources/expertcarinsights/resource-1b0mdpi/values-vs-goals (downloaded 3rd September 2025).

Hayes, S. C., Strosahl, K. D., & Wilson, K. G. (1999). *Acceptance and commitment therapy: an experiential approach to behavior change*. Guilford Press.

Hayes, S. C., Strosahl, K. D., & Wilson, K. G. (2016). *Acceptance and commitment therapy: the process and practice of mindful change* (Second Edition). Guilford Press.

Health Care and Professions Council (HCPC). (2024). *Standards of conduct, performance and ethics*. Health & Care Professions Council.

Henretty, J. R., & Levitt, H. M. (2010). The role of therapist self-disclosure in psychotherapy: a qualitative review. *Clinical Psychology Review*, 30(1), 63–77.

Holt-Lunstad, J. (2024). Social connection as a critical factor for mental and physical health: evidence, trends, challenges, and future implications. *World Psychiatry*, 23(3), 312–332.

Horton-Salway, M. (2007). The 'ME bandwagon' and other labels: constructing the genuine case in talk about a controversial illness. *British Journal of Social Psychology*, 46(4), 895–914.

Jason, L. A., Melrose, H., Lerman, A., Burroughs, V., Lewis, K., King, C. P., & Frankenberry, E. L. (1999). Managing chronic fatigue syndrome: overview and case study. *AAOHN Journal*, 47(1), 17–21.

Lavin, T. (2015). ACT: the live better series – gratitude and self-compassion. *YouTube*. https://www.youtube.com/watch?v=vO0sz3di2IA

Maes, M., & Twisk, F. N. (2010). Chronic fatigue syndrome: Harvey and Wessely's (bio) psychosocial model versus a bio (psychosocial) model based on inflammatory and oxidative and nitrosative stress pathways. *BMC Medicine*, 8(1), 35.

Maksoud, R., Magawa, C., Eaton-Fitch, N., Thapaliya, K., & Marshall-Gradisnik, S. (2023). Biomarkers for myalgic encephalomyelitis/chronic fatigue syndrome (ME/CFS): a systematic review. *BMC Medicine*, 21(1), 189.

Murphy, R., & Harris, B. (2025). Can current post-traumatic growth models capture the lived experience of life with a fluctuating chronic illness? Towards a new model. *British Journal of Health Psychology*, 30, e70003.

National Institute for Health and Care Excellence (NICE) (2021). *Myalgic encephalomyelitis (or encephalopathy)/chronic fatigue syndrome: diagnosis and management (NG206)*. London: National Institute for Health and Care Excellence. https://www.nice.org.uk/guidance/ng206

Notarte, K. I., Catahay, J. A., Velasco, J. V., Pastrana, A., Ver, A. T., Pangilinan, F. C.,…, & Fernández-de-Las-Peñas, C. (2022). Impact of COVID-19 vaccination on the risk of developing long-COVID and on existing long-COVID symptoms: a systematic review. *EClinicalMedicine*, 53.

Philip, K. E., Owles, H., McVey, S., Pagnuco, T., Bruce, K., Brunjes, H.,…, & Hopkinson, N. S. (2022). An online breathing and wellbeing programme (ENO Breathe) for people with persistent symptoms following COVID-19: a parallel-group, single-blind, randomised controlled trial. *The Lancet Respiratory Medicine*, 10(9), 851–862.

Pinquart, M., & Forstmeier, S. (2012). Effects of reminiscence interventions on psychosocial outcomes: a meta-analysis. *Aging & Mental Health*, 16(5), 541–558.

Porges, S. W. (1999). Regulation of the autonomic nervous system. *The Integrative Neurobiology of Affiliation*, 6, 5–82.

Radford, G., & Chowdhury, S. (2016). *ME/CFS research funding: An overview of activity by major institutional funders included on the dimensions database*. Action for ME: Bristol, UK.

Smyth, N., Ridge, D., Kingstone, T., Gopal, D. P., Alwan, N. A., Wright, A.,…, & Chew-Graham, C. A. (2024). People from ethnic minorities seeking help for Long Covid: a qualitative study. *British Journal of General Practice*, 74(749), e814–e822.

Tedeschi, R. G., & Calhoun, L. G. (1996). The posttraumatic growth inventory: measuring the positive legacy of trauma. *Journal of Traumatic Stress*, 9(3), 455–471.

The Medical Staff of the Royal Free Hospital. (1957). An outbreak of encephalomyelitis in the Royal Free Hospital Group, London, in 1955. *British Medical Journal*, 2(5050), 895.

Thoma, M., Froehlich, L., Hattesohl, D. B., Quante, S., Jason, L. A., & Scheibenbogen, C. (2024). Why the psychosomatic view on myalgic encephalomyelitis/chronic fatigue syndrome is inconsistent with current evidence and harmful to patients. *Medicina*, 60(1), 83.

Vandenbogaart, E., Figueroa, M., Winston, D., Cole, S., Bower, J., & Hsu, J. J. (2025). Preliminary evaluation of a mindfulness intervention program in women with long COVID dysautonomia symptoms. *Brain, Behavior, & Immunity-Health*, 44, 100963.

Wang, S., Li, Y., Yue, Y., Yuan, C., Kang, J. H., Chavarro, J. E.,…, & Roberts, A. L. (2023). Adherence to healthy lifestyle prior to infection and risk of post–COVID-19 condition. *JAMA Internal Medicine*, 183(3), 232–241.

Wessely, S., David, A., Butler, S., et al. (1989). Management of chronic (post-viral) fatigue syndrome. *The Journal of the Royal College of General Practitioners*, 39(318), 26–29.

Westminster Hall Debate Tessa Mund MP. (20 November 2025). https://www.meresearch.org.uk/westminster-hall-debate-on-me-19-november-2025/.

Chapter 3

Living and working as a system

Complex dissociative disorders in clinical psychology

Sam Fletcher

Introduction

When I[1] began learning more about complex dissociation, I recall how difficult it was to find information about it from people who experienced it. When I did find any examples, they upset the (my) system as the focus was generally on how awful it was, the terrible consequences, and the traumatic circumstances by which it had arisen. As the dutiful intellectualising psychologist, I read academic papers and books, and while they helped me understand the processes, which were important to me, it was very clinical and didn't really match my felt experience. I had certainly internalised the negative stereotypes of dissociation seen in the media and fictionalised accounts. None of these clinical or sensationalised media accounts resonated with me. It caused a lot of dissonance in my mind, leading to periodic cycles of denial and acceptance of my experience. I was a regular person with a job, family, friends, and hobbies, and I existed outside of my mental illness. In order to do this, I was a master of compartmentalisation, which undoubtedly resulted from my dissociative experiences, and for which I am very grateful, but life was hard. There didn't seem to be much hope for a life well lived in the literature I read. The shame and self-stigma I felt, driven by dominant invalidating narratives, kept me quiet about my experience. It still does to a large extent.

When I tentatively told my psychologist about the 'thoughts not under conscious control' (I don't think I let her use the word parts for several months), it was a leap of faith I hadn't expected to make. I didn't know if I would ever feel safe enough to share my experiences. I was worried my experience would be dismissed as psychosis, which I had experienced in my 20s – although I wonder now if it was psychosis or actually dissociation. Or worse, that I was making it up. I worried about the impact on my career if I shared these experiences. It was incredibly confusing that my experience was largely undescribed in any of the teaching I had received during my training, or even by fellow patients. I hadn't realised that generally others did not experience their inner world as I did.

Complex dissociative disorders represent discontinuity of integration and control over cognitions, consciousness, behaviour, and bodily movements.[2] For me, when things in the world start to look the wrong size or colour or start moving in

DOI: 10.4324/9781003636014-4

a way they should not, it's a sign I am beginning to dissociate and experiencing derealisation. If we think of dissociation as being on a continuum and a natural tendency of the human brain, perhaps this is similar to seeing shapes in the clouds when you are absentmindedly gazing at the sky. With depersonalisation, my body feels like it's made of wire covered in cotton wool, and I'm not sure where I end and the world begins. I also experience distinct parts/identities as part of my system with varying levels of amnesia between them/us.

In the US, there is a growing network of clinicians who openly write and present about their experience of dissociation. In her book Dissociation Made Simple, Dr Jamie Marich interviewed over 40 contributors who identified as having dissociative experiences within a phenomenological framework (Marich, 2023). I attended one of Dr Jamie Marich's trainings on Navigating Self-Disclosure and came away from this hopeful to bring more authenticity to my life and be less compartmentalised about the different aspects of it. I have struggled to find similar dialogues amongst therapists in the UK, however.

There is the development of some excellent work in the UK with regard to dissociative disorders more broadly. Carolyn Spring is an author, trainer, and speaker who writes beautifully about her experiences of having a dissociative disorder and produces resources for both survivors and professionals. When bits of her writing resonated with us, it offered a chink of hope. The Dissociative Disorders Alliance, a new charity in the UK by and for people living with complex dissociative disorders, is beginning to grow. The Complex Trauma and Dissociation Clinic (CTAD) makes thoughtful and informative YouTube videos about dissociation from a clinician's perspective, and The CTAD Clinic and The Pottergate Centre deliver training in the UK. However, there remains an inconsistency regarding whether there is any knowledge/recognition of dissociative disorders in specific UK health services. There certainly remains the them/us narrative within these spaces, and it at times feels uncomfortable and sometimes isolating to sit in both of these.

Despite the difficulties in accessing appropriate support, recognising and treating dissociative disorders works (Myrick et al., 2017), but it can take 5–12 years in treatment before a dissociative disorder diagnosis is made (Brand, Loewenstein & Spiegel, 2014). I had nine hospital admissions and had been trialled on 21 different medications before I was treated appropriately for a dissociative disorder and began to understand my experiences. Research suggests that lifetime prevalence for dissociative disorders ranges from 0.4% to 1.5% (Sar, 2011; Brand et al., 2016; Kate, Hopewood & Jamieson, 2019; Simeon & Putnam, 2022) – comparable with bipolar disorder and schizophrenia. I feel a sense of injustice that a condition with equivalent rates to psychosis is so poorly provided for and misunderstood in the National Health Service (NHS). Some clinicians believe they will never come across patients with this experience in their career. This is a discourse I have recently sat with in my current work life and bravely but quietly whispered the prevalence rates and more recent thinking on the condition. It has been hard, at times, to work within a system that does not always validate my experiences, even amongst colleagues who work with complex trauma. Encountering people who might reject the concept of dissociative identities/complex dissociation has sometimes led me to question the validity of my own experience and doubt my professional voice. If clinicians do not believe a condition exists, few will be willing to engage in service development and research related to it. It is one of the reasons I wanted to write this book chapter: to situate a misunderstood experience within a well-established theory. We are not serving our patients by perpetuating disbelief.

Judith L. Herman, MD, Trauma and Recovery

I first read *Trauma and Recovery: From Domestic Abuse to Political Terror* (1992) by Judith Herman (MD) in my 1920s, then revisited and discovered my dusty 2001 edition when I was completing my clinical psychology training. I was surprised to find scribbles all over the margins that may or may not have been mine. I would never have known in my 1920s how significant Herman's description of the stages of recovery from trauma would be for me/us. The fact that my 2001 copy is 292 pages long and the more recent 2022 edition has 469 pages reflects the developments that have occurred over the past 30 years and also the enduring relevance of this way of conceptualising healing from trauma.

Herman is a professor of psychiatry at Harvard Medical School and co-founder of the Victims of Violence Program at the Cambridge Hospital (US). Among some of her achievements are two award-winning books. She is a recipient of the Lifetime Achievement Award from the International Society for the Study of Trauma and Dissociation (ISSTD), received the Women in Science Award from the American Medical Women's Association, and is a distinguished Life Fellow of the American Psychiatric Association. She is thought to be one of the first to use the term Complex Post-Traumatic Stress Disorder (Herman, 1992), which was later introduced to the ICD-11. Her human and accessible way of speaking about difficult topics has helped me make sense of my experiences at several points in my life.

In Trauma and Recovery, Herman (1992) discusses collective forgetting/episodic amnesia that occurs periodically in relation to researching and advancing understanding of the impact of trauma. She suggested that this happens due to the difficulty we have in acknowledging and accepting that humans can inflict atrocities on others. This would certainly fit with the denial of the prevalence rates of dissociation. To acknowledge more accurate rates of dissociative disorders means acknowledging the extent to which humans can hurt one another and the impact of this on the continuity of the self. It has always resonated for me on a micro level as well as the global experience. There has been repeated forgetting from me and my parts over the course of my life. The dance of denial is easy to fall in and out of, particularly when colleagues and my treating healthcare professionals deny the existence of dissociative disorders.

Complex dissociative disorders usually result from developmental trauma, and as is often described in the context of Complex Post-Traumatic Stress Disorder; dissociation was a necessary and incredibly important cognitive strategy at the time of the trauma to survive, particularly where physical escape was not a possibility.

However, over time, it becomes less helpful to be so fragmented and dissociative (Boyer, Caplan & Edwards, 2022).

Herman (1992) outlines three stages of recovery from trauma: establishment of safety, remembrance and mourning, and (re)connection with everyday life. Thirty-two years after she wrote Trauma and Recovery, Herman published *Truth and Repair: How Trauma Survivors Envision Justice* (2023), where she describes a fourth and final stage of recovery from trauma – Justice. A collective responsibility we all have to seek justice.

Herman draws parallels between her conceptualisation of stages of recovery with the work of the French psychiatrist and philosopher Janet (1886), combat trauma (Scurfield, 1985), Post Traumatic Stress Disorder (Brown & Fromm, 1986) and the field of dissociative disorders (Putnam, 1989). Descriptions of the stages translate well when supporting patients with dissociative disorders, and the social and political context of her descriptions reflects a shift away from shaming the individual to a collective need to redress atrocities that lead to traumatisation.

Herman explains, 'Like any abstract concept, these stages of recovery are a convenient fiction, not to be taken too literally. They were an attempt to impose simplicity and order to a process that is inherently turbulent' (Herman, 1992, p.155). Herman's stages of recovery always appeared to me to represent a non-blaming, compassionate aid to living a complete and fulfilling life following traumatic experiences.

Safety

To begin the process of recovering from trauma, Herman (1992) describes the process of establishing a sense of safety and security in the survivor's external environment and inner world. The foundation of later stages of recovery is the development of safety and restoring control.

People must first be physically safe from harm, have their basic needs adequately met, develop supportive and safe interpersonal relationships, and enter a therapeutic alliance that respects trust and choice. With complex dissociative disorders, all parts have to feel safe and to trust the therapist and in the therapeutic process. For me, there was certainly a sense that all parts were checking my psychologist out to see if she could be trusted, and it took time to feel safe enough for things to start shifting in therapy. Internally, therapeutic work involves enhancing emotional regulation, reducing the intensity of symptoms, and developing strategies to manage intrusive memories, hyperarousal, and dissociation. Establishing a sense of stabilisation, re-establishing daily routines, and developing skills restoring a sense of agency is crucial. With more awareness of the things required to help my parts feel safe came a need to build in more routines/habits that helped all the parts. Herman explains, '*It is often tempting to overlook the requirements of safety and to rush headlong into the later stages of therapeutic work*' (Herman, 1992, 1997, 2015, 2022, p.249).

Recovery from trauma is not linear, and people may return to different stages as life dictates or when new information becomes available to the person. This is particularly true for the safety stage, as other stages of recovery may be destabilising, necessitating a return to the strategies developed at this stage. For me, different parts required different things to feel safe at different times, and different external and internal triggers destabilised each of them, which was incredibly confusing early on in trying to make sense of my experience.

Running alongside the denial/acceptance spiral for me was a deep need to understand my experiences so I could feel safe enough to begin processing my traumas. Perhaps this was a desire for clarity in an experience that was incredibly confusing, or perhaps it came from my role as a psychologist wanting to understand the theoretical base for my experience. As though understanding why this experience was happening would give validity to it. It was a source of distress that I couldn't find the right words to describe my experience, and it felt like shifting sands below my feet. In part, this was related to internalised shame and stigma surrounding complex dissociation, but also the parts had their own language and way of sense-making. Different theoretical frameworks describe the experience of separate parts of the self, such as Structural Dissociation (Van der Hart, Nijenhuis & Steele, 2006), Internal Family Systems (Schwartz, 1995), and Schema Therapy (Young, 1990). The most dominant in relation to these, and framed within the ISSTD guidelines, is Structural Dissociation. Using the language of structural dissociation initially helped me start to understand my multiplicity; however, latterly I prefer to use different ways to conceptualise my experience. The language felt shaming, and some of the narratives around these central theories did not fit with my clinical style of appraising theories and theorists. Finding the right language was incredibly important because it gave ownership over my lived experience. The right language, on my terms, provided some containment and a sense of safety to what was previously overwhelming.

I recall reading a paper my psychologist gave me about resourcing the parts, which explained that the only limits are the client and therapists' imagination to develop a sense of safety for all parts. Related to this, Fraser's 8-phase Dissociative Table Technique (Fraser, 1991, 2003) was incredibly helpful for me/us to enable a form of communication to help know what the parts needed. I came across this technique in my own Eye Movement Desensitisation and Reprocessing Therapy (EMDR) training. This is a structured technique to begin internal interaction, where imagery is used to invite parts to a room or meeting place to sit around a table together. For me, it was a way to begin to find out what the parts needed to feel safe, and it is something we revisited throughout therapy.

I now have an elaborate inner world of things to help the parts feel safe. Externally, the parts have things too. Recognising and acknowledging that I had younger parts allowed me to provide them with things in my everyday life. Things for them in the house, favourite foods, or a trip out of their choosing sometimes. It certainly helped intrusive spending. There were times I had to change my passwords on shopping apps and sometimes delete them, as parts were making purchases without my awareness. Meeting their needs means they have been thought about and considered, and ultimately meet the needs of the whole system. The struggle for them to be heard and the intrusions on my everyday life are fewer. There were definitely some negotiations needed regarding this book chapter and whether it felt safe to write about my experience, given the views of many of my colleagues. Some parts were fiercely against writing in 'non-work' time when they were meant to be able to do their own things. Some felt it was our duty to let people know they do not understand the experience, and some felt deep shame that I would share this intimate information. The use of Sam Fletcher as a pseudonym was negotiated as a compromise. I hope to feel safe enough to use my own name in the future.

Living as a system with little internal communication can be confusing, chaotic, and destabilising. Often, the usual tasks of everyday life can feel overwhelming, making the stage of stabilising routines difficult. We worked with an occupational therapist who helped us develop strategies to keep on top of day-to-day living, establishing habits, routines, and hacks to meet the needs of all the parts but also get basic life tasks done.

The parts hold different elements of my traumas and have different life experiences, so they all need different things to feel a sense of safety. They all communicate in different ways, and it was trial and error to know what they needed and what to do to give them that. It seemed to be slow progress, figuring all this out, and the remembering/forgetting dance I have been in all my life got in (and still sometimes gets) in the way when I have to 'realise' something I'd forgotten I'd already realised.

Remembrance and mourning

The second stage of recovery in Herman's model involves transforming traumatic memories to integrate them into the survivor's life story and give words to experiences. With dissociation, particularly, it can be difficult to have a coherent narrative, and so this stage supports the parts to process trauma memories and bring the narrative together. As Herman describes: '*Out of the fragmented components of frozen imagery and sensation, patients and therapist slowly reassemble an organised, detailed, verbal account, orientated in time and historical context*' (Herman, 1992, 1997, 2015, 2022, p.256). With dissociative disorders, often this will need to be done by and with different parts as they bring their differing experiences to the front. By doing this, the survivor can put words to their experience, reclaim a sense of authorship over their life that has meaning and perspective.

It has at times been helpful for me to be able to understand my experiences according to the diagnostic criteria, to make sense of and give words to what was going on at a very chaotic time in my life. Using the language of diagnosis and exploring it academically initially gave me some distance to tolerate exploring around the edges of my felt/lived experience, but it took a long time to be able to find words to fit my experience that I felt comfortable using. There was a fear that putting any words to my experience within therapy would acknowledge something that couldn't be unsaid. However, naming my experiences allowed healing to begin.

Herman (1992) described the descent into mourning as the most necessary and dreaded task of this stage of recovery, with a frightening and timeless quality. It involves grieving not only the traumatic events but also the consequences throughout life and for those with early trauma, of what was never theirs to lose. It allows for the expression of associated feelings that may have been denied for many years. It is easy to intellectualise the 'telling' of trauma experiences, particularly as a clinician. However, the stage of remembrance and mourning brings the meaning of events, related emotion, and sensation into the re-processing of memories.

Complex dissociation adds another layer of confusion to therapy, and it can be more difficult to disentangle everything. Once there was an acceptance of my dissociative experience, there was a huge outpouring and scramble from some of the parts to be at the front, to tell their story and to be heard. From others, there was a reluctance to be seen or even go to therapy. It makes sense that they all felt differently about it, but one consensus was the grief when felt experiences were shared. Having their experiences acknowledged made some of them very much more present, and I would often get blended with them without the ability to recognise that was what was happening. I cycled through clarity/overwhelm/destruction/denial/repair many times. I once found a box of things in my attic that I had very little recollection of, where some of the parts had been trying to communicate for years, which sent me down a spiral of confusion and grief for the missed opportunities for healing earlier in life.

Some days, I would want to try and understand and listen to the parts and feel so connected to them. I would feel empathy and was excited about what I could learn from them, what I could do for the parts, and make sense of things that had never made sense before. Then other days, I hated the idea. Self-stigma dismissed the whole concept of complex dissociative disorders, and I would slip back into denial. I would be overwhelmed with how difficult it was to be in touch with all these hurt and traumatised parts living inside me. I was scared to identify as someone who experienced such fragmentation because of what it said about me and how people would perceive me. I worried about the impact on my career if people 'found out'. I was very much coloured by the negative portrayals of the condition. How could I openly share an experience I knew many colleagues did not believe? It felt embarrassing, and there was a deep sense of shame to talk about these experiences, particularly when I was in touch with younger parts, as I had never spoken to anyone about them, and I didn't know how other people would respond. It meant that externally, we felt quite disconnected when we were trying so hard to connect, and it added additional layers of grief.

According to Herman (1992), this stage of recovery is never fully complete, as new challenges arise at different stages of life. However, a shift towards hope and energy occurs when the survivors' life story is reclaimed. For me (and my system), this was reclaiming the life stories of all the parts, and while this has been difficult at times, it has been a joy to experience.

Reconnection

Herman (1992) explains that empowerment and reconnection are the core experiences of recovery. In the final stage, the task is to rebuild a meaningful life beyond trauma. Reconnection involves reclaiming agency, experiencing a renewed sense of identity, and often developing, re-establishing, or deepening relationships. For me, in addition to deepening relationships between the parts, it was also about integrating the experience of having parts into my life and work. When I spoke about my experience of having parts with my close friends, it was such a relief, and their compassionate and accepting response was incredibly freeing. I hope this acceptance will become more commonplace in clinical practice.

It's fun to be in touch with some of the parts. It's also been interesting to see how their experiences change. I thought they would remain the same way indefinitely, and I would just find ways to cope, but they haven't. Some of them have learned new things and been able to update to know that I have a different life now. It's nice experiencing them learn new things. One part feels very clever that she can access the knowledge I have gained as an adult, and she likes to express her preference for Janet over Freud. Some of the parts are fiercely protective, others sensible, joyous, or mischievous, and I can draw on those experiences too when everybody isn't so dissociated away.

I am never lonely living as a system, and being part of a team to tackle life experiences collaboratively is incredibly helpful. Many of the parts have different perspectives on topics, and we often use this to consider decisions, where in the past, I would often be frozen with indecision and confusion. Recognising that competing wishes/desires/beliefs are coexisting helps unstick us and opens up opportunities to try new things or different ways of being.

Greater communication between the parts has meant that we are able to share the enthusiasm everyone has for their interests. Allowing the parts to engage in activities that interest them has meant many of the parts have been able to experience them too. For example, many of the parts enjoy nature, and one in particular likes spotting and photographing fungi. This is one of the few activities that many of the parts can participate in together. We often have the most useful internal dialogues when walking through woods. Which is interesting when you consider that Shapiro (2001) began developing the concept of using bilateral stimulation in EMDR when out walking in a park. Perhaps the bilateral stimulation when we walk in the woods helps regulate or process the content of our internal conferences.

Herman's (1992) conceptualisation of recovery from trauma and the move towards reconnection maps onto the guidelines for treating complex dissociative disorders published by The International Society for the Study of Trauma and Dissociation (International Society for the Study of Trauma and Dissociation [ISSTD], 2011, third Ed., in revision). These guidelines also describe a phase-oriented treatment approach, including: (1) establishing safety, stabilisation, and reduction of symptoms; (2) confronting, working through, and integrating traumatic memories; and (3) integration and rehabilitation of the identity. For me, integration has involved getting to know my parts, the roles they played, what their needs are, and meeting those needs so I can live a full life with more coherence, kindness, and fewer intrusions of dissociative experiences. Integration for us is (re)connection, communication, and collaboration with all the parts. As the parts started to experience connection and compassion for each other, they facilitated each other's journey towards recovery and provided support to the whole system at times of distress.

Integrating internal worlds and external roles

Writing this chapter prompted me to reread my PhD thesis in Cognitive Psychology, which I completed before my clinical training. Ironically, the topic was memory processes, and one of the final chapters of my thesis starts with the quote '*A retentive memory may be a good thing, but the ability to forget is the true token of greatness*' (Hubbard & Hubbard, 1923). I was interested in references to literature suggesting that there was no widespread empirical evidence uncovering marked differences in the memory processes of traumatised and non-traumatised individuals (see Rubin, Berntsen & Bohni, 2008). I discuss the oft-reported notion that emotional memories are remembered with greater clarity and accuracy, referred to as the modulation hypothesis (McGaugh, Chaill & Roozendaal, 1996).

Much of my thesis discusses the various ways in which memory is universally fallible and vulnerable to reconstruction. It was difficult in therapy to be comfortable with the intangible nature of the parts' experiences when there was also a part that held these very academic theories and would use that to invalidate our internal experience and add waves of cognitive dissonance.

During the writing of this chapter, I was considering whether my understanding had changed or whether this still maps onto my experience. Herman discussed George Orwell's 'Doublethink' from his novel 1984 (Orwell, 1949); the ability to simultaneously hold two opposing thoughts and beliefs without cognitive dissonance. Was that at play when I was writing my thesis perhaps? I also sometimes wonder whether a different part or different parts were around during my PhD days, as my research team.

When I decided to become a clinical psychologist, I questioned whether my experience of mental illness would be detrimental to my career. When I had to take significant periods off from work, I didn't know if I would ever be able to go back. I became very unwell when the traumatised parts of me were activated, and I didn't know if I would return from that place. Moving towards increased conscious awareness of the different parts of my system at times made it more difficult to keep the parts as separate as they had been, and I sometimes felt less confident about my ability to manage competing demands coming from a number of parts simultaneously. I recall a time period where there was difficulty navigating and negotiating wearing 'work clothes', resolved by a compromise of wearing fun socks. Ultimately, connecting with all parts and giving them what they needed to be seen, heard, and helped brought me back to myself/ourselves.

I don't think experience of mental illness necessarily makes people better clinicians, but I think it does give a different and sometimes helpful perspective. The compartmentalisation that is intrinsic to dissociation has also been incredibly helpful in my focus at work, and in holding multiple perspectives simultaneously.

I found connecting with the parts to give them what they need left more room and space to enjoy work. I also feel my journey towards a more compassionate internal experience has translated into a greater capacity for holding others with compassion.

I was treated in the same organisation I worked in, which, at times, was incredibly difficult, particularly when I knew colleagues doubted the validity of complex dissociative experiences. It was crucial, however, to connect with my parts and invite them into my everyday life in a way that meets their needs and the needs of the whole system to live a more coherent life both in and out of work. I reflected at the conclusion of my therapy with my psychologist on the experience of being colleagues while also in a patient/therapist relationship. When we saw her at work outside the therapy room, some of the parts would later express confusion about why she was not there just for us. My psychologist observed that we often used the knowledge of our profession to our advantage in having a shared language and understanding to build on, and ultimately, this helped my recovery.

The legacy of controversy, stigma, and negative portrayals as barriers to recovery

The controversies related to the repressed memory/false memory debates, labelled the 'memory wars' from the 1990s (Crews, 1995), in combination with the stigmatised portrayal of dissociative disorders, have led to widespread disbelief and erasure of dissociative experiences to this day. When I come across current literature that expresses this, it can still sometimes rock the sense of safety and stability that came with understanding my system and that we fought so hard to achieve. Few clinicians question that depression and anxiety are 'real'. We don't expect those people to prove these experiences; why are dissociative disorders considered differently? Brand et al. (2016) expressed that even after four decades of work, a developing and authoritative evidence base, unsubstantiated myths about dissociative disorders still abound.

In 2020, the British Psychological Society published a position paper regarding clinical psychologists with lived experience of mental health difficulties (Hogg & Kemp, 2020). This supported the unique and valued contribution that lived experience of mental health difficulties brings to individuals working within clinical psychology. There are certainly more clinical psychologists discussing and sharing their experiences of mental health difficulties. In an anonymous online survey, two-thirds of qualified clinical psychologists disclosed that they had personal experience of mental health difficulties (Tay, Alcock & Scior, 2018). However, the paper cites that more than half of the respondents were reluctant to disclose to colleagues and superiors, and clinicians discussing their experience of dissociative disorders still seems to be lacking in the UK, which can feel professionally isolating at times.

Marie and Miles (2008) found that perceived dangerousness was more strongly associated with schizophrenia (which is often conflated with dissociative disorders) than depression or substance abuse/dependence. Tay et al. (2018) also suggest that mental health difficulties that are more visible, or perceived as more dangerous, also attract higher levels of stigma. There are often stereotypical views portrayed in the media that those with dissociative disorders are dangerous (see the movies Split and Fight Club). These issues make it difficult for people to talk about their experiences, and it has certainly impacted my willingness to disclose my experiences. However, it is only by opening a dialogue that we can shift narratives surrounding dissociative disorders.

Dissociative disorders are sometimes considered fad diagnoses or driven by a 'TikTok generation' appropriating symptoms seen on social media despite the published prevalence rates. I found this narrative particularly difficult to sit with when I was at the beginning of the process of making sense of my experiences. It was invalidating and would often send me back into the spiral of denying my experience. Some of my experiences ARE odd and unusual and make no sense out of the context of a dissociative disorder. I would feel shame in allowing some of the younger parts to express themselves. For example, as a bookish clinician, it would be embarrassing if people saw some of the (excellent) collections of Teenage Mutant Ninja Turtles we had if I hadn't got the chance to put them away when an unexpected visitor called. This was a recurring theme during my therapy; allowing expression for the younger parts, which felt freeing and healing, but shameful when I would come across something that said it might be 'wrong'.

My parts have different likes/wants/needs/strengths, and one particularly enjoyed researching descriptions of dissociation seen in literature for over 200 years to counter the idea that this is a new concept. There are varying thoughts about the origins of the experience and description of dissociation, whether it be the physician Benjamin Rush in the early 1800s, descriptions in the novel Moby Dick by Herman Melville in the 1850s, or the French psychiatrist and philosopher Pierre Janet in the 1880s. Michelle Proust, the French novelist, critic, and essayist, gave rich descriptions of dissociation in his novel Swann's Way, published in 1913. There was a sense of relief in my system on discovering the concept of dissociation had longevity in literature and academia.

An invitation to colleagues

I remember being in hospital, not being believed that I didn't remember how I was detained under the Mental Health Act, that I didn't know where I was, what had happened or that I couldn't remember the last few days. I experienced no sense of safety either internally, because I was so confused about my experience, or externally, as the healthcare professionals supporting me were unable, or unwilling, to acknowledge what was going on. Having dissociative experiences is upsetting and distressing in its own right. When you try to make sense of it by talking to a healthcare professional, and you are disbelieved, it is doubly heartbreaking. The negative impact it had on me was huge. It was transformative when I met a clinician who responded to my experiences and was able to provide appropriate treatment, and when I spoke to others who lived as a system. I want other people who experience dissociative disorders to be able to access this too, to create a life that includes the richness and fullness that comes with knowing your parts.

Few specific pathways for dissociative disorders exist in the NHS to enable this to happen, and there are currently no UK NHS treatment guidelines, which perpetuates the view that it is a rare phenomenon. At this time, South London and Maudsley NHS Foundation Trust remains the only NHS organisation to host a service for clients with dissociative disorders in the UK. A recently published book, *Working with Dissociation in Clinical Practice: Guidance for Mental Health Professionals and Multidisciplinary Teams* (Ed. Crockford, Goodwin & Langthornem, 2026), supported by The Association of Clinical Psychologists UK (ACPUK), represents a shift towards more widespread recognition. The book brings together experts by occupation and experience to offer practical strategies and processes for working with dissociative patients in a non-stigmatising and balanced way. I hope that the voice of lived experience practitioners will become more present in these dialogues.

It is an injustice that people are not able to access support and treatment that works. In Herman's recent book *Truth and Repair: How Trauma Survivors Envision Justice (1992),* her description of justice as the fourth and final stage of recovery resonated with me, particularly as a clinician who has experienced systemic abuse, both developmentally and within some of the treatment I received in services. These experiences have certainly led me to be a strong advocate for my service user population, at least in part, because so many in my system can understand what it is like not to be heard. This stage conceptualises reparative justice as a responsibility of us all, particularly those in positions of power, inherent in our role as clinicians. Herman (1992) asserts that trauma is not just an individual wound but a social rupture. Healing can't be done privately, in isolation, but needs social acknowledgement and to be recognised as a collective responsibility to seek justice. If experiences of complex dissociation are denied, minimised or silenced, this is not possible. To embody the justice Herman envisions, clinicians need to be witnesses, collaborators, and participants in repair – not gatekeepers or sceptics. For me, sharing my experiences as I have in this chapter is another step towards reparative justice for me, all my parts, and others who have dissociative experiences.

I invite colleagues to listen to their patients with openness and to hold space for experiences that don't always align with familiar frameworks based on outdated views of dissociative disorders. This enables us to contribute to a culture of practice that is kinder and more compassionate, supporting patients in reclaiming agency and integrating their experiences into a broader life narrative.

Believing patients' experiences is an act of kindness, but also a clinical intervention in its own right and a first step towards restorative justice. How can we support our patients if we don't believe their experiences? Recognition of dissociation and those who live with it should not be optional; it is an ethical and compassionate choice our profession must make.

Notes

1 I will generally write from a first-person perspective as me/I, the clinician writing this chapter. However, I will also talk about us/we/they/them when discussing my parts and us as a collective.

2 The main diagnostic manuals that describe Dissociative Disorders are The Diagnostic and Statistical Manual of Mental Disorders, fifth edition (DSM-5) and The International Classification of Diseases – 11 (ICD-11).

References

An online educational program for individuals with dissociative disorders and their clinicians: 1-Year and 2-year follow-up. *Journal of Trauma Stress*, 32(1), 156–166.

Boyer, S. M., Caplan, J. E., & Edwards, L. K. (2022). Trauma-related dissociation and the dissociative disorders: Neglected symptoms with severe public health consequences. *Delaware Journal of Public Health*, 8(2), 78–84.

Brand, B. L., Loewenstein, R. J., & Spiegel, D. (2014). Dispelling myths about dissociative identity disorder treatment: An empirically based approach. *Psychiatry*, 77(2), 169–189.

Brand, B. L., Sar, V., Stavropoulos, P., Krüger, C., Korzekwa, M., Martínez-Taboas, A., & Middleton, W. (2016). Separating fact from fiction: An empirical examination of six myths about dissociative identity disorder. *Harvard Review of Psychiatry*, 24(4), 257–270.

Brown, D. P., & Fromm, E. (1986). *Hypnotherapy and Hypnoanalysis* (1st ed.). Hillside, NJ: Lawrence Erlbaum Associates.

Crews, F. (1995). *The Memory Wars: Freud's Legacy in Dispute*. New York: The New York Review of Books.

Crockford, H., Goodwin, M., & Langthornem P. (2026). *Working with Dissociation in Clinical Practice: Guidance for Mental Health Professionals and Multidisciplinary Teams.* Routledge: Oxon – New York.

Fraser, G. A. (1991). The dissociative table technique. A strategy for working with ego states in dissociative disorders and ego-state therapy. *Dissociation*, VI(1), 205–213.

Fraser, G. A. (2003). Fraser's "dissociative table technique" revisited, revised: A strategy for working with ego states in dissociative disorders and ego-state therapy. *Journal of Trauma & Dissociation*, 4(4), 5–28.

Herman, J. L. (1992). Complex PTSD: A syndrome in survivors of prolonged and repeated trauma. *Journal of Traumatic Stress*, 5(3), 377–391.

Herman, J. L. (1992, 1997, 2015, 2022). *Trauma and Recovery*. Basic Books: New York.

Herman, J. L. (2023). *Truth and Repair, How Trauma Survivors Envision Justice.* Basic Books: London.

Hogg, C., & Kemp, N. (2020). *Statement on Clinical Psychologists with Lived Experience of Mental Health Difficulties*. Leicester: The British Psychological Society, Division of Clinical Psychology.

Hubbard, E., & Hubbard, B. (1923). *Selected Writings of Elbert Hubbard: His Mintage of Wisdom, Coined from a Life of Love, Laughter and Work.* New York: W. H. Wise & Co.

International Society for the Study of Trauma and Dissociation. (2011). Guidelines for treating dissociative identity disorder in adults, Third Revision. *Journal of Trauma & Dissociation*, 12(2), 115–187.

Janet, P. (1886). Les actes inconscients et le dédoublement de la personnalité. *Review of Philosophy*, 22(2), 212–223.

Kate, M. A., Hopwood, T., & Jamieson, G. (2019). The prevalence of dissociative disorders and dissociative experiences in college populations: A meta-analysis of 98 studies. *Journal of Trauma & Dissociation*, 21(1), 16–61.
Marich, J. (2023). *Dissociation Made Simple*. North Atlantic Books: Berkely, CA.
Marie, D., & Miles, B. (2008). Social distance and perceived dangerousness across four diagnostic categories of mental disorder. *Australian & New Zealand Journal of Psychiatry*, 42(2), 126–133.
McGaugh, J. L., Cahill, L., & Roozendaal, B. (1996). Involvement of the amygdala in memory storage: Interaction with other brain systems. *Proceedings of the National Academy of Sciences of the United States of America*, 93(24), 13508–13514.
Myrick, A., Webermann, A., Loewenstein, R., Lanius, R., Putnam, F., & Brand, B. (2017). Six-year follow-up of the treatment of patients with dissociative disorders study. *European Journal of Psychotraumatology*, 8(1), 1344080.
Orwell, G. (1949). *Nineteen Eighty-Four*. London. Penguin Classics.
Putnam, F. (1989). *Diagnosis and Treatment of Multiple Personality Disorder*. Gilford Press: New York.
Rubin, D. C., Berntsen, D., & Bohni, M. K. (2008 Oct). A memory-based model of post-traumatic stress disorder: Evaluating basic assumptions underlying the PTSD diagnosis. *Psychological Review*, 115(4), 985–1011.
Sar, V. (2011). Epidemiology of dissociative disorders: An overview. *Epidemiology Research International*, 2011(1). Article ID 404538. https://doi.org/10.1155/2011/404538
Schwartz, R. C. (1995). *Internal Family Systems Therapy.* New York: Guilford Press.
Scurfield, R. M. (1985). Post-trauma stress assessment and treatment: Overview and formulations. In Figley, C. R. (ed.), *Trauma and Its Wake: The Study and Treatment of Post-Traumatic Stress Disorder.* New York: Brunner/Mazel, pp. 219–256.
Shapiro, F. (2001). *Eye Movement Desensitization and Reprocessing: Basic Principles, Protocols, and Procedures* (2nd ed.). New York: Guilford Press.
Simeon, D., & Putnam, F. (2022). Pathological dissociation in the national comorbidity survey replication (NCS- R): Prevalence, morbidity, comorbidity, and childhood maltreatment. *Journal of Trauma & Dissociation*, 23(5), 490–503.
Tay, S., Alcock, K., & Scior, K. (2018). Mental health problems among clinical psychologists: Stigma and its impact on disclosure and help-seeking. *Journal of Clinical Psychology*, 74(9), 1545–1555.
Van der Hart, B., Nijenhuis, E. R. S., & Steele, K. (2006). *The Haunted Self: Structural Dissociation and the Treatment of Chronic Traumatization.* W. W. Norton & Company: New York and London.
Young, J. E. (1990). *Cognitive Therapy for Personality Disorders: A Schema-Focused Approach.* Sarasota, FL: Professional Resource Exchange, Inc.

Resources

Beacon House. https://beaconhouse.org.uk
Carolyn Spring. https://www.carolynspring.com/
Clinic for Dissociative Studies (CDS). https://clinicds.org.uk
Complex Trauma & Dissociation Clinic (CTAD). https://www.cheshirepsychology.com/ctad-clinic/
Dissociative Disorders Alliance (DDA). https://thedissociativedisordersalliance.org.uk/

Dr Jamie Marich. https://www.instituteforcreativemindfulness.com/about-dr-jamie-marich/
South London and Maudsley NHS National Trauma and Dissociation Service. https://slam.nhs.uk/service-detail/service/trauma-and-dissociation-service-280
The Pottergate Centre for Dissociation and Trauma. https://dissociation.co.uk/

Chapter 4

The embodied therapist – meaning-making with Merleau-Ponty

Helen Molden

Introduction

The story of how it starts is never the same. For some, it is present from birth, or even before, in the intergenerational and epigenetic story. For others, it is an acute trauma or an abrupt eruption of the mind and body asserting itself in a novel, in an alarming and unwelcome way. Or a gradual onset of mysterious happenings that morphed into symptoms, an entity that could not be ignored, then a diagnosis (or perhaps not) delivered by a medical professional. With every exacerbation or flare up, the lived experience of disability can be exhausting, unpredictable, scary, and more.

As humans, we bring our own sense of meaning-making, with many layers. In seeking therapy, we look to understand something of that story, in exploration with another, engaged in supporting that process. You could say to lay down a psycho-geographical map, which can support the client in moving forward. As a psychologist and psychotherapist with lived experience of disability, for me this story-making remains complex, a mix of the personal and the professional. For those with lived experience of disability, each story contains a wealth of emotions, pain, and expertise, alongside the demands of their condition.

As a counselling psychologist and integrative psychotherapist, I have worked with clients across their lifespan, based in hospitals, primary care, and in the community. This has often emphasised the impact of living with challenging physical health, e.g. working with young people living with Type 1 diabetes, or home-visits to support those living with MS. I often introduce a metaphor that I have found useful, that living with a disability can be like having a demanding member of the family who snuck in, uninvited and (at least initially) unwelcome, but is there every day, even before you open your eyes on waking.

Within this chapter, I share something of my own story-making process and how that informs my work, through the theoretical lens of Merleau-Ponty who put the body at the centre of his view of the self and its relationship to the world. He was a French philosopher and phenomenologist (1908–1961), as well as a lecturer on child psychology and education, political journalist, active in the resistance movement against Nazi-occupied France, economist, and author.

DOI: 10.4324/9781003636014-5

The existential philosophers who promoted phenomenological ideas, mainly in the first half of the twentieth century, each had their own interest, focusing on the descriptive approach of everyday experience at the core of phenomenological theory. Husserl, for example, was concerned more with the intra-individual (1913/1982), Sartre the existential (1943/2003). However, Merleau-Ponty offers an important and distinctive approach. Merleau-Ponty's (1945/2012) concept of the "lived body", known in the text as "corps vécu", highlights the embodied self as the primary way of being-in-the-world, with intersubjectivity at its core.

As a clinician, I have been drawn to the ideas put forward by Merleau-Ponty (1945/2012) as they have a landscape-like bottom-up quality, which I find useful for reflection. While the medical model segments into an ontological duality of mental or physical health, living with an illness or disability is an overall process impacting your whole body, mind, and sense of identity. You are both a mind and a body that act as one intentional breathing entity, within an ever-changing context. Any disruption to how we work and act in the world is a disruption not just to how we function, but also to the processes by which we create meaning in our lives. The dilemma (whether client or therapist) is how to acknowledge and process the disruption and create a new meaning for the embodied self that works for you.

Below, I look at how some elements of that process, including acceptance, agency, and autonomy, can play out in the therapeutic relationship, when living with disability is in the phenomenal field. The phenomenal field is a way of describing the world, and its people and objects, as it appears to us. I argue that three key phenomenological concepts by Merleau-Ponty are useful here. Firstly, around the lived body, the corps vécu, as subject, emphasising lived experience and autonomy over diagnostic categories; secondly, reflections around intersubjectivity and the healing dynamic; and thirdly, the idea of the body as a creative and adaptive agent. In combination with practices from acceptance commitment therapy (ACT) and compassionate-focused therapy (CFT), these aspects of theory form the bedrock of my clinical practice and self-care.

I will examine the usefulness and limitations in the phenomenological approach posited by Merleau-Ponty, the challenges and moments of connection between therapist and client that can occur when either, or both, live with visible or hidden disability. I argue that in its very emphasis on the intertwined nature of human experience and the world, these ideas offer a theoretical framework for the co-creating of a psycho-geographical map to benefit those living with disability, such that the whole self can be seen and explored. The phenomenological idea, initiated by Husserl (1913/1982), of returning to the phenomena – things as they are in the world – provides a touchstone in the here-and-now that can often helpfully cast doubt on mainstream assumptions about disability, e.g. around loss, usefulness, function, and appearance.

As a psychologist, I work alongside the medical model – the predominant model that holds power within the NHS and healthcare services. It is reductionist, seeking to isolate and address the immediate symptoms causing distress. It does so within an economic structure with limited resources for meeting expanding healthcare demands. While it can undoubtedly be improved, I am not arguing that it should be summarily discarded. Rather that, taken alone, as both an explanatory and therapeutic model, its spotlight is too narrow. Merleau-Ponty's (1945/2012) phenomenological framework, an embodied relationally constructed view of disability, can contribute an important additional layer. It offers validation to the therapist living with disability and their clients, both in its emphasis on diverse modes of embodied being, and its querying of pathologising medical norms.

Happily, we are hearing more in general discourse of the diversity and heterogeneity of peoples' lived experience of living with disability or a chronic health condition. We no longer need just to look to the seminal text by Susan Sontag (2002) for guidance on navigating the *dual kingdoms of the well and the sick* at the beginning of "*Illness as Metaphor*" (2002, p3). Writers and campaigners such as Frances Ryan (activist and journalist for *The Guardian)* and actor Liz Carr (known amongst other roles for her regular character in BBC crime drama Silent Witness 2013–2020) cover important debates from pragmatic issues such as transport, healthcare, and jobs to assisted dying.

Clinicians who have become insider-experts through their own health challenges and disability have made important contributions, for example Dr Grace Spence Green's (2025) excellent *To Exist As I Am* where she speaks of some of the terrifying, scary, and isolating moments in facing life post-incident, with a spinal injury (p19ff). What struck me reading it is how early in the process as a patient, Spence Green (2025) feels she must manage others' emotions and response to what has happened – family, friends, and healthcare professionals, in particular, one healthcare worker who is seemingly speechless at the visible traumatic outcome in caring for Grace. This plays out while she is coming to terms with her own process and functioning in the here and now of living with recovery and disability.

Spence Green (2025) also comments on the way in which society cannot seem to view living with a disability from a neutral standpoint, as just part of everyday normal experience (p154). Instead, there is a pressure "*that I must do something extraordinary that proves I still have value in society...it must be something grand. I must overcome my disability, be tragically triumphant. There is no space for mediocrity here*" (p147).

The academic and "Alice" biographer Professor Robert Douglas-Fairhurst (2023) writes with great perspicacity and acuity on his life changes due to a diagnosis of MS, in *Metamorphosis: A Life in Pieces*. Offering the reader an engaging way into his material, with Lewis Carrollian backwards chapters, he interweaves the personal with the professional, showing how the tacit trust in our own bodies can be degraded both gradually and then suddenly, as a progressive condition gains hold.

Douglas-Fairhurst (2023) makes similar points to Spence Green (2025) about the experience of being in hospital. For example, despite the kindness of staff, as a patient hooked up to machines, autonomy and some identity can feel lost within the machine system, and too often the healthcare professionals' gaze is that of the other solving a puzzle.

Resistance

My story started with day-dreaming and dissociation. Looking back, I now see that early on at school, I made an unconscious decision to tune out my body as much as possible. It was frightening and unpredictable with dizzy spells, as well as continual coughs, mucus, and infections. At university, sick again, but trying to keep up with my philosophy classes, I welcomed and played with the idea of retreating purely to an intellectual realm, the so-called Brain in a Vat (BIV) argument, popularised by the philosopher Hilary Putnam (1981). Perhaps this life, including difficult health episodes, was all just sensations fed by computer, a somatic reduction. After all, Western philosophy has long sought to prioritise the rational or the mind, seen as early as the Greek philosopher Plato c. 375 BCE as being superior to the more morally suspect and unreliable body (Phato, 2014, 2007). Using dissociation, I minimised the continual respiratory infections, balance issues, ear pain, and fatigue and with it, diminished many aspects of the embodied.

But the foul productive cough, so difficult to mask, would not let up. Not to mention much of life I just dropped out of, from doctoral training, work events to innumerable family and social fun times, and just everyday life. Clearly, I was just unlucky to be so seemingly susceptible to respiratory and sinus bugs, with frequently burning lungs and fatigue.

Purely by chance, working as a psychologist in a large hospital, I discovered my mysterious symptoms were jigsaw pieces of a systemic genetic condition that impacts ciliary function, especially in key places such as the lungs, reproductive, and sinus systems. Between the exhaustion of family responsibilities and reluctance to consider myself a caring professional, as needing support, it took several years to accept that this condition, primary ciliary dyskinesia (PCD), best explained my story. And with resistance finally subsiding, I returned to the writings of Merleau-Ponty, first met at university, and his bottom-up approach of curiosity of the things themselves.

Merleau-Ponty's (1945/2012) insistence that I return to the embodied view of the self entailed sitting down at the table to have a real conversation with that unwelcome family member alluded to earlier. The one that shows up every day uninvited, in different forms, throwing plans and spontaneity, into dispute. One that would require me to change my job, lifestyle, and attitude to medicine to look after myself.

Below, I outline something of my oscillating response to Merleau-Ponty's lived body challenge, how it helps in navigating a world, and clinical practice as a psychologist living with a (largely hidden) condition that requires daily attention in different ways (medication, physiotherapy, exercise, medical aids, self-care for emotional health). This alongside my appreciation and gratitude for the regular NHS PCD clinics and support from my partner and sons. Please note that examples below drawn from clinical work are abstractions for illustrative purposes, not specific to any individual or given set of circumstances, exceptions are where they relate to my own condition.

Rediscovery – the lived body – corps vécu

However, the story started, by the time you reach the middle parts, on the medical model, the process consists of pulling apart, of seeing what works, what doesn't, and what can be done about it. When someone arrives at therapy, usually, the body has already been segmented, broken up, by the medical model in its attempts to gain control. These are useful (often vital and life-saving functions), but they are not the whole story.

This first section of the theoretical framework looks at how Merleau-Ponty's (1945/2012) active embodied engagement in the world sees the "lived body" as a subject with its own agenda, which he describes as "*projects*". The sense of agency is figural from the beginning as we see from this quotation which outlines the essential function of the body as a "*vehicle of being*" busy with "*projects*" as the main way of the self-engaging with and meaning-making in the world: "*The body is the vehicle of being in the world and, for a living being, having a body means being united with a definite milieu, merging with certain projects, and being perpetually engaged therein*" (p171). These projects are not defined by any normative or default sense, and neither is the world. Philosophically, the world is already there prior to reflective thought, not an entity created through our consciousness. Merleau-Ponty (1945/2012) writes that phenomenology is "*a philosophy for which the world is always 'already there' before reflection begins....*" (Preface, plxxxiii).

With clients, and initially for myself, there is talk of "previously...and since" usually with an urgent sense of wanting to go back to normal. As a therapist with lived experience of disability, to establish a good working alliance, I find it is important to listen, repeatedly check in, clarify, and understand the details of the disruption, and the client's understanding. And in listening, to ourselves and clients, Merleau-Ponty's (1945/2012) bottom-up approach invites us to reunite the whole – piece by piece, thing by thing, event by event with the many emotions attached, a welcome emphasis on the lived experience.

Philosophically a corrective to Cartesian dualism and detachment, with its split mind and body, Merleau-Ponty (1945/2012) offers a description-focused approach "*Phenomenology involves describing, and not explaining or analysing*"' (Preface, plxxi), the latter phrase following Husserl who first outlined phenomenological ideas. This is knowledge through perception, over scientific explanation, which frames our sense of our minds and bodies, and the gestalt of their interaction, differently from that offered by the realism and idealism that dominates Western philosophy. Perception, thought, and action are not imposed on the body by a detached mind as sense data but experienced through it. Later on, in the Phenomenology of Perception his main work to outline these ideas, Merleau-Ponty (1945/2012) uses a metaphor to emphasis the body's centrality "*One's own body is in the world just as the heart is in the organism: it continuously breathes life into the visible spectacle, animates it and nourishes it from within, and forms a system with it*" (p209).

The body is instrumental, a way of engaging with the world, which mean actions have intention but an essential openness or incompleteness as we make sense of the world: "*the unfinished nature of phenomenology and the inchoate style in which in proceeds are not the sign of failure; they were inevitable because phenomenology's task was to reveal the mystery of the world and the mystery of reason*" (Merleau-Ponty 1945/2012, Preface, pp.lxxxiv–lxxxv). Thus, thinking in terms of psychological formulation, actions that might be seen as protective or perpetuating factors are always situated in a world of, for example "I may be supported by others (or not)", "I may have resources to help me (or not)", making up a complex nuanced subjective story. Plus, that story has a continual feel, an incompleteness which sits with our ability to not know, and for that to be ok. In returning to the phenomena as experienced, we return to ourselves, the patient as an embodied-being-in-the-world, an emphasis that can often be lost in anonymity of the medical model.

Just as for clients living with a disability (visible or hidden), recognising diverse modes of being in the world, from an embodied self, can be validating for me as a psychologist living with a disability. It reminds me that the "lived body" experience which clients bring to therapy is always varied and positional in its viewpoint. It emphasises the detail required for the collaborative work, when we consider that most lived experience of disability, and illness exacerbations of it, are diffuse, experienced differently at different times as we go through the lifespan.

The philosopher Reynolds (2017) has summarised, "*Merleau-Ponty, in his early critiques of objectivism and intellectualism and across his oeuvre, consistently pushes against reductions of the body that fail to attend to the multiplicity of its always meaningful relations*" (p419). This again emphasises the novelty of what Merleau-Ponty was doing by placing the embodied experience as not just central to phenomenology but always in relationship to self and other. I am arguing that his framework of meaning creation through the lived body both expands description and helps to undermine the pathologising norms that ascribe an experience of disability as automatically categorised with loss, pain, harm, and vulnerability. The latter being what Reynolds terms as the "*ableist conflation*" (Reynolds, 2017, p421), an attitude and set of assumptions around disability that have historically held power within social discourse.

For therapists and clients with lived experience of disability or health conditions in a world essentially structured for normative bodies, the act of their experiences being acknowledged and shared helps shake the dominance of pathological, *less-than* presentation often reported by clients, negotiating the NHS system.

The above point has recently been explored by the work of the philosophy professor Carel (2016) who uses autoethnography to extrapolate from her own experience of lung disease in her philosophical analysis of chronic illness. Carel argues that the phenomenological approach offers a crucial extra layer as it can augment what she terms the naturalistic or objective medical approach.

Both are valid explanatory models, useful depending on the context and therapeutic aims and goals, though Carel (2023) goes further than my earlier proposal of Merleau-Ponty's (1945/2012) framework as a contributory layer to the patient narrative in her suggestion the "*biomedical model is incomplete for care*" (Carel, 2023). However, I concur with Carel that the phenomenological approach can give patient and therapist a comprehensive insight into how the patient "*encounters (the) body as painfully-lived*" (Carel, 2023), not just a focus on dysfunction and limitations.

In contrast, the medical model by its nature reinforces the sense of less than or loss, with the language often one of fighting, of battle of "*living with the enemy*" (Owen, 2014). Within this there can be an objectification and potentially a disavowal of parts that break down, as if they are somehow no longer part of us, or at least not seen as being in any use to us. This might even include parts vital to our processes but with which we have little or no direct experience. The philosopher and medical doctor Leder (2023) in The Healing Body makes the valuable point that so many of our embodied aspects are outside our direct experience, i.e. I have no conscious knowledge of how my liver works – I cannot see it or feel it – I just know that it is there working ...until an issue arises in bloodwork or other symptomology. Leder's (2023) book is the final in his trilogy where he explores a variety of existential healing responses to bodily change and breakdown, including Merleau-Ponty's ideas. Instead of objectifying parts of our embodied self (direct or indirectly experienced) that no longer function as they once did, a wider range of emotions, thoughts, and behaviours can be explored through a more forensic level of description.

For example, a self-compassionate inquiry as to how my ear feels and connects to the world, in its muted, pressured, and painful state, reminds me that to be a good enough therapist, I do not need perfect hearing. Intentional listening happens as a whole-body experience (including technology provided by hearing aids). Sometimes I will use a soundscape creative activity (e.g. close your eyes and for five minutes draw or mark everything you hear on a page, using variety to delineate each sound and positioning, then reflect on this, what is figural, what less so) as a way of grounding myself before clinic, a useful checking-in exercise.

Within therapeutic work, clients bring many themes around bodily sensations, autonomy, and environment, e.g. within conditions such as diabetes, gastrointestinal, or cardiac aspects of the lived body, where technology is essential to the processes by which the body functions. In "My World" pictures where children are asked to draw whatever is important to them and represents things that make up their world, I am struck by how many children with Type 1 diabetes draw worlds full of technology, usually in greys and blacks – big images of items that puncture, wound, incessantly spew out numbers, and keep them alive.

A theoretical approach such as the "lived body" encourages more curiosity around meanings of the nexus of technology and body – in what ways might it add and detract from activities that matter to the young person in their daily life? It allows for a "both...and" continuum and exploration, highlighting the multiplicity of meanings around subjective experience.

However, in considering objects meeting with the embodied self, and in particular items that support living with disabilities, Merleau-Ponty (1945/2012) has drawn criticism. His exposition of the blind man's cane as being no longer an object for the blind man but part of his body is a core part of his conveying the essence of the nexus of embodiment and objects imbued with meaning;

> The blind man's cane has ceased to be an object for him, it is no longer perceived for itself; rather, the cane's furthest point is transformed into a sensitive zone, it increases the scope and the radius of the act of touching and has become analogous to a gaze.
>
> (pp176–177)

While Reynolds (2017) sees Merleau-Ponty's centrality of the body in experience as emphasising multiplicity in the creation of meaning, he also holds that Merleau-Ponty's "*treatment of disability vacillates between committing and undermining the ableist conflation*" (p422). He argues convincingly that Merleau-Ponty misconstrues key aspects of the blind man's experience, by coming from an ableist perspective, e.g. by minimising the social dimension of visual impairment, by underestimating the "*radicality of this disability in its world creating capacity*" (Reynolds, 2017, p424) and by his choice of an able-bodied simulation (if a person with sight was to simulate the use of a cane).

These criticisms highlight important and valid points. However, I think that Merleau-Ponty's (1945/2012) explanation, embedded in the mid twentieth century, with its examples, *is* a reasonable enough attempt at a lived experience of disability. For me, Merleau-Ponty is both trying to understand and promote how the lived body holds a multiplicity of meaning with the objects around it. He would resist the idea, I think, that his explanation of the cane and its incorporation within the embodied self is enough. Rather, it is positional, incomplete, and contextual.

Thus, I can both exist in the world with hearing that has many aspects – where I feel cut off, lost, less than, and left out, but also where I feel included, technology feeding signals through my ear to my brain. Plus, there is the multiplicity of meanings according to my "*projects*" as Merleau-Ponty (1945/2012) describes our intent, e.g. listening out for my baby niece as she goes to sleep, or a thrilled/scared response with hairs on the back of my neck feeling the thrum if not the whole sound of the two-note entrance watching the beginning of Jaws in the cinema.

In fact, we have, Merleau-Ponty (1945/2012) argues, two aspects to our experience of bodies as objects. One is the habitual body (pre-reflective) which is our typical automatic bodily processing to daily events and objects. We also have an actual body (reflective) mode, which comes into play when conscious focus is needed. Lived experience of disability, I would argue, gives you something of a superpower to toggle consciously between these modes at will.

While many people ordinarily pay remarkably little attention to the somatic level of lived experience, living with a disability entails that aspects of daily life require extra time, behaviour shifts, and careful thought, and often a shift into a reflective mode. Within the therapy, this recognition of awareness, opening up of space, and considering choices in our responses is something which can be hard to explore. Yet most clients living with a disability have an implicit sense of this; they (and caregivers) are skilled in it. This is a useful skill to practise in combination with defusion in ACT, where the client is encouraged through experiential exercises to sit with the uncomfortable piece, allowing it to be alongside, rather than fight and reject it, freeing up energy for things in life that matter to them (as detailed by Russ Harris, 2021).

Reconnect – intersubjectivity and the healing dynamic

The main goal in therapy is to raise awareness, for the client to be better empowered to make choices towards what matters to them. Meeting the client in session is a co-created interpersonal event, collaborating towards the client's therapeutic aims. The embodied intersubjectivity emphasised by Merleau-Ponty (1945/2012) offers a valuable position from which client's specific dilemmas, e.g. how to respond to the other's gaze, dealing with difference, can be explored in detail within the therapeutic relationship –

> Thus we must rediscover the social world, after the natural world, not as an object or sum of objects, but as the permanent field or dimension of existence: I can certainly turn away from the social world but I cannot cease to be situated in relation to it.
>
> (p379)

Merleau-Ponty's (1945/2012) phenomenological approach views me as one object in a phenomenal field of objects that I encounter, each imbued with meaning. There is no Cartesian separateness as in *cogito ergo sum* where there must be the "I" that must exist to be doing the apprehending, but instead

> The true cogito is not the private exchange between thought with the thought that I am having this thought, for they only unite through the world. The consciousness of the world is not established upon self-consciousness, but they are strictly contemporaries.
>
> (p399)

Other objects have their own positionality and perspective, but there is a unitary view: self, other, and world belong together; we are simultaneously both subject and object.

As the meaning we attach to ourselves is always body-based (for Merleau-Ponty, it can be no other way), this means knowledge is gained not just through the cognitive or intellectual realm but also held through an intentionality expressed in our every action in the world. To give an example, in this picture of the boy looking at the cake-box below (see Figure 4.1), a phenomenological approach might emphasise: the forward reaching aspect of the arms and shoulders crouching with intent over the box, the fine motor skills in the fingers unpicking the ribbon, the open lips and hunger response within the stomach as we imagine the mouth salivating at the thought of the chocolate eclair inside, the stomach and intestines tightening, the eyes fully focused downwards on the task of undoing the ribbon to gain access to the firmness of the box rigidity, the left ear slightly leaning to the side to take in any possible threat from a sibling predator keen to share, and so on…

This phenomenological approach, for me as a psychologist, reminds me that therapeutic meaning-making is beyond a cognitive, behavioural, or even socio-emotional exercise. It is a firmly somatic one – "*The phenomenological world is not pure being,*

Figure 4.1 Photo: © Helen Molden 2016.

but rather the sense that shines forth at the intersection of my experiences and at the intersection of my experiences with those of others through a sort of gearing into each other" (Merleau-Ponty 1945/2012, Preface, plxxxiv). This includes both (1) using my embodied self within the therapeutic relationship pragmatically to capture the client's experience, and (2) in collaborative sense-making of their developing narrative.

For example, if it is a child using a wheelchair, ensuring that they have space to play and move about, express themselves fully, or leave as they wish. While a client might have slower movements due to MS or less dynamic facial movement due to Parkinson's, their intentionality is expressed in other ways – frustration in a flicker of a foot or joy in how they hold their hands. As a psychologist with hearing loss, I will often lean in or try to catch a client's face as they turn away as reading lips and facial expression is extra important to me. I have a sense of how fatigue might be experienced, from my own embodied situated perspective, but fully appreciate the need to take in my client's – where are the similarities? where the differences? where the nuances?

A lived experience of disability has given me layers of my somatic story, as it would for anyone who has aspects of their body that they struggle with, e.g. breathing, moving, eating, recognition, and responding to instincts. As therapist, this means having an active sense and curiosity around how the somatic holds and presents for my client at each session. How stories of courage, pain, frustration, anger, and rejection are felt and exist in the body, including transferentially within the therapeutic relationship.

I observe how my client is sitting, moving, where today they hold their stomach, protecting their stoma, or how a client sits with nervousness and retroflecting, throbbing in and around their throat in response to our work around anxiety and where it shows up. I also use somatic pieces that I have learnt over the years, from compassion-focused therapy (CFT) e.g. a kind heart exercise such as those developed by Kristin Neff at The Self Compassion Institute www.self-compassion.org), or consideration of a membrane metaphor for boundary pieces, as opening and closing rituals or practises for myself as a therapeutic practitioner – an important aspect of self-care in a day of sessions.

In supporting the client in consideration of their authenticity, autonomy, and agency in facing their own challenges, dilemmas, and working towards what matters to them, I would argue that the therapist must also attend to their own process and how their lived experience of health challenges is within the therapeutic relationship. This lived experience might co-create both a useful healing relational dynamic or potentially could be a barrier or limiting factor.

I had my own therapy during my counselling psychology and integrative psychotherapy training, and subsequently, which has been vital (how stories around health show up intergenerationally and, for me, how my breathing signature has been shaped by my experiences). It enables me to bracket off my own story, but also to hold and reflect what might be useful. I take time to reflect on all these aspects and continue to build my thinking through supervision and conversations with colleagues.

When you, their therapist, are a person who has also dealt with daily difficulties with your health, this can be a permission-giving aspect for the client. I am both someone wanting to know their story, and someone who knows something of health struggles, but, crucially, not their experience. I have often found that in coming to therapy, this might be the first place where a client has had someone offer a safe space and a conversation that begins, "*Tell me more about that…*". This can have a powerful impact in the same way that a therapist modelling their own errors or mistakes, whether small or large, can offer a real-world example ("they made that error and the world carried on…"), and this is good for clients who experience challenges of perfectionism.

Merleau-Ponty's (1945/2012) intersubjective position reminds us we are not as separate as we might sometimes think, feel, or behave. I have found this a useful framework for encouraging or developing client advocacy (or your own as a psychologist) – asking for needs to be respected, even if they cannot be met easily, can be something that a client, experiencing depression and negative rumination, can find hard or even impossible, lost within the strands of a story with many challenging turns within a normative system. Emotions such as guilt, shame, or anxiety or low mood can obviate accessing the medical, educational, and social input and support required. Working with a therapist with a sense of this process, across a lifespan, can encourage clients to advocate for what they need reminding them of their position of "expert by experience" (EBE).

Reflecting on my practice over the years means that I have moved from active avoidance of discussion around my own health issues to now a greater level of self-disclosure (mainly as a one-off process, as part of the initial therapeutic contract, covering any issues such as the likelihood of frequent respiratory infections and impact on the work). Ethical practice is important here – if I am not well enough to be present and show up for my client, I will say so, not just mask and push through, as perhaps I once did in training. With improved daily self-care in combination with medical advice, the regularity and frequency of infections have slowed, and I am grateful for a welcome outcome of more stability, as Carel (2016) describes the "*health within illness*", periods of stability where tougher aspects of ill health, e.g. hospitalisations, are less figural.

However, living with a chronic condition entails unpredictability and unreliability. For psychologists, where consistency and reliability are key to working with clients in a long-term model, this can bring up feelings of guilt, shame, and more. Additionally, if you live with a disability, this can be a job in and of itself, e.g., daily physiotherapy, ensuring you have the correct medications and medical kit, travel and transport arrangements, financial implications, and more.

Ultimately, for me, this meant moving into independent practice, where I have more control over my time. While this felt a harsh compromise for me initially (I had wanted to remain working within a hospital setting, working in paediatrics), leaning into the autonomy has worked out well, led me to innovate, and connect with others on a variety of projects that are important to me.

Recreate – the "lived body" (corps vécu) as a creative and adaptive agent

In this final section, I want to focus on the way Merleau-Ponty (1945/2012) could not conceive of our lived bodies as other than reaching out towards the world and shaping it. His emphasis on "*projects*" and agency echoes much of what we as clinicians are supporting our clients with as they negotiate the different parts of their own psycho-geographical map of what is important to them. Seeking psychological flexibility and using metaphor and image are central to both ACT and CFT. Each contains elements and practises which are helpful in developing skills around compassion and flexibility, while remaining focused on meaning-making and values.

One artist who captures the essence of Merleau-Ponty's understanding of the subject-object experience in the phenomenal realm was the surrealist Leonora Carrington (1917–2011), who lived most of her life in Mexico. She was British-born but fled her family's expectations in the 1930s, ending up living with many of the key figures in the Surrealist movement in France, Spain, and Portugal. She experienced a period of major depression in her 20s, prior to fleeing to the USA and finally Mexico. Her writings, artwork, and sculpture around her experiences are vividly drawn and valuable in helping us to understand a breaking down of boundaries within these experiences.

Carrington shows us how important aspects of what it is to be human intermingle with and gain their essence and meaning from the objects around them. The latter might be human (her immediate family, whom she resisted, or her close connection with her sons), animal (her love for horses), or parts of the house (candlesticks, tables, pieces of life traditionally seen as domestic that appear to come to life in her paintings). In her paintings, e.g. Self Portrait (Inn of the Dawn Horse, 1938) the phenomenological flow between space, house, nature, human body, animal, magical elements, and more is clear.

Here, the many relational aspects of the phenomenal realm are revealed through details such as anthropomorphic chair legs, reflected in the high-heeled boots of the self-portrait. Or hinted at in echoes of her voluminous hair in the hyena and horse's bodies and movement. Similarly, the sculptural piece, the delicacy in the anthropomorphised features of the Minotaur's Daughter, beautifully illustrates possible layers of meaning – strengths and vulnerabilities – of a creature trapped by family expectations.

Meaning-making in sessions is created not just by talking therapy but through art, play, music, and therapy within the natural world. I hope I have shown how the phenomenological approach is useful in its very questioning of the duality between mind and body, between human and non-human, is more easily dissolved. When living with a hidden disability, I have found that clients have gained in exploring tensions that exist around being seen and understood through creative means. In some sessions, encouraged to create a sand tray or explore a theme through drawing, e.g. "meeting people when I feel ill, but on first appearances, look fine", the turn-taking between the client and I takes on a natural flow, and energy, towards the aim of exploring what lies behind that theme. Our hands move quickly, picking up or pointing towards aspects of the creation.

In session, using an umbrella as a cricket bat or a tiny tin as a sailboat, when working with young people with functional neurological disorder (FND), we will work out through play how conversations with adults and children might go, so that despite limited mobility and fatigue, they can join in alongside their team. A young client may demonstrate their hurt and pain, showing me how the puppet dislikes invasive tests and needles. The puppet's furry body, squishy tummy, and longer limbs react when the child enacts the medical procedure. Similarities and differences between their own and the puppets are noted, and a young client may express compassion and courage for the puppet and, I gently, suggest, for themselves also. We may discuss how intricate feelings connect and tough thoughts emanate according to different aspects of the lived body experience of treatment, and data points to inform medical staff (and concerned parents/carers). The gaps where the overwhelming feelings and thoughts start to get bigger, anxiety in the embodied experience reduces, and more time is spent at school, play, or wherever is important to that child, alongside demands of day-to-day living.

This interconnectedness includes the outdoor world. I have found nature to be hugely supportive when strange, painful, and difficult things are happening. The powerful ongoing strength of leaning your back or hand against a tree, for as long as you want, and sensing it not just as another thing in the world but as an object, like you, in its intentionality. While we are centrally located in our phenomenal field, and our knowledge is perspectival through our capacities and boundaries, so the tree is in its field and perspectives. A session of walk and talk therapy when working with a client with mobility issues can be empowering, energizing, and calming. We can go at the pace they choose, where we stop is a mutual negotiated process. While I act as a guide, and ask questions that invite connection, the client can decide where to stop, when to go on, with me alongside in a parallel process.

One of the criticisms that has been levelled at Merleau-Ponty's (1945/2012) embodied phenomenological approach is that he pays insufficient importance to the socially-constructed aspects of being a human in this self-other-world landscape, e.g. race, gender, and class. However, as philosopher such as Weiss (2015) has eloquently argued, it is precisely his suggestion that gender, race, or ability within bodies is not innate, or a fixed feature, that helps to "*overturn accepted notions of normalcy, naturalness and normativity*". It opens the possibility, I think, of the either/or, or both...and ambiguity (in contrast to operating in a more fixed mode either unconsciously or consciously), which is so helpful as an explanatory model when working as a therapist.

Holding a space for the ambiguity and more open conversations can be permission-giving for clients, especially in consideration of how bodies change over time and lifespan.

> Whether it is a question of the other person's body or of my own, I have no other means of knowing the human body than by living it, that is, by taking up for myself the drama that moves through it and by merging with it.
>
> (Merleau-Ponty, 1945/2012, p292)

Merleau-Ponty is encouraging us to apply a phenomenological attentiveness, a descriptive and enquiring curiosity, and respond creatively to how we ourselves engage with the world. This can only be through our bodies, and similarly of those around us. We have moved beyond the active promotion of eugenics in the nineteenth and twentieth centuries. However, these ideas are still supported and negotiated in laws and attitudes throughout the world, operating at the level of what has been termed "*velvet eugenics*" by the bioethicist Rosemarie Garland-Thomson (2024, para 5). She highlights hidden and conscious assumptions, fuelled by consumer and medical demands in technology growth, when she states

> If the broadest ethical goal of any medical technology is to improve human lives, we must untangle some of the aspirations of eugenics from the enterprise of genetic technology and other medical interventions aimed at bringing all humans to a standard, "normal" form and function.

By loosening the rigidity and boundaries around the interpersonal and objects in the world, Merleau-Ponty (1945/2012) is shaking the established ideas of his time around physical, social, cognitive, and moral norms, and the pull to the "less-than". The phenomenological curiosity behind this approach remains vitally important now in the evolving debate around what it is to be human in a tech-based economy. It focuses on choice and autonomy, allowing greater choice in my and your story, than the "less than" default.

A further criticism of Merleau-Ponty's (1945/2012) approach could be that he is too vague – that his intersubjectivity and first-person descriptive perspective do not lend themselves to a structure of where I begin in comparison to the rest of the phenomenal realm. This may be true if we are looking to the philosophical standards of empiricism, but my argument is that we need this extra layer of the narrative when considering life across the embodied experience. As humans, we all experience mortality, with our story of birth, death, and everything in with great variation. But with our somatic skin in the game (in comparison say to an AI therabot), we have that existential sense of how it is to be in a crisis or challenging moment, where health and future are uncertain.

Reflecting on psychologists I have known who have lived with serious health conditions and navigated clinical practice, I remind myself that this is something that therapeutic practitioners have always faced. For example, the psychoanalyst Donald Winnicott's (1978) The Piggle, published in his famous paper on the work he did with a child known as The Piggle was during a period of immense physical health distress (cardiac disease and ocular pain). This is well summarised by Brett Kahr (2024) in his recent biography of the man, amongst other key figures in British Psychoanalysis, where he comments, "*A man of considerable sturdiness, Donald Winnicott managed to access his professionalism, his playfulness, and his joy for living, in order to transmit these qualities to The Piggle, in spite of his own quite significant medical struggles*" (p91).

I began by emphasising the multiplicity of meanings within our lived body, which has implications for how we create and hold our own psycho-geographical maps as we go through life. It is my contention, after the privilege of years of collaboration in several clinical settings, that Merleau-Ponty's centrality of the lived body as instrumental in the self-body-world relationship offers a valuable guide for therapist and client, especially combined with mainstream psychological models such as ACT and CFT. It goes beyond the medicalised objective view of placing the locus of attention within this or that symptom, and beyond the dual identities of living with disability and the normative body. As a psychologist with lived experience of health concerns and painful disruptions to daily life, I also know in an embodied sense that things will be in a different place this time next year. As such, I have the privilege of holding the hope until such time and possibility as a client can affirm their own capability, agency, and autonomy in the future.

Acknowledgements

The ideas above are explored with thanks and gratitude to the clients and colleagues I have worked with and whose stories I have heard, in the NHS, community, and private practice, as a therapist and supervisor.

References

Carel, H. (2016). *The phenomenology of illness*. Oxford University Press.

Carrington, L. (1937–1938). *Self-portrait (Inn of the Dawn Horse)* [Oil on canvas]. Metropolitan Museum of Art, New York, NY. https://www.metmuseum.org/art/collection/search/492697

Douglas-Fairhurst, R. (2023). *Metamorphosis*. Penguin Random House.

Garland-Thomson, R. (2024, August 26). *Enhancing future generations with CRISPR is a road to a new eugenics, says ethicist Rosemarie Garland-Thomson*. LiveScience. https://www.livescience.com/health/genetics/enhancing-future-generations-with-crispr-is-a-road-to-a-new-eugenics-says-ethicist-rosemarie-garland-thomson. Excerpt adapted from Velvet eugenics: In the best interests of our future children? In N. Baer (Ed.) *The promise and peril of CRISPR* (pp. 153–171). John Hopkins University Press.

Harris, R. (2021). *When life hits hard.* New Harbinger Publications.

Husserl, E. (1982). *Ideas pertaining to a pure phenomenology and to a phenomenological philosophy: First book: General introduction to a pure phenomenology* (F. Kersten, Trans.). Springer. (Original work published 1913).

Kahr, B. (2024). *Hidden histories of British psychoanalysis*. Karnac Books.

Leder, D. (2023). *The healing body: Creative responses to illness, aging and afflictions (studies in phenomenology and existential philosophy).* Northwestern University Press.

Merleau-Ponty, M. (2012). *Phenomenology of perception* (D. A. Landes, Trans.). Routledge. (Original work published 1945).

Owen, R. (2014). *Living with the enemy*. Routledge.

Plato. (2007). *The republic* (D. Lee, Trans.; 2nd ed.). Penguin. (Original work c. 375 BCE, middle period).

Plato. (2014). *Plato's Phaedo: A translation of Plato's Phaedo* (R. S. Bluck, Trans.). Routledge. (Original work c. 375 BCE, middle period).

Putnam, H. (1981). *Reason, truth and history.* Cambridge University Press.

Reynolds, J. M. (2017). Merleau-Ponty, world-creating blindness, and the phenomenology of non-normate bodies. *Chiasmi International: Trilingual Studies Concerning Merleau-Ponty's Thought, 19*, 419–434.

Robinson's Podcast. (2023, May 23). *Havi Carel: The phenomenology of illness* [Audio podcast episode]. In *Robinson's Podcast* (No. 93). YouTube. https://www.youtube.com/watch?v=c7xT5cTq7Jc

Sartre, J.-P. (2003). *Being and nothingness* (H. E. Barnes, Trans.; 2nd ed.). Routledge. (Original work published 1943).

Sontag, S. (2002). *Illness as metaphor*. Penguin Classics.

Spence Green, G. (2025). *To exist as I am*. Wellcome Collection.

Weiss, G. (2015). The normal, the natural, and the normative: A Merleau-Pontian legacy to feminist theory, critical race theory, and disability studies. *Continental Philosophy Review*, *48*(1), 77–93.

Winnicott, D. W. (1978). *The piggle: An account of the psychoanalytic treatment of a little girl* (I. Ramzy, Ed.). Tavistock Publications.

Chapter 5

The influence of early script development on the experience of disability as a counselling psychologist

A Transactional Analysis framework

Susan Jacques

Introduction: what is meant by the term 'script' in Transactional Analysis?

'Eric Berne, (1910-1970), the founder of Transactional Analysis (TA)' proposed that 'each person decides in early childhood how he will live and how he will die, and that plan, which he carries around in his head wherever he goes is called his script' (1972, p.31). Providing a detailed account of the concept of *life script* within (Transactional Analysis; TA) is beyond the scope of this chapter, as ideas continue to evolve and shape our understanding on this creative concept that offers valuable insight into how we perceive ourselves, others, and the world. In considering the everyday use of the term script, drawn to Eric Berne (1961), who in his book *Transactional Analysis in Psychotherapy*, suggests an analogy between life scripts and Aristotelian principles of a Greek tragedy. The play's composition comprises a multitude of characters with the protagonist playing the leading role, the plot infamously embodying complexity, ambiguity, and depth. In this play of life is the customary task of the characters grappling with universal lived experiences whilst contending with their own internal battles or conflict. The characters' 'life scripts' or 'cognitive structures' are a means by which they learn to navigate and organise their world. The substance of the characters and plot is relatable, as in these compelling narratives are tales of discord, adversity, and resilience in which people learn to circumnavigate their world. There are endless attempts at achieving greater happiness, or fundamentally for many Transactional Analysts, a bidding to become 'script-free'. How is this achieved? For Berne, this requires that a person must 'close the show and put a better one on the road' (Berne, 1976, p140), the essential components of this task involving significant behavioural changes to primarily alter intrapsychic beliefs and bodily responses. For Erskine (2010), an influential figure in TA, the process is one of 'internal reorganization and new integration of affective and cognitive structures, undoing physiological retroflections, decommissioning introjections, and consciously choosing behaviour that is meaningful and appropriate in the current relationship' (p4).

Berne (1961) postulated that these Aristotelian concepts are a depiction of a real-life 'script' that he earlier referred to as a 'transference, [often] split up into

DOI: 10.4324/9781003636014-6

acts, exactly like the theatrical scripts which are intuitive artistic derivatives of [these] primal dramas of childhood' (p116). At the very essence of the primal dramas, the script protocol, is a host of suppressed emotions that motivate an individual's script decisions or early beliefs about the self, others, and the world. Based on the protocol, the script uncompromisingly leads the person's behaviour and relationships, and this 'unconscious life plan' as Berne (1961) termed, decides from a young age, the path that is to follow. A central part to this path, Berne postulated, involved adopting an 'existential position' in 'order to justify a decision based on early experience' (Berne, 1964), a position that defines one's sense of OKness or not OKness.

Claude Steiner, who made a substantial contribution to our understanding of life scripts in TA stressed the decisive role of early childhood experiences and decisions in sculpting an individual's core beliefs and future pathway (Steiner, 1974). For Steiner, these unconscious life scripts have an 'onset, a course and an outcome' (p23). In reviewing Berne's early definitions of script, Steiner (2010) notes how a script directs a person's behaviour much like a director does with his actors. A crucial element to his assertion is that the person and his audience are habitually under the illusion of autonomy, unknowingly repeating feelings that feed the very substance of their script which time and again restrict their existential growth. Erskine et al. (2011) noted how for Berne, many often create a storyline which constrains their identity by forming 'self-repeating patterns' which Erskine noted is the source of unnecessary suffering in relationships.

Scripts according to Berne's (1961) are embedded in the realm of transference and are at the core of 'adaptations of infantile reactions and experiences' (p116). Both Berne (1972) and Erskine (1980) refer to script as decisions created as 'survival' tools in childhood which have life-long impact outside of awareness. In referring to the notion of script decision, Steiner further (1974) describes a process of the young person, applying and navigating their adaptive resources, and altering their expectations in the hope they match with the realities of the home environment.

The role of the parents in script formation in Berne's definition of script is evidenced throughout his work. With his reference to the notion of parental introjects, Berne, alongside other theorists in the field of TA (Goulding & Goulding 1976, 1979; Steiner, 1971, 1974), viewed script formation akin to a series of 'injunctions' or negative prohibitions, 'passed on' by parents which alter a child's future behaviours. For example, as a practicing psychologist, I have seen how such injunctions can have a significant effect on how a person relates to their experience of a disability when the injunctions reinforce the limitations of their chronic condition. Examples include being passed on the injunction of 'don't make it' which can typically hinder recovery and adjustment. Clients may doubt their own capabilities by reason of these internal messages (Cole, 1993), and unconsciously self-sabotage their achievements.

Goulding and Goulding (1979), who were credited with developing the concept of injunctions, referred to them as: 'messages from the Child ego state of parents, given out of the circumstances of the parents' own pains, unhappiness, anxiety, disappointment, anger, frustration, secret desires' (p34). The very notion of injunctive messages deriving from the Child ego state of parents is further supported by Steiner (1974). Erskine (1980) goes one step further when discussing script formation by suggesting that not all life scripts are based on parental injunctions or script decisions and considers how 'unconscious conclusions' are decisively located in real-life experience. Furthermore, unlike Berne, Erskine (1980) prompts us to consider the notion that script decisions can be made at any developmental age.

Additionally, Roberts (1983) invites us to reflect on how individual scripts interface with cultural scripts, noting how injunctions are tacitly transmitted through culture and family. He further claims that: 'All cultures promote scripts by virtue of the fact that cultures value certain persons more than others' (p253), offering valuable consideration of the duality of script and disability alongside the concepts of 'Otherness' and prejudice.

Erskine and Zalcman's (1979) later termed 'Script System' model further supports the notion of a self-perpetuating intrapsychic organisation which is maintained over time, with decisions, introjections, and reactions unconsciously manifesting in core beliefs, behaviours, and reinforcing memories. The script system was created with the aim to analyse how the script is functioning in life today, in contrast to a historical perspective which Berne largely devoted attention to. Part of this script system is script beliefs, which can arguably be viewed as 'a condensed expression of an unexpressed life story' (Erskine, 2010, p292), that motivate self-regulation and form part of a meaning-making process. What's more, Erskine so aptly describes how 'the intrapsychic dynamics of the script system serve to keep the original needs and feelings that were present at the time of script formation out of awareness, whilst also maintaining a semblance of attachment with others' (Erskine, 2010, p292).

Lastly, in the 'Script System' there are reinforcing memories-emotional memories of past experiences that come to the fore when engaging in rackety displays (substitute behaviours) and serve as a reinforcement of script beliefs to corroborate the scripts validity. Significantly, the model formulates a process in which a person in script upholds certain emotional and behavioural experiences and reflects a time in which unmet needs are not addressed.

Berne's theory of script evolved over the course of his life, and it was evident that he was caught in his own impasse about the notion of personal autonomy and the authority of life script (Cornell, 1988). On one side of the fence, we sit with Berne's notion of embedded 'script electrodes' which strips the individual of any tools to make autonomous choices. Here, script theory views the individual as a product rather than a product-maker of his script (Cornell, 1988). Berne also notably held a pessimistic view of people's aspiration to seek autonomy, that is, the burden of the script surpassed a person's longing for self-determination (Cornell, 2010). On the other side, we see in Berne's later writings that there were some playful attempts at affording the individual with a sense of agency and a level of resourcefulness that implied a process of natural individuation and a move towards the freedom to choose and express one's feelings from the array available, stemming from either the Child, Parent or Adult ego states (Berne, 1964; Steiner, 1974).

Prior to attending to the conundrums of game analysis, Berne positioned the concept of script in a more fluid way (English, 1988). There was arguably the prevailing assumption amongst his peers that his definition typically adopted a distinct deterministic flavour which overtime declined in popularity. Both Cornell (1988) and English (1988) were keen to highlight how script theory gradually evolved into a linear, more restrictive perspective which emphasised psychopathology over healthy lived experience. Indeed, when addressing scripts, English (1988) stressed how 'our ability to conceptualise and generate scripts is one of the exciting manifestations of being human and having a creative drive' (p297). What's more, English (1988) articulated how scripts have the potential to surpass the frequent negative role they are assigned and can instead provide a map for the process of meaning-making.

Further consideration in the (TA) literature has been given to the notion of script as a 'normal, necessary human process of meaning-making' (Newton, 2006), whilst placing script in the context of an everchanging non-pathological process that is subject to change (Loria, 1995). The reader will discover how I give value to the content of submissions proposed by Loria (1995), Newton (2006), Erskine (1980), English (1988), and Cornell (1988), as they irrefutably validate the notion of my own script, which has not only been mutable but also offered a deep process of self-understanding. It will become evident that my own internal battle as a psychologist with lived experience of a disability has presumed a process of experiential sense-making, unconsciously drawing from the very essence of my life script as a way of offering predictability and safety, but irrevocably offering a surprisingly level of perspicacity.

Deconstructing a 'disability script'

Drawing attention to the concept of life script in TA, I have been dynamically informed by the numerous theoretical accounts which have been instrumental in aiding understanding and allowing for the formulation of my 'unique script system'. In deconstructing my script through a TA lens, I illustrate in the chapter how an ongoing meaning-making process comprised a shift from a place of intrapsychic conflict and shame about my condition, to a place in which the uncontaminated part of my Adult feels free to make autonomous choices (Berne, 1972). One component of this process was that it allowed for the integration of self-acceptance and the capacity to navigate my condition in more adept ways.

I invite the reader to join me on a discursive process which focuses on what I shall term my 'disability script', or more specifically, my 'epilepsy script' – a subset of my script that has unequivocally carried significant weight in my personal and professional identities. 'The chapter employs Eric Berne's analogy of life paralleling a Greek play, journeying the reader through a transference drama in which I position my experience of epilepsy within established TA theories on 'life script'.

As the story unfolds, I share how I discern new meanings in my life in relation to my epilepsy and reflect on ways this impacts my clinical practice, including ways it may enter the transferential relationship between client and myself as a practitioner.

The practice of stepping into my disability script with conscious awareness and further re-evaluating my script through the therapeutic relationship formed part of a dynamic process of development towards what I shall term 'script refinement'. This is not a process characterised by the foregoing need for adaptation or desire for 'sameness', but the capacity to make self-governing decisions in relation to my epilepsy script. Therefore, it does not 'inhibit spontaneity or limit flexibility in problem-solving and relating to people' (Erskine, 1980, p106).

The inciting incident: a diagnosis of epilepsy

Epilepsy may be defined as a disorder of the brain characterised by a persistent predisposition to produce epileptic seizures (Gavvala & Schuele, 2016). Seizures are abrupt bursts of neuronal activity that momentarily disrupt the brain's function and may cause isolated or combined sensory, cognitive, and emotional symptoms (Fisher et al., 2017). The clinical features of seizures differ depending on the area of the brain they originate from, the onset, and the underlying neuroanatomy (Gavvala & Schuele, 2016; Fisher et al., 2017). Around 50 million people worldwide experience epilepsy, thus making it one of the most common neurological diseases globally (World Health Organisation [WHO], 2024).

I was diagnosed with epilepsy in my early teens. To paraphrase Berne (1972), this was a time in which I witnessed the 'dramatic nature of my script come into full bloom'. However, as a young child, I experienced frequent episodes of impaired awareness, behaviour, sensation, and movement, otherwise known as focal seizures-seizures that originate from one part of the brain. Uncontrolled surges of electrical activity in my brain result into fleeting moments of what are to be described as mistaken feelings of familiarity, or déjà vu, there being consistent incongruence between what I thought I had seen and what I experienced. These ineffable and somewhat uncompromising experiences at times engendered confusion and fear in both myself, and in my close relationships, arguably because what is unknown and unexplainable is often met with disquiet and negative bias.

At a familial level, judgements were irrefutably located in transgenerational messages. At a cultural level, I argue that it is society that defines the social contract on how a disability such as epilepsy is construed, that is, whether it is met with unease, if it is to be 'feared', and ultimately whether it feeds into what Berne (1972) termed a person's 'losers' or 'non-winning script' (pp203–205). As a young woman, I was forced to navigate my way through this debilitating condition of which I had little understanding. Despite the 'trap of social adaptation', the crucial question was: 'did I feel the freedom to be myself?' (Mazzetti, 2010). On reflection, I allowed myself to be controlled by my script for many years, and thus what ensued was a culmination of racket feelings, or substitute feelings such as internalised shame and guilt, feelings that I believe I was given the permission to express.

Explicit changes that followed a new diagnosis of epilepsy included being part of a treatment plan that involved long-term health-care support and significant self-education on a condition that neurologists made tireless attempts to control. The seizures were persistent, and overtime were having a noticeable impact on the quality of my life. Underneath the iceberg of relative normality was a mosaic of physical, cognitive, and emotional stress that included fearing the risk of injury from a fall, cognitive shortfalls such as impaired memory, and learning to navigate the adverse effects of anti-seizure medication, which at its minimum was chronic fatigue. It is my view that such effects were frequently held at a somatic level in which there was a vicious cycle of fatigue and tension followed by increased seizures. Ligabue (1991) reminds us that the body holds 'injunctions and adaptive decisions', so for me, where certain thoughts and feelings lacked a voice, the body often spoke volumes.

One study by Tombini et al. (2024), which focused on resilience and psychosocial factors in adults with epilepsy, found consistently that people with epilepsy reported a significantly worse quality of life. This was owed to factors such as seizure frequency and due to it being a highly stigmatised condition. Furthermore, 'resilience', as it relates to positive adaptation to the adverse effects of seizures, positively correlated with self-compassion. However, I intuitively became somewhat adept at discounting myself. My narrative took the form of 'Why can't I be like others?', resulting in a moderated self-worth. My Parent ego state thus instructed me to meet society's standards to be 'normal' (Sugarman, 1979), and a key element of this was downplaying my symptoms.

I identified that my relationship with epilepsy involved a process of bargaining. On the one hand, I was forecasting a morbid trajectory of medication after medication and witnessing little change, and, on the other hand, experiencing a part of the self that was curious about this 'abnormal wiring of the brain'. The seizures frequently journeyed me somewhere extraordinary – it was an ephemeral but rather captivating perceptual and emotional shift devoid of language. What was apparent however was that the term 'disability' was not part of my narrative, despite being immersed in a process of medicalisation of epilepsy. I become aware that overtime I had internalised a negative belief system connected to a fear of difference and the 'unseen reality of being the other' (Turner, 2021). Questions around my physical and emotional health came to the fore, fearing the potential disabling and detrimental effects that epilepsy may have on the quality of my life. Here was a condition that involved frequent exposure to irrepressible episodes of losing control over my body. As a person who was starting to live a life with an experience of this unseen disability, there begun what was a deep-seated search for meaning.

Cornell (1988) and English (1988) both discuss script in the context of making meaning in life, and purport that major script decisions can be made at any stage of life. Notably for Cornell, confronting life challenges and experiencing 'failure' will habitually nurture more restrictive, and dysfunctional components of a script, but their very essence is not pathological, in that they form part of a process of 'ongoing psychological construction of reality' that is open to change (Cornell, 1988).

Through therapeutic exploration, I recognised that I was making several attempts to make sense of my diagnosis, and it required giving meaning to my thoughts, feelings, and behaviours (Erskine et al., 2011) and significantly understanding where I felt 'stuck'. From one standpoint, I had my Adult telling my Child that it was fine to be who I am, and from the other, my script was dictating the need to adapt through a process of denial. Further, as a result of my diagnosis, I began to question if people would start to view me in a different light given the general lack of awareness of epilepsy as a condition. Belanger and Laube (1979) in reflecting on the process of discounting from the non-disabled person identified that it classically occurs from the others' contaminated adult as they struggle to process the reality data available to them. Moreover, they are often afraid of the 'other', in this case 'the person with a disability', and what we see is the non-disabled person subsequently retreating to their Child ego state. This effectively results in rejecting what is feared and further restricts freedom of movement for the disabled person.

The extraordinary nineteenth-century Russian novelist Fyodor Dostoevsky who himself had a diagnosis of epilepsy faultlessly captures the ethereal experience of a seizure in his own description:

> For several instants I experience a happiness that is impossible in an ordinary state, and of which other people have no conception. I feel full harmony in myself and in the whole world, and the feeling is so strong and sweet that for a few seconds of such bliss one could give up ten years of life, perhaps all of life.
>
> (Dostoevsky, 1995/1848, p8)

For Dostoevsky, adversity was translated into artistic opportunity, and his struggle with epilepsy also gave him a profound understanding of human suffering and resilience. However, for a long time, my epilepsy script habitually held me in a binary position which oscillated between incitement of genuine curiosity and a denial of its very existence. The perpetual struggle has been achieving the task of integrating all aspects of my disability and what it symbolises, that is, holding and accepting it in its entirety, the good, creative aspects, and the not so good parts. My understanding of this 'splitting process' can be located in the need to survive and protect, and this implicated a process of projecting parts of the self that were deemed to be 'bad' outwards onto the external world, thus creating a world that was at times perceived to be unfair, unjust, or unsafe. What's more, my epilepsy script conclusions focused on feeling 'less than', and feelings of being misunderstood were consistently being confirmed. Hargaden and Sills (2001) contextualise this need to split as a means of managing repeated misattunement in the child's environment and referred to what Melanie Klein (1986) termed as the splitting of the 'undigested experiences'. Hargaden and Sills (2001) argue that because of this process, the Child remains both 'incomplete and unintegrated'.

The rising action: feeling 'Not-OK'

As aforementioned, Berne (1962) wrote about 'existential life positions' in TA, and fundamental to the concept was the notion that subjects of all positions are components of the polarity I-Other, and their co-ordinates are particulars of the polarity OK-not OK (Steiner, 2012).[1] According to Steiner (2012), the OK/not-OK concepts are closely linked with the script and a person's sense of meaning and purpose in the world. The concept of OKness for Berne was rooted in our early decisions about ourselves and others, most notably our parents and the world at large, and these decisions are likely to remain cemented unless otherwise consciously altered. Core methods that work with changing life scripts in Transaction Analysis include Script Analysis, Redecision Therapy, Ego State work, Game Analysis, and Cognitive Restructuring. All involve a process that moves from awareness to effective change and re-creating a life 'unshackled by the outdated constraints of the negative script' (Widdowson, 2016, p19).

Essentially, Berne's theory on OKness can be located in his theory on games (Steiner, 2012), but the concept was considerably more developed by the likes of Harris (1969) and Ernst (1971). Harris (1969), in particular, brought the concept to life with his assertion that the life position: 'I'm not OK-You're OK' is an inherent universal position. Harris paints the negative component in this position as feeling inferior and at the 'at the mercy of others', classifying the other as superior and dominant. I propose that a crucial component of my epilepsy script was the complex interplay of the discounting from others, and the unwavering discounts towards the self-both elements Belanger and Laube (1979) assert are central to the Not-OK position.

A crucial component of the 'I'm not OK-You're OK' position is the strong desire for strokes or recognition, and this is achieved by the very simple act of being cared for. Benjamin (2004, 2018), in reflecting on the concept of intersubjectivity supports the notion of an inherent desire for recognition and to be 'seen and met' for who we are, that is, as separate and distinct subjects. This space of recognition for Benjamin embodies mutuality where two people adeptly coexist, a space of equality that embraces difference and acceptance. However, what happens as Moores and Oates (2024) suggest when this space is split into unequal parts and is characterised by relationships full of misunderstandings; or where there are barriers to be seen for who we are? (Benjamin, 2004), in these scenarios predicts power imbalances resulting into binary splitting of good and bad or, significantly, OK-Not OK.

The Not-OK part Harris (1969) suggests are the conclusions a child has about himself. One way of living out this position according to Harris is to live out a life script. He purports that the life script 'confirms the Not OK and is written unconsciously by the Child' (p44). In addition, the script might necessitate withdrawal behaviours since its unbearable to be in the presence of OK people. Alternatively, we live out the position by the constant seeking of strokes from a big Parent, a task that arguably is never really accomplished.

The notion of one's 'subjective experience of worthiness' (Zivkovic, 2023) for Berne was conceptualised using the analogy that 'every human being is born a prince or princess' (Berne, 1966, p289), until faced with the restraints of repeated early experiences and the 'civilizing process' in which we may be subjected to the persona of a 'frog'. In these unfortunate circumstances, instability and insecurity ordinarily prevail. Harris (1969), who challenges Berne's concept that every child is born believing he is 'OK', paints a picture of child for whom a one down position is the starting point, the child figuring out ways to make sense of his world whilst making ongoing conclusions about his parents and his surrounding environment.

Instrumental to my epilepsy script development has been what I shall term a 'fragile sense of OK-ness' which I locate in a complex set of introjected messages about epilepsy as a disability.

This fragile sense of OKness is the crossroads between parental injunctions rooted in fear and cultural scripts on epilepsy as a stigmatised condition. The consequences of this interface led to partial views about myself and my sense of equality, unequivocally promoting residual feelings of 'less than' (Roberts, 1983). My fragile sense of 'OK-ness' can be appositely described as conditional in that I was only ever OK 'if' I accommodated to what was seen to befit the current environment. Parry (1979) interestingly detailed how OKness invariably performs the function of *being* and not of *doing* and highlights its conditional flavour in that 'until' a person is responded to in an OK way, their experience of life is potentially one of struggle and vulnerability. Harris (1969) aptly refers to 'living out the Not OK position by a counterscript with borrowed lines from the Parent' (p44). Within this idea sits a compliant person for whom strokes are paramount, and thus, there is a habitual lifetime commitment to gaining approval.

It is notably Berne's (1962, 1966) 'I'm not OK, you're OK' position that has mostly been played out from my younger self through to my adult experience and has been largely responsible for my script beliefs and behaviours; the need is subsequently projected, and there is a deep desire to be like the Other. I further advocate the idea that the position of 'I'm not OK, you're OK' supports a conditional OKness which can be understood in the context of failure to meet the needs of the internal object (Zivkovic, 2023). In my own lived experience, the conditional OK-ness is compounded by a rigid 'Try Hard' driver which at its best resulted in creativity, and at its worst meant overcompensation (Widdowson, 2026). Furthermore, my epilepsy script was often characterised by bouts of inauthenticity in my attempts to survive what was both my own and collective projected realities (Turner, 2021).

Evident in this stage are modicums of parental, societal, and cultural injunctions and script decisions rooted in lived experience which overtime have fed into an unconscious epilepsy script, a script often marred by self-doubt and shame. Through deep exploration of early experiences and valuable personal insight, I recognise that my epilepsy script has been expressed at an affective, physiological, and relational level through feelings of confusion, minimisation, physical tension, and a desperate desire to belong. Habitually operating from my

Child ego state, there has been a desperate need to meet others' expectations. My decisions, whilst habitually rooted in survival and a need to 'fit in', intuitively served to maintain a 'less than' script in that by playing down my disability, I was under the illusion that 'difference' was not a feature of the self. In fact, my ineffectual relationship with my epilepsy served to reinforce its associated stigma by the very fact of silencing it. The workings of my script system created a cycle of 'unconscious adaptation' and a desire for what was essentially conditional acceptance. In this was an attempt to achieve psychological predictability whilst defending my script decisions in my day-to-day adult life, endeavouring to create a reality that was both familiar and one that fit neatly into my subjective understanding of epilepsy. However, in playing out my epilepsy script, most noticeable at times of shame or embarrassment, I unconsciously engaged in behaviours that advanced me closer to my 'script payoff' (Berne, 1961).

The interlacing of my disability with a sense of 'otherness' was a component of my internalised subjective experience from an early age as I attempted to navigate an environment that viewed epilepsy as otherworldly or peculiar. Since its inception dating back to Ancient Greece, the term epilepsy has transposed from being associated with mysticism and divinity to a sacred disease embroiled with demonic possession (Magiorkinis et al., 2010). In the initial scene of my own Greek drama is a young teenager for whom feelings of difference were customary. My sense of Okness was not about an inherent sense of badness, but about being different. However, I awaited ongoing acceptance. Furthermore, feelings of difference were incessantly being reinforced at both an implicit and explicit level, through overt judgmental comments to covert misattunement and expressions of fear. All the whilst my unique script system was unconsciously being strengthened through negative beliefs about myself and my condition, both as a way of providing a 'creative process of meaning-making' (Erskine, 2010) and affording a predictable model for life and relationships.

In this chapter of my life, I was now subtly forced to confront ableist norms and practices, and what's more, find a place in a society that positioned epilepsy in a Not OK position. Belanger and Laube (1979) refer to the concept of a reaction cycle in the context of ableism based on the perpetuation of discounting from others and discounting towards ourselves, and it is evident in my story that both served to propagate a Not OK position.

Aldridge and Stilman (2024) in their paper on neurodivergent script decisions capture the very essence of how 'implicit ableism' is often navigated by the person who feels 'less than', where a desire to belong often 'leads the marginalised other to accept a compromised position' (p57). My own compromised position was to initially minimise my epilepsy and place it behind closed doors as a means of maintaining ego strength and self-regard (Belanger & Laube, 1979). All the whilst I was draining my resources to survive the emotional and physical impact that my seizures presented me with, pushing against a wall titled 'intractable epilepsy'-seizures that despite multiple medications attempts insisted on staying put. My survival strategy thus involved developing substitute ways of achieving strokes (Steiner, 1974) and repressing my authentic feelings through what was an unconscious fear of rejection. Little was I aware that this would serve to promote repeated rackety feelings and displays that carried the definitive theme that epilepsy was not OK or acceptable.

The climax: meeting a crossroad both personally and professionally

'In order to go through life, we need to kill off, [sic] a part of ourselves which is deemed unworthy by society that suggests that we go through life in a constant state of inauthenticity' (Turner, 2021).

Having an 'unseen disability' afforded the opportunity for my epilepsy to be effortlessly compartmentalised, in that what isn't visible can at some level be shut off. Moores and Oates (2024) refer to Berne's script in the context of the need to protect unfamiliar parts of the self from increased harm. Minikin (2021) detailed how scripts, whilst serving a somewhat creative purpose, can simultaneously have negative consequences in that the predictability is often created under an oppressive arrangement. As previously noted, these split off unintegrated parts of the self in the past facilitated protection but not without consequence. Baskerville (2022) notes with great perspicuity how the part of the self that performs this task 'finds a way to survive by intuiting at a deeply unconscious level how to adapt…' (p237), and this certainly mirrors the path that followed. In essence, my Adapted Child continued to follow the path of needing acceptance, and this pointed the way for a need to conform to a 'dominant collective narrative' so that I could veer away from anything that represented otherness or difference (Minikin, 2021). Turner (2021) described a process of 'killing off that which is deemed wrong by the system or by the subject' (p105), and my epilepsy script unquestionably reinforced this demand.

In discussing the principles of privilege and normativity, Minikin (2021) refers to the position of 'almost OK', a position manufactured by the dominant group and imposed on those who are marginalised. The acceptance of an almost OKness by the 'less than' group, she argues, comes at a cost, the aftermath is feeling anxiety, conscious and unconscious, whilst those with the louder voice retain their authority. I propose that by accepting the position of 'almost OK', it overtime diminished my authenticity. Navigating my way through clinical practice required making the decision to downplay my unseen condition within the workforce to minimise any distractions and not cause any undue attention. My script was incessantly informing me that 'psychologists and epilepsy do not appear on the same tableau'. Furthermore, my self-appraisal became reliant upon what was deemed acceptable by the prevailing narrative to promote feelings of inclusion.

The 'hunger' to be recognised I posit is a healthy, fundamental human need and is closely linked to Berne's (1964) reference to the need for a sense of belonging, and what's more, promotes the opportunity for strokes. However, I believe that our need for acknowledgement and reassurance from others when embedded too deeply thwarts the potential for human growth. Furthermore, it carries both an adaptive and acquiescent function (Cornell, 2010) that has the potential to augment the very substance of our 'script system' and ultimately, as mentioned, lead to our 'script payoff'.

On further reflecting on Minikin's (2021) arguments on our 'desire to belong', she makes the valuable point that our responses to external messages are contingent on our given state of mind, on our sense of self and overall level of inner 'groundedness'. On the occasions when I was likely to step out of my epilepsy script, for example, when surrounded by like-minded people, I recognised that I had the ability to hold my disability with an inner conviction, and shameful feelings, be it ephemeral, were averted. However, the components of my internal orchestra that desired to belong meant that I would often revert to a 'default life position' (Widdowson, 2026), that is, to my 'fragile sense of OKness'. One way of formulating this experience is that I had made the 'despairing decision' as a child (McNeel, 2010) that 'something was wrong with me' and my attempts to be defiant against this decision were often dismissed by such deeply held beliefs.

I am acutely drawn to the metaphor Cornell (2010) refers to in his paper on 'Aspiration and Adaption' when he refers to 'a cage door opening from which a man has a choice only to walk out if he wishes' (p243). This metaphor elucidates what was my conflicting relationship with epilepsy, a composite of my occasional desire to leave my script behind and experience freedom and authenticity, and the opposing state of staying in a place that felt both familiar and predictable but that curtailed a sense of spontaneity. This dilemma appears to parallel Berne's own battle between his belief in a human's desire for self-actualisation and growth, or *physis* (Clarkson, 1992), and the passive more pessimistic view of the individual who lacks mastery and competence to achieve self-enhancement (Cornell, 1988). I began to question the implications this line of thinking had for someone like me who has a long-term, incurable health condition. For example, what level of authorship do I have over my script? If it is always evolving as Cornell (1988) and English (1988) detailed, is it open to refinement and progress in later life? Significantly, what are the clinical implications of my epilepsy script on my work with clients?

Berne's contribution to our understanding of the concept of script was evidently prolific, but as Erskine et al. (2011) expressly mentioned, the psychotherapeutic applications of his theory were severely lacking in his writing. However, Berne (1961) did refer to the practice of 'script analysis' in which he proposed that the task of therapy was to release the individual from the compulsion to repeat early script-bound scenes so that: 'control of the individual's [client's] destiny can be shifted from Child to Adult', from archeopsychic unconsciousness to neopsychic awareness (Berne, 1961, p117). Berne argued that script analysis involved the gathering of material until the nature of their script is fully grasped by the client, acting as an enabler to the breaking free of self-limiting patterns and achieving autonomy.

In TA practice, the *life script* functions as an essential component to the understanding of a person's unconscious long-term life plan; they grant access to the kind of world a person has been living, the people they are, and the quality of relationships they have formed (Erskine, 2010). Understanding and evaluating these scripts with clients aids the exploration and understanding of self-defeating, often purposeful behaviours rooted in parental injunctions, script decisions, and 'unconscious conclusions' from lived experience. I would argue that it is vital in the exploration of a 'disability script' that 'cultural transmissions of injunctions' (Berne, 1972) are considered, and any potential moral underpinnings attached to a person's experience of 'disability'. For example, important questions include: were there any social expectations relating to their disability that may have been internalised as part of their Cultural Parent? Have they in anyway felt devalued by their experience of having a disability (Drego, 1996).

The two worlds of being a disabled person and a psychologist practitioner were now meeting, and a host of conundrums were being confronted. I now began to question how this scripted self that was a measure of protection was going to show itself transferentially through the therapeutic relationship. As Baskerville (2022) eloquently puts it: 'did I dare to dialogue about difference with clients should it arise in the therapeutic space?' (p241). Through ongoing personal and professional development, I was increasingly becoming more adept at recognising and understanding my own internalised oppression relating to distorted messages about epilepsy, located at an individual and cultural level. I was thus developing greater tools for tapping into transference and countertransference dynamics as they relate to disability. My clinical experience has afforded the opportunity to work with clients who describe themselves as having a disability, and it has been a space through which open exploration about the challenges of 'difference' has occurred. I believe that due to my own lived experience of disability, this therapeutic space that exists between myself and my client is unique, in that here is the meeting of two subjective realities that have an instant commonality-they have likely encountered struggle, and at times knowingly encountered 'other esteem' for which they may have learnt to compensate (Roberts, 1983). However, for the benefit of the client, it was vital that I was not addressing this commonality from a place of scripty views on disability. In other words, did I remain stuck in my impasse on disability and therefore feel less free to have open, 'uncontaminated' reflections?

As a psychologist with epilepsy, the push and pull between the need to adapt and to conform to the forces of my script versus the desire to sit comfortably with my own 'version' of OKness were frequently brought into question. At both a conscious and unconscious level I had internalised a set of beliefs about epilepsy through a set of introjected injunctions, such as 'don't belong' and 'don't be important', and through a culture's value system that both judged and feared epilepsy as a disability. Yet I was entering into a profession that prides itself on being in a space with our clients grounded on principles of self-acceptance and equality. Here was a disabled woman who had learnt to 'fit in', and in the process 'lose my [her] authentic sense of identity' (Hargaden & Sills, 2002). It was therefore essential to the therapeutic process that I actively attended to the parts of my epilepsy script that were characterised by denial and internalised shame.

I was further aware that I was faced with the dilemma of whether, in the service of the client, to disclose my unseen disability. Disclosure may provide a model of vulnerability and instil a level of trust in the therapeutic relationship. However, it was brought to my attention that my script at times took me to a place where I questioned if this would simply induce fear in my client given that epilepsy as a condition still felt so misunderstood. In addition, I questioned how power differentials may play out in the therapeutic space. Would disclosure create a Child/Parent dynamic that would reinforce the 'less than' part of my script? I had lived in an 'other' space for most of my life, but as a white, professional woman, I became curious about who, if anyone, held the power in the room.

Baskerville (2022) in addressing the concepts of intersectionality and identity, invited me to ask a thought-provoking question when considering my disability script in the therapeutic space, and that is: 'What parts of me are welcome here?'. In understanding and integrating the split off parts that constitute my epilepsy script, I have overtime developed the tools that allowed for an 'internalised sense of OKness' (Hargaden & Sills, 2002). As a result, I embodied an inner self-acceptance which laid the foundation for authentic discourse around difference and otherness to occur safely within the therapeutic frame. By no longer feeling ashamed about my epilepsy, it not only fostered personal growth and resilience, but also created the space for empathy and connection with clients who have typically remained silent about their own disability due to external stigma, the internalising of negative attitudes, and systemic discrimination.

Prior to this awareness I had unconsciously consented to the position of 'almost OK', that for all its downsides, was a compromised position that did not 'deconstruct or threaten the norm' (Minikin, 2021). This entailed at times minimising or outrightly rejecting the impact my seizures had on my emotional and physical well-being. Yet lurking beneath was a professional woman who, when forced to confront the realities of her seizures, experienced a level of inner vulnerability. Seizures dictated that I took extra time to rest between clients, more time to complete tasks, and permission not to overcompensate to prove my capabilities. For both my personal and professional well-being, it was not merely the time to 'open the cage door' but to leave it open and move out of script.

Denouement

> Awareness means the capacity to see a coffeepot and hear the birds sing in one's own way, and not the way one was taught.
>
> (Berne, 1964, pp158–159)

As above-mentioned, there are clear divergences in opinion within the TA literature with regards to the degree of agency and self-creation the individual has in the formation of their life script, and arguably, the extent to which the individual has the capacity to change their script in pursuit of autonomy. Berne's thinking around the individual's capability for adjustment and adaptation diversified, and at times presents as confusing. On the one hand, his notion of script was flavoured with a deterministic value in which the individual had the challenging task of realising that their lives had thus far been restricted by parental programming flavoured by the 'the illusion of autonomy' (Cornell, 1988). It appeared that the move away from this proved at best challenging. On the other hand, Berne (1972) recognised the child's capacity to make choices, and whilst not specifically referring to the idea, implied the possible attainment of a 'healthy script', albeit caught in what Cornell (1988) aptly refers to as a continuous enthrallment of transgenerational drama. For Berne, the ultimate goal of TA was to achieve 'autonomy' or for a client to 'redesign their own life story' (Allen & Allen, 2005). This meant developing the tools for self-governance, responsibility, and moving away from patterns that longer proved helpful. Berne (1964) significantly noted how the execution of autonomy is brought about by the release or recovery of three capacities: awareness, spontaneity and intimacy.

It is evident from my unfolding narrative that the internalisation of a collection of disability script messages from parental injunctions and cultural scripts undoubtedly mapped my relationship with epilepsy in a dynamic and composite way. My disability script has been pivotal in acting as a buffer against shame, and under the guise of masking and minimisation helped to navigate my way through a series of life challenges and promote feelings of safety in an otherwise 'overstimulating world' (Scherch, 1979). In this sense, my epilepsy script offered me the platform for security, self-identification, and a means to organise my reality (see Cornell, 1988; English, 1988). Increasingly however I accepted that the lens through which I understood my experience of epilepsy was both surplus and outdated and no longer served a healthy function in the construction of my reality. I progressively became 'aware' that such a script, unless examined for its resourcefulness, would continue to be limiting. The process of 'refining' my script I argue has not involved direct elimination of old 'faulty' script messages but instead a mindful altering of my relationship with them at several levels. As the character Socrates in Dan Millman's book *Way of the Peaceful Warrior* (1980) aptly refers: 'the secret of change is to focus all your energy not on fighting the old, but on building the new' (p130). The focus for me was on creating a new relationship with my epilepsy rather than resisting the old script messages.

One of the main principles behind a new, meaningful way of being with my epilepsy can be understood in terms of Cornell's (2010) notion of resilience. The process of change was one of 'intrinsic motivation' and desire to gain a sense of both agency and competence, and this was invaluable to personal growth. In clinical practice with our clients, this means attending to what Cornell (2010) referred to as 'the dialectic tensions within the script' (Cornell, 2010, p249) as it provides the opportunity to redirect energy from writhing with the past to consciously recognising the freedom to choose and express feelings from those available.

Change has been incremental and has entailed deep exploration of transference and countertransference dynamics and strong interpersonal relatedness. Through increased awareness of my lived experience of epilepsy, I have highlighted numerous accounts of limited feelings of 'OKness', but arguably other times of increased ego strength as I learnt to shift my frame of reference from defining myself as an unworthy person to someone who is 'unique'. Stepping out of my disability script has involved negotiating ways of relating with my epilepsy experience that served to promote accepted ways of being with myself whilst moving away from an adaptive system that chiefly assumed a Not-OK position (Belanger & Laube, 1979).

I maintain that changes to my script beliefs are an ongoing process, but there has evidently been script refinement at a behavioural, intrapsychic, and affective level. For example, through intrapsychic exploration within therapy, I have learnt to sit 'alongside' epilepsy as a condition, rather than hold it in a place of opposition. As noted, this implies a decontamination of my script beliefs as they no longer 'narrow my frame of reference' (Erskine, 1980). In addition, script refinement has entailed a deeper understanding and changing of relationship patterns which I propose has been a two-way process. As I have become less combative towards my condition and become open to new ways of relating to it, it has demystified how I relate to others about my condition- I have begun to interact with others in a game-free, authentic way. A part of this process involved standing outside of myself and appreciating others' perceptions, despite at times being wrapped in misunderstanding and fear. In line with Allen and Allen (2005) on their relational view of autonomy, I contend that moving out of script towards a place of self-empowerment also involved a process of 'unfolding and expanding in and through {my} relationships with others' (p257), and this has involved for example open discussion about my epilepsy with people and fighting prevailing assumptions through active engagement in group discourse.

The task of 'refining' my epilepsy script and moving towards a place of autonomy has undoubtedly been characterised by ongoing, mutable life changes. Personal growth and potential {physis} as Erskine (2013) argued forms part of an 'internal thrust to challenge acquiescence' (p6), and as a disabled person with a script that at times questioned the notion of self-worth and self-governance, this task proved challenging. Oates (2021) in addressing the notion of neurodivergence and difference captures an important ingredient to moving out of my script which has involved 'differentiating myself from the norm in accounting for my different needs and ways of expression' (p70). That is, giving myself the permission to be myself without naming such differences as deficits. In addition, it is undeniably good practice as a psychologist to be aware of 'difference' as it enters the therapeutic space. Being open, curious and receptive to difference within my clients promotes attunement to potential internalised ableism that may have shaped the client's sense of self (Moores & Oates, 2024). Piccinino (2018) goes one step further and refers to positive ways the therapist can provide permission to the client to be themselves, to stand out and be autonomous, thus encouraging the process of self-fulfilment.

I believe that becoming conscious of my script was concomitant with a sense of regaining control and making healthy decisions that were no longer at the service of my script beliefs. I, for example, carried the message that my entire identity was linked to my epilepsy, illustrated by the common belief that I 'am' my epilepsy' rather than I 'experience' epilepsy. What's more, the integration of both the OK and the not OK aspects of my epilepsy has permitted a greater acceptance of the self, with a move away from a narrative that defines 'me' as the problem, to a place in which I can confidently hold dichotomous feelings about my epilepsy with increased 'authorship and autonomy' (Brajović Car, 2025).

Sugarman (1979), in detailing his experience of stuttering, shares how he shed the negative features of his earlier life script as he began to make choices, choices that were no longer enveloped in racket feelings of shame and helplessness. He describes how a 'symbiotic relationship' became a 'position' where his own self was OK, but his condition was not, and thus the 'alley dialogue' that previously prohibited permission for him to be himself no longer dominated. Sugarman's (1979) account accurately reflected my own experience with my disability. I had overtime 'collected stamps' that resulted in the internalisation of judgments and discounts which led to avoidance of talking about my epilepsy through fear of rejection. Overtime however, I no longer became tied to the pattern of my script, but instead, my Adult learnt to communicate with my Child that 'I am OK' (Sugarman, 1979). As Harris (1969) so aptly wrote: 'To know one's own Child, to be sensitive to one's Not OK feelings, is the first requirement for Adult data processing' (p90).What's more, my new contract now recited: 'I can be different from you, and you can be different from me' and this difference is welcomed on both sides'.

Conclusion

My life script has been part of a meaning-making process that has informed both my personal and professional development as a counselling psychologist and has been subject to increased positive change. In line with Newton's notion of script (2006), I propose that 'each of us creates our own continuous explanatory narrative that gives meaning to the past, provides a problem-solving blueprint for the present, and predicts the future' (p186). What's more, I advocate that these narratives are multiple and encompass numerous characters which are fundamental to the rich tapestry of life. Key components to the refinement of my epilepsy script included being part of a collaborative relationship that promoted open discourse about my disability, a space of discovery, compassion, and de-shaming. What's more, this sets the scene for the belief that as counselling psychologist with lived experience of epilepsy, I have the capacity to find a voice that is uniquely my own.

Note

1 The four existential positions include: (1) I am OK, You're OK; (2) I am OK, you're not-OK. (3) I am not-OK, you're OK. (4) I am not-OK, You're not OK.

References

Aldridge, B., & Stilman, R. (2024). Unmasking Neurodiversity: Revisiting the Relationship between Core Self and Sense of Self to Examine Common Neurodivergent Script Decisions. *Transactional Analysis Journal*, 54:1, 47–62. DOI: 10.1080/03621537.2024.2286576

Allen, J.R., & Allen, B.A. (2005). *Therapeutic Journey: Practice and Life*. Oakland, CA: TA Press.

Baskerville, V. (2022). A Transcultural and Intersectional Ego State Model of the Self: The Influence of Transcultural and Intersectional Identity on Self and Other. *Transactional Analysis Journal*, 52:3, 228–243. DOI: 10.1080/03621537.2022.2076398

Belanger. E., & Laube, J. (1979). Discounting the Disabled. *Transactional Analysis Journal*, 9:1, 47–50. DOI: 10.1177/036215377900900111

Benjamin, J. (2004). Beyond Doer and Done to: An Intersubjective View of Thirdness. *The Psychoanalytic Quarterly*, 73:1, 5–46. DOI: 10.1002/j.2167-4086.2004.tb00151.x

Benjamin, J. (2018). *Beyond Doer and Done to: Recognition Theory, Intersubjectivity and the Third*. Abingdon: Routledge.

Berne, E. (1961). *Transactional Analysis in Psychotherapy*. New York: Grovc Press.

Berne, E. (1962). Classification of Positions. *Transactional Analysis Bulletin*, 1:3, 23.

Berne, E. (1964). *Games People Play*. London: Penguin Random House.

Berne, E. (1966). *Principle of Group Treatment*. New York: Oxford. University Press.

Berne, E. (1972). *What Do You Say after You Say Hello?* London: The Psychology of Human Destiny. Transworld Publishers.

Berne, E. (1976). *Beyond Games and Scripts*. New York: Grove Press.

Brajović Car, K. (2025). Autonomy and Intimacy: A Critical Psychology Perspective. *Transactional Analysis Journal*, 55:3, 276–287. DOI: 10.1080/03621537.2025.2510882

Clarkson, P. (1992). *Physis in Transactional Analysis Journal*, 22:4, 202–209. DOI: 10.1177/036215379202200402

Cole, M. (1993). Injunctions and Secondary Gains in Chronic Pain Patients. *Transactional Analysis Journal*, 23:4, 191–194.

Cornell, W.F. (1988). Life Script Theory: A Critical Review from a Developmental Perspective. *Transactional Analysis Journal*: 18, 270–282.

Cornell, W.F. (2010). Aspiration or Adaptation? An Unresolved Tension in Eric Berne's Basic Beliefs. *Transactional Analysis Journal*, 40:3–4, 243–253. DOI: 10.1177/036215371004000309

Dostoevsky, F. (trans. by Alan Myers). (1995/1848). *White Nights and Other Stories*. London: Penguin Books/Penguin Classics.

Drego, P. (1996). Cultural Parent Oppression and Regeneration. *Transactional Analysis Journal*, 26:1, 58–77. DOI: 10.1177/036215379602600111

English, F. (1988). Whither Scripts? *Transactional Analysis Journal*, 18, 294–305.

Ernst, F. H., Jr. (1971). The OK Corral: The Grid for Get-on-With. *Transactional Analysis Journal*, 1:4, 230–239.

Erskine, R., & Zalcman, M. (1979). The Racket System. A Model for Racket Analysis. *Transactional Analysis Journal*, 9(1), 51–59.

Erskine, R. (1980). Script Cure: Behavioural, Intrapsychic and Physiological. *Transactional Analysis Journal*, 10:2, 102–106.

Erskine, R. (2010). *Life Scripts. A Transactional Analysis of Unconscious Relational Patterns*. London: Karnac Books Ltd.

Erskine, R., Tosi, M.T., O'Reilly-Knapp, M., Napper, R., English F., & Stuthridge, J. (2011). Life Scripts: Definitions and Points of View. *Transactional Analysis Journal*, 41:3, 255–264.

Erskine, R. (2013). Vulnerability, Authenticity, and Intersubjective Contact: Philosophical Principles of Integrative Psychotherapy. *International Journal of Integrative Psychotherapy*, 4:2, 1–9.

Fisher, R.S., Cross, J.H., & French, J.A. (2017). Operational Classification of Seizure Types by the International League against Epilepsy: Position Paper of the ILAE Commission for Classification and Terminology. *Epilepsia*, 58:4, 522–530.

Gavvala, J.R., & Schuele, S.U. (2016). New-Onset Seizure in Adults and Adolescents: A Review. *JAMA*, 316:24, 2657–2668.
Goulding, R., & Goulding, M. (1976). Injunctions. *Decisions and Redecisions Transactional Analysis Journal*, 6:1, 41–48. DOI: 10.1177/036215377600600110
Goulding, R.L., & Goulding, M.M. (1979). *Changing Lives through Redecision Therapy*. New York: Grove Press Inc.
Hargaden, H., & Sills, C. (2001). Deconfusion of the Child Ego State: A Relational Perspective. *Transactional Analysis Journal*, 31:1, 55–70. DOI: 10.1177/036215370103100107
Hargaden, H., & Sills, C. (2002). *Transactional Analysis: A Relational Perspective*. Hove: Brunner-Routledge.
Harris, T.A. (1969). *I'm OK-You're OK*. New York: Harpur and Row.
Klein, M. (1986). *The Selected Melanie Klein* (1. Mitchel/ Ed.). London: Penguine Books.
Ligabue, S. (1991). The Somatic Component of the Script in Early Development. *Transactional Analysis Journal*, 21:1, 21–30. DOI: 10.1177/036215379102100104
Loria, B. (1995). Structure Determinism and Script Analysis: A Bringing Forth of Alternative Realities. *Transactional Analysis Journal*, 25, 156–168.
Magiorkinis, E., Sidiropoulou, K., & Diamantis, A. (2010 Jan). Hallmarks in the History of Epilepsy: Epilepsy in Antiquity. *Epilepsy & Behavior*, 17:1, 103–108. DOI: 10.1016/j.yebeh.2009.10.023
Mazzetti, M. (2010). Eric Berne and Cultural Script. *Transactional Analysis Journal*, 40, 3–4, 187–195.
McNeel, J.R. (2010). Understanding the Power of Injunctive Messages and How They Are Resolved in Redecision Therapy. *Transactional Analysis Journal*, 40:2, 159–169. DOI: 10.1177/036215371004000211
Millman, D. (1980). *Way of the Peaceful Warrior*. Tiburon, CA: J. P. Tarcher/Houghton Mifflin.
Minikin, K. (2021). Relative Privilege and the Seduction of Normativity. *Transactional Analysis Journal*, 51:1, 35–48. DOI: 10.1080/03621537.2020.1853349
Moores, J., & Oates, S. (2024). What Is Psychological and What Is Neurological? A Political and Phenomenological Exploration of Neurodivergent Identity and Encounters with Thirdness. *Transactional Analysis Journal*, 54:1, 63–77. DOI: 10.1080/03621537.2023.2286575
Newton, T. (2006). Script, Psychological Life Plans, and the Learning Cycle. *Transactional Analysis Journal*, 36:3, 186–195. DOI: 10.1177/036215370603600303
Oates, S. (2021). What If My 'I'm OK, You're OK Is Different from Yours? Could the Inherent Optimism in Transactional Analysis Be a Form of Compulsory Ableism? *Transactional Journal*, 51:1, 63–76.
Parry, T.A. (1979). To Be or Not to Be Ok: The Development of the Child Ego State. *Transactional Analysis Journal*, 9:2, 124–130. DOI: 10.1177/036215377900900217
Piccinino, G. (2018). Reflections on Physis, Happiness, and Human Motivation. *Transactional Analysis Journal*, 48:3, 272–285. DOI: 10.1080/03621537.2018.1471293
Roberts, D.L. (1983). Cultural Scripts: The Problem of Supremacy. *Transactional Analysis Journal*, 13:4, 253–254. DOI: 10.1177/036215378301300415
Scherch, R.O. (1979). How Come We Don't See What We See: An Operational Theory and an Exercise about Frame of Reference, Redefinition and Discounts. *Transactional Analysis Journal*, 9:4, 251–254. DOI: 10.1177/036215377900900405
Steiner, C. (1971). *Games Alcoholics Play*. New York: Ballantine Books.
Steiner, C. (1974). *Scripts People Live*. New York: Grove Press.

Steiner, C. (2010) 'Scripts, then and now', in Erskine, R.G. (ed.) *Life Scripts: A Transactional Analysis of Unconscious Relational Patterns*. London: Karnac, pp. 203–216.
Steiner, C. (2012). The OK Position: Freedom, Equality, and the Pursuit of Happiness. *Transactional Analysis Journal*, 42:4, 294–297. DOI: 10.1177/036215371204200408
Sugarman, M. (1979). From Being a Stutterer to Becoming a Person Who Stutters. *Transactional Analysis Journal*, 9:1, 41–44. DOI: 10.1177/036215377900900108
Tombini, M., Narducci, F., Ricci, L., Sancetta, B., Boscarino, M., Quintiliani, L., Lanzone, J., Straffi, M., Di Lazzaro, V., & Assenza, G. (2024). Resilience and Psychosocial Factors in Adults with Epilepsy: A Longitudinal Study. DOI: 10.1016/j.yebeh.2024.109746
Turner, D. (2021). *Intersections of Privilege and Otherness in Counselling and Psychotherapy*. London: Routledge.
Widdowson, M. (2016). *Transactional Analysis for Depression: A Step-by-Step Treatment Manual*. Oxon: Routledge.
Widdowson, M. (2026). *Transactional Analysis—The Basics*. New York: Routledge.
World Health Organisation (WHO). (2024). https://www.who.int/news-room/fact-sheets/detail/epilepsy https://www.who.int/news-room/fact-sheets/detail/epilepsy
Zivkovic, A. (2023). OKness Revised: Analysis and Evolution of Berne's Concept of OKness, the Basic Positions, and the Related Reenactments of Berne's Internal World in the Transactional Analysis Community. *Transactional Analysis Journal*, 53:3, 286–300. DOI: 10.1080/03621537.2023.2214420

Chapter 6

Seeing an autistic psychologist in the mirror

An attachment perspective on autistic identity and experience

Emma Bede

Introduction

Choosing a thesis topic for my clinical psychology training, I knew that I wanted to do research with autistic adults. I had a background in working with autistic people, and chose to do so wherever possible, for reasons I couldn't really pin down beyond the simple fact that I found them easier to work with than other people; they understood me, and I understood them. It would take me nearly 20 more years of working with autistic people to recognise that this sense of ease was because I was also autistic. I could write that it took me decades to identify my own autism "despite all my training and experience", but in fact it was *because of* that supposed professional expertise that I failed to recognise myself in what I knew from diagnostic criteria and research that autism was meant to be like. When I encountered autistic people – even though I met them in circumstances where they were in the "othered" categories of patient, client, or research participant – I recognised something of myself, found a shared worldview and communicative style, and felt a connection. The DSM-IV diagnostic criteria in place at that time (American Psychiatric Association, 1994) talked about "marked impairments" in nonverbal communication, "a lack of spontaneous seeking to share enjoyment", and "a lack of social or emotional reciprocity"; the words "stereotyped" and "repetitive" and "inflexible" and "abnormal" echoed through the criteria, in ways that didn't connect at all with my experience. Descriptions of what autistic people were supposed to be like – unempathic, lacking insight into other people's minds, socially indifferent (see Baron-Cohen, 1990; Chevallier et al., 2012) – felt in many ways the opposite of myself, and certainly far removed from what a therapist or clinical psychologist should be like. I knew that I was socially awkward and anxious, and sometimes misread situations, and said the wrong things; I found reassurance and even joy in order and routine and repetition, and I echoed words and phrases that pleased me; I was perceived as different and as aloof, and I was bullied, and partly for these reasons I struggled with my mental health. The world could be confusing and overwhelming to me, but my brain and body were fizzing with colour and energy and meaningful connections, not DSM-IV's "nonfunctional routines". I felt deep and powerful emotions and was hypersensitive to others' moods and to shifts

DOI: 10.4324/9781003636014-7

in the emotional temperature of social situations, even if other details could elude me. I was fascinated by people and tried hard to make the interpersonal connections that I longed for, learning by focused observation the implicit social rules that others were following, and the patterns of words and facial expressions and gestures that would allow me to be (sometimes tentatively) accepted by other people. If I had "qualitative impairments in social interaction", it certainly wasn't for lack of trying, and surely at least some of the responsibility needed to rest with the people who were policing me out of the social relationships that I was trying so hard to create. I did succeed in forming some intense and long-lasting friendships – all of whom were subsequently found to be undiagnosed neurodivergent people. I had warm and loving relationships with relatives, without the mutual incomprehension that I encountered so often with outsiders. It was hard to be me, but the problem seemed to exist in the space between me and most other people, not intrinsically in me, although the world appeared very keen to tell me a different story.

Autism and attachment

For my thesis research, I settled on the idea of exploring attachment patterns among autistic adults. There was already a large body of research and theorising on autistic children's attachments: many of the earliest writers about autism characterised autistic children as entirely lacking normal attachment relationships. Some clinicians blamed the parents, the mothers in particular, who they perceived as cold and emotionally unavailable, and believed these failings had made the children autistic (e.g. Bettelheim, 1967). Others blamed the children. For example, Kanner (1943, p. 250) wrote that "these children have come into the world with innate inability to form the usual, biologically provided affective contact with other people". This latter idea remained explicit in the diagnostic criteria until DSM-III (American Psychiatric Association, 1980) and was implied even as late as DSM-IV-TR in phrases like "children with this disorder may treat adults as interchangeable [or] may cling mechanically to a specific person" (American Psychiatric Association, 2000). But contrary to these preconceptions, research generally shows that autistic children without other developmental delays demonstrate secure attachments at a rate largely consistent with children following a typical developmental trajectory. Those who are autistic and are also developmentally delayed are less likely than non-autistic developmentally delayed children to be classified as secure (Rutgers, Bakermans-Kranenburg, van IJzendoorn & van Berckelaer-Onnes, 2004); this is not the case for non-autistic children, where developmental or cognitive delay makes no difference to attachment security. In other words, there is something specific about the combination of autism with cognitive delay that interferes with attachment. It has been suggested that perhaps autism is intrinsically disruptive to the formation of secure attachments, but that children with more advanced cognitive (and verbal) skills are somehow able to use those skills to compensate, using effortful cognitive strategies to find a pathway to attachment security in the absence of the typical subconscious, affective pathway.

There is comparatively little research available on autistic adults' attachment representations. Given a hypothesis that children were forming attachments through some kind of cognitive effort, I wanted to listen to people who could tell me about their experiences in their own words. From where I sit now, 20 years later and aware of my own neurodivergence, it is hard to accurately remember the thought processes that led me to that point, but what strikes me from here is how that instinct is reflected in the shifts in my own understanding of autism, and in the transitions that have taken place within academic and clinical thinking over that period of time (see Dekker, 2020; Kras, 2009; Leadbitter, Buckle, Ellis & Dekker, 2021). The increased willingness and ability to hear directly from autistic people – as clinicians, researchers, and active participants and collaborators in research rather than subjects – has been slowly transforming our conceptualisation of autism (Fletcher-Watson et al., 2019; Happé & Frith, 2020; Pellicano et al., 2022; Stark et al., 2021). This move towards more accurately understanding autistic people's internal experiences carries an interesting echo of the literature on mentalisation – the ability to think about other people as having minds (Fonagy, Gergely, Jurist & Target, 2002) – that is central to the exploration of autism and attachment.

Mentalisation is at the heart of some important differences between the ways that we think about children's and adults' attachment patterns. Children's attachment behaviours are understood largely as a pragmatic response their specific caregivers' behaviours and capabilities; you can't be securely attached to an unavailable or unreliable parent (Bowlby, 1969). However, by adulthood, we are assumed to have amalgamated our various experiences of attachment figures' behaviour into a single internal working model of attachment, with expectations about how others will perceive and respond to us (Bretherton & Munholland, 1999). In simple terms, we learn the answers we expect to receive to the questions of "am I lovable?" and "are people trustworthy?" The Adult Attachment Interview (AAI; George, Kaplan & Main, 1996) particularly focuses on an adult's ability to reflect on and make sense of whatever they experienced in childhood, good or bad. In adulthood, attachment security is the ability to think coherently about your attachment relationships, whatever actually happened in them, and to hold your caregivers accurately and compassionately in mind regardless of how well they were able to do that for you.

This concept of accurately holding other people in mind as thinking beings has been given many names. The broad term "mentalisation" covers the moment-to-moment intuitive and mostly non-conscious processes that allow us to understand other humans in terms of their mental states (Fonagy et al., 2002); "reflective function" refers to ways of measuring mentalisation specifically within the context of attachment (Fonagy, Steele, Steele & Target, 1997). In looking at interactions between parents and children, different researchers have tried to capture the ways in which a parent is (or is not) able to hold the child and their experiences and emotions in mind, and respond appropriately, using terms such as parental sensitivity (Ainsworth, Blehar, Waters & Wall, 1978), emotional availability (see Bretherton, 2000), and mind-mindedness (Meins, 1997). Fundamentally, they are describing the parent's ability to correctly perceive their child's internal states and to reflect them back to the child in a manageable form. When the parent manages to do this, the child has the experience of being accurately and lovingly held in mind by the parent: "This person knows me and understands me, so they are able to meet my needs". In addition, the child learns something about recognising and responding to their own internal states. Imagine a parent saying to a crying toddler, "Were you frightened by that noise? It's OK, it was only a lorry going past, it won't hurt you – come and have a cuddle". In this tiny interaction, the child is learning names for their feelings, finding out about the causes of emotional reactions and about mistaken beliefs, being offered helpful strategies to manage their own difficult feelings, and (re)discovering that their parent is available and willing to look after them. Thousands of small exchanges like this are the building blocks not only of a secure attachment, but also of the child's ability to understand their own and others' minds, and their ability to perceive, understand, and regulate their own emotions. These specific behavioural interactions – rather than, for example, simple genetic inheritance – are the basis of attachment transmission, meaning that securely attached parents will generally have securely attached children (Sette, Coppola & Cassibba, 2015).

Autistic internal experiences

Within autism research, there has been an interest for many years in theory of mind, which is a very similar concept to mentalisation, though generally focused specifically on conscious cognitive problem-solving about other people's minds, captured in formalised tests such as false belief tasks and social stories (Baron-Cohen, Leslie & Frith, 1985; Premack & Woodruff, 1978). Autistic people's different patterns of responding in these tasks have historically been viewed as a lack of capacity for empathy and perspective-taking, with one prominent autism researcher going so far as to base entire theories around the presumption of autistic people's "mind-blindness" (Baron-Cohen, 1990). Another has written that

> The most general description of social impairment in autism is lack of empathy. Autistic people are noted for their indifference to other people's distress, their inability to offer comfort, even to receive comfort themselves. What empathy requires is the ability to know what the other person thinks or feels despite the fact that it is different from one's own mental state at the time... Even able autistic people seem to have great difficulty in achieving empathy in this sense.
>
> (Frith, 1989, pp. 144–145)

This was the model of autism that I was taught: autistic people have minimal ability to understand other people's thoughts or emotions and are in any case uninterested in trying to do so. I didn't recognise myself in that, and honestly, as an aspiring clinical psychologist – or even as someone trying to be a decent human being and member of society – it might have been extremely damaging to claim to belong to a group who apparently had those characteristics, which were not just absolute and irreparable skills deficits, but also framed autistic people as perhaps amoral, and possibly even inhuman (Chapman, 2018; Moran et al., 2011; Sun et al., 2022).

Over the last two decades, there has been a powerful movement towards centring the self-reported lived experiences of autistic people, and these tell a very different story about the autistic experience than those described above. Key concepts have been introduced into the literature and research by neurodivergent people, including monotropism (Murray, Lesser & Lawson, 2005), neuroqueer (Walker, 2021; see also Zurn, 2024), and even the term "neurodivergence" (Asasumasu, 2015; Botha et al., 2024). As part of this movement, an autistic researcher, Damian Milton, identified and named the "double empathy problem" (Milton, 2012): autistic people's behaviour doesn't make sense to non-autistic people, not because autistic people lack empathy, but because of mutual incomprehension between autistic and non-autistic people who think and experience the world in fundamentally different ways. This might at times lead autistic people to behave in ways that seem unempathic to neurotypicals, but it equally leads non-autistic people to perceive and treat autistic people in ways that are harsh, dehumanising, and harmful (Lim, Young & Brewer, 2022; Sasson et al., 2017; Shaw et al., 2024). In fact, although the double empathy problem describes a two-sided communication problem between brains that speak different languages, my personal and clinical experience would lead me to argue that autistic people are far more aware of this and work harder to bridge the gap, due to a lifetime steeped in neurotypical culture and being encouraged, or actively trained, to accommodate non-autistic people's preferred styles of communication and interaction.

Ironically, the diagnostic criteria in their various evolutions over the years are a fairly good demonstration of the double empathy problem. They focus on the observable behaviours of autistic people, repeatedly label them as strange and aberrant, and either lack curiosity about the internal experiences underlying them, or make wildly inaccurate assumptions about autistic people's motivations, intentions, and emotions. I didn't recognise myself in the diagnostic criteria because they were effectively written by a non-autistic person with a clipboard, observing autistic people's behaviour from a distance and noting down everything that seemed odd or incomprehensible. It didn't help that, at that time, the DSM-IV insisted that autism and ADHD were mutually exclusive diagnoses. We now know that a very significant proportion of people who meet criteria for one of those diagnoses will, like me, meet criteria for both (see for example Rong, Yang, Jin & Wang, 2021). There was obviously far less understanding of the unique profile many people now call AuDHD (autism plus ADHD) at that time when the diagnostic manual declared it impossible, which was yet another barrier to people recognising themselves in the criteria, or being recognised by professionals, because of inaccurate assumptions about their internal worlds.

Many autistic people have noted that the current diagnostic criteria are most accurate when viewed as a description of a distressed autistic person – social withdrawal, clinging to routines, sensory overload, and stimming. But they also muddle together autistic distress and autistic joy: am I echoing verbal phrases because I'm overwhelmed and have lost the capacity to use spontaneous speech, or am I delighting in the texture of my favourite phrases, and maybe connecting with another autistic person who shares my pleasure in this? Am I fixating on a specific topic because I am burnt out by the demands of everyday life and need to rewatch familiar TV or play meaningless phone games to recalibrate my brain and body, or am I immersed in a deep and satisfying interest that lights me up inside more than anything else I could possibly be doing right now? If the very lowest ebbs and the most beautiful moments of my experience are all jumbled together in these criteria as examples of disorder, deficit and abnormality – and, more importantly, if the experts given the task of describing me can't even tell the difference between my distress and my joy – how can I ever be accurately seen by anyone who knows autism though the lens of these criteria? If I am being described to myself by someone who doesn't understand me; should I decide that they are wrong, or that I am?

Attachment relationships as a place to see ourselves

One of the concepts that interested me when I started to learn about attachment is that our first relationships are not just places where we go to seek safety, but they are also the places where we learn about our own and other people's internal experiences (Jurist & Meehan, 2009). Our caregivers have the job of holding up a mirror to us that reflects us back accurately, though compassionately coloured by the flattering light of unconditional love. But that mirror can be distorted by the caregivers' own anxieties and experiences, by their beliefs about the world, by their lack of availability or their attention being consumed by other things. This isn't to blame them – they may be struggling with their own physical or mental health, with meeting the family's basic survival needs, or protecting their children from domestic violence; they may in turn have been profoundly shaped by the mirrors their parents held up to them. But the impact on the child is a distorted reflection, magnifying their perceived faults and what is most "difficult" about them, and concealing parts that the caregiver doesn't understand or can't work out how to love. In my therapy work, clients often find this mirror metaphor useful for understanding the ways that their own self-image, their perceptions of other people, and their behaviour in relationships, have been shaped by their own early relationships – in a way that doesn't blame their own "faulty thinking", or focus too heavily on parental failings that it's too late to fix now.

Using this model based in attachment and mentalisation, we can conceptualise the therapeutic relationship as holding up a more accurate and compassionate mirror to the client in front of us. Sometimes the focus of our work is on the relationship itself as the vehicle for change (in psychodynamic or cognitive analytic therapy, for example, mapping out the patterns of how the client expects to be experienced and expects to relate to others; Lemma, 2003; Ryle & Kerr, 2020). Sometimes the focus is on examining and adjusting unhelpful ideas that might have been learnt through the original distorted mirror (in CBT or ACT; see for example Beck, 2020;

Harris, 2019). Sometimes the heart of therapy is simply holding up this new mirror and making space for the client to process the experience and respond in new ways (the concept of unconditional positive regard in person-centred therapy seems to capture something very similar to this idea; Rogers, 1961).

In my own research (Taylor, Target & Charman, 2008), I asked autistic adults about their early childhoods and their experiences of being parented, and the most common responses are still what I often hear now as a therapist: "they loved me but they didn't understand me", or "they wanted to do the best for me, but what they did wasn't what I needed". The mirrors that were held up to these people were often well-intentioned, but still distorted by their attempts to reflect back a neurotypical child who just wasn't there, or by caregivers' struggles to understand and meet the needs of a child who didn't behave like the ones described in the parenting books, or by parents' own undiagnosed and unsupported neurodivergence and struggles with mental health and everyday life. As a therapist working in neurodiversity-affirming ways, my aim is to hold up a mirror that offers the possibility of more accurate and helpful reflections, not distorted by the kinds of assumptions and misunderstandings that still shape the diagnostic criteria. This kind of therapy supports people to accurately perceive their own needs, and the particular ways in which their bodies and brains operate and compassionately encourages them to pay attention to their internal experiences rather than pushing past them in pursuit of masking or fitting in (Flower et al., 2025; Hartman et al., 2024).

As therapists, we know that a collaborative and warm therapeutic relationship is the foundation of any effective therapy, and are used to holding this in mind, but what has become more apparent to me in my clinical practice is how much assessment and diagnosis can also be helpfully conceptualised in this way. When I work through the assessment process with people, and when it results in an autism diagnosis and a formulation of how the issues someone brought to an assessment can be understood through the lens of autism, it is surprisingly common for the client to reflect back that they feel understood in a way they have never felt before. This is less about the relatively short time I've spent getting to know them, and more about having an explanatory framework, in seeing them as autistic, that organises what they have told me so I can offer a new and more accurate mirror to reflect them back to themselves. The illusion of being known better than ever before is actually the impact of seeing themselves reflected back in a newly coherent way that makes sense of what felt like chaos and that brings structure and focus to what was blurred and incomprehensible.

Being autistic and a psychologist

Where do I sit in this process as an autistic psychologist, assessor, and therapist? It's important to acknowledge the complexity of making self-disclosure decisions, and the differences these could make to therapeutic relationships and to clients' self-concepts (Audet & Everall, 2010; Robertson et al., 2025). I make client-by-client, session-by-session decisions about whether to disclose to clients explicitly that I am neurodivergent, to imply it, or to avoid referencing it. But whether or not clients know I am autistic, the fact that I am shapes the mirror that I hold up to the people I work with. As hard as we might (or might not) try to be blank slates, as psychologists we are all human beings, and our assumptions and reactions and micro-expressions are influenced by the human life experiences that we bring to our work (Carn, undated; Welton, 2018). When I hold a mirror to my clients, it is affected by my history and daily existence as an autistic person, and I believe that makes a better mirror for my autistic clients, which helps them to feel accurately perceived and compassionately held in mind.

I notice that this process of mirror-holding changes me too. I work hard and consciously to be actively neurodiversity-affirming and inclusive in the ways that I reflect back to clients. Autistic people are more likely to identify with marginalised genders and sexual orientations and relationship models (George & Stokes, 2018), are more likely to experience chronic illness and disability (Cashin, Buckley, Trollor & Lennox, 2018), and autistic people of colour experience more acute discrimination at the intersection of those two social marginalisations (Jones, Botha & Sasson, 2025). I have grown up steeped in these prejudices, the ones that marginalise me as well as the ones that privilege me. I cannot undo that or extract myself and my clients from the unjust world we live in, but I can choose to actively push against it, to educate myself and relearn the language I use, and choose to listen to other stories than the ones presented to me as the defaults, the social norms. But in actively taking this neuroaffirming stance with clients, training myself to hold the mirror that I wish they had been able to see in their early years, some of it inevitably reflects back onto me. I catch glimpses of myself in the mirror I am holding and see my own differences and struggles in that compassionate light.

There are risks inherent in this sense of being better understood, the biggest one being that people have the illusion of being seen perfectly, in a way that we all crave on some level, and which is never fully possible in the real world. The leap from feeling misunderstood to feeling understood puts people at risk of confusing the mirror with the person, imagining that the therapist is able to perceive them perfectly in a way that nobody ever really can, instead of recognising that their experience has been transformed by the new lens, not the person holding it. This is particularly acute when someone's past experience or self-concept has been strongly coloured by criticism or shame, and for the first time they are being offered acceptance just as they are (Cruwys et al., 2023; Smith, 2015).

Being accurately and inaccurately seen

As human beings who are working as therapists, we also run the risk of perceiving sameness where there is only really similarity – of seeing ourselves in our clients, of distorting the mirror we hold by reflecting our own selves and experiences in it. When you navigate the world as autistic – and more broadly, as neurodivergent or disabled or minoritised in any way – you constantly experience yourself as other and different, in a world whose defaults are neuronormativity

(Benson, 2023), heteronormativity (Ward & Schneider, 2009), white normativity (de Bruijn, Emmen & Mesman, 2025; Plaisime, Jipguep-Akhtar & Belcher, 2023), and so on. Through finding scraps of representation, and self-recognition, you can cobble together a sense of yourself in the world, whether that's neurodivergent people seeking out ND-coded characters in fiction, or Black parents hunting for dolls that look like their children, or queer or trans people obsessively following the career paths of LGBTQ+ politicians or celebrities, or wherever it is that you find the little fragments of the world that reflect your face back to you in some small way, instead of only showing you what's possible for people who are not quite like you. We have a fundamental need and desire for connection, for seeing ourselves in others and being accurately seen.

Prior to getting a diagnosis, I had not fully anticipated the complexity of decisions about "coming out" as autistic in professional contexts. I had some anxiety about whether clients would perceive me as a competent therapist if they knew I was autistic, and some ideas about how I might handle this (Beagan, Sibbald, Pride & Bizzeth, 2022; Turnock, Langley & Jones, 2022). I gave relatively little thought to the potential reactions of my clinical psychology colleagues. I assumed that they would understand autism well enough to respond with compassion and empathy; those are, after all, not only necessary professional prerequisites, but also supposedly something that the neurotypical majority can do better than I can. However, in practice, I have become extremely cautious and self-protective in professional spaces, except for specific groups where I know most people work in neurodiversity-affirming ways, or when people are explicit in signalling their awareness and/or open-mindedness. This is not just anxious over-caution, but a deliberate strategy in response to prejudices and harmful behaviour that I have witnessed and directly experienced from fellow professionals. There is always a risk that someone's "knowledge" or beliefs about autism actually get in the way of them seeing and understanding me, just as my own "knowledge" prevented me from accurately seeing myself for so long. If someone has a deficit-based understanding of autism like that embodied in the diagnostic criteria, as I previously did, then inviting them to look at me through the lens of autism may distort their perception of me, or alternatively, they may flatly refuse to do it and tell me I am not autistic. The question I am always asking myself is this: if this person has a box in their head labelled "autism", and I don't fit neatly into it, will they expand the box to accommodate me, or will they shrink me to fit me into the box? It is interesting to think about cognitive dissonance theory in this context, and the many ways in which humans use cognitive strategies to avoid having to change their minds (Festinger, 1957).

A reflection that makes sense

Like so many neurodivergent people, I have a horror of even trying to fit into a box, of being limited and defined by a specific category, and not accounting for all the other aspects of people's identities – how I might have more in common with someone else who is also a parent or a professional or the same age as me, or how my whiteness or accent or physical health might advantage me relative to someone else with the same diagnosis. But even at the start of that previous sentence, I've grouped myself into the category of neurodivergent people, put us all into this box even while saying none of us wants to be in there. There is something valuable in finding similarity with other people, if we can do so without reducing everyone to that one shared characteristic. Rather than a box, I return to the idea that knowing about my autism shows me a mirror that reflects me more accurately than other mirrors I may have been offered. I bring my whole self to the mirror, with all the complex intersections of relative privilege and disadvantage and lived experience, and see all of that reflected back to me in ways that make sense. All the things about me that the neurotypical world told me were deficits make sense when they're seen through a lens of neurodivergence; and, far from being incompatible with being a therapist, these exact things are some of my best assets as a psychologist. I can tolerate really long silences, I ask awkward questions, I'm puzzled by the social rules that say certain subjects can't be spoken about, I run away from empty small talk and towards the intensity of deeper topics, and I may fail to see the supposedly obvious but can often bring a totally unexpected perspective. These things make me a misfit in neurotypical social situations, but I find similarity and connection with other neurodivergent people, and I also thrive in the specific and very socially weird setting that we call therapy (Carter, 2025).

Conclusion

In putting myself forward to write this chapter, I wrestled with two dilemmas: one, whether it feels safe to position myself publicly as autistic, to a professional (and presumably largely neurotypical) audience; and two, whether I really belong in a book about disabled psychologists. I still don't know whether I think of my own autism and ADHD as disabilities, or as a neurotype that is socially marginalised (and therefore disabling), and I don't know whether other people with very different lived experiences of disability would be comfortable with me using the label of disability for myself. The questions of identity and belonging persist in these two worries: will I be accurately perceived by these social groups, whether the group called psychologists or the group called disabled people? And will they recognise me as similar enough to belong with them, or will other facets of my self exclude me? Of course, questions of social exclusion and of trying to conceal my differences in order to fit in are fundamental to the autistic experience. How much of this anxiety is genuinely not belonging, and how much is a lifetime of being told I don't belong, and self-protective anticipation of rejection? In some ways nothing has changed: I still see versions of myself reflected in other people's eyes, whether that's direct or implicit feedback, or witnessing the conversations that some clinical psychologists have about neurodivergent people when they haven't noticed that we're in the room too, or reading books and papers that still cling to deficit models, or seeing news and social media making wildly inaccurate claims about causes of and cures for autism. Humans are intrinsically relational creatures, and it's probably inevitable, and psychologically healthy, to keep looking to others for feedback. The difference that has come with identifying as autistic, and that continues to evolve over time, is perhaps just an ability to recognise the subjectivity and multiplicity of identities; to see the mirrors, as well as the reflections.

References

Ainsworth, M. D. S., Blehar, M. C., Waters, E., & Wall, S. (1978). *Patterns of attachment: A psychological study of the strange situation.* Hillsdale, NJ: Erlbaum.

American Psychiatric Association (1980). *Diagnostic and statistical manual of mental disorders* (3rd edition). Washington, DC: American Psychiatric Association.

American Psychiatric Association (1994). *Diagnostic and statistical manual of mental disorders* (3rd edition). Washington, DC: American Psychiatric Association.

American Psychiatric Association (2000). *Diagnostic and statistical manual of mental disorders* (4th edition – text revision). Washington, DC: American Psychiatric Association.

Asasumasu, K. [posting as "sherlocksflataffect"] (2015). PSA from the actual coiner of 'neurodivergent'. *Tumblr post.* Available from: https://sherlocksflataffect.tumblr.com/post/121295972384/psa-from-the-actual-coiner-of-neurodivergent

Audet, C. T., & Everall, R. D. (2010). Therapist self-disclosure and the therapeutic relationship: A phenomenological study from the client perspective. *British Journal of Guidance & Counselling, 38*(3), 327–342.

Baron-Cohen, S. (1990). Autism: A specific cognitive disorder of "mind-blindness." *International Review of Psychiatry, 2*, 81–90.

Baron-Cohen, S., Leslie, A. M., & Frith, U. (1985). Does the autistic child have a 'theory of mind'? *Cognition, 21,* 37–46.

Beagan, B. L., Sibbald, K. R., Pride, T. M., & Bizzeth, S. R. (2022). Client-centered practice when professional and social power are uncoupled: The experiences of therapists from marginalized groups. *The Open Journal of Occupational Therapy, 10*(4), 1–14.

Beck, J. S. (2020). *Cognitive behavior therapy: Basics and beyond.* New York: Guilford Publications.

Benson, K. J. (2023). Perplexing presentations: Compulsory neuronormativity and cognitive marginalisation in social work practice with autistic mothers of autistic children. *The British Journal of Social Work, 53*(3), 1445–1464.

Bettelheim, B. (1967). *The empty fortress: Infantile autism and the birth of the self.* New York: The Free Press.

Botha, M., Chapman, R., Giwa Onaiwu, M., Kapp, S. K., Stannard Ashley, A., & Walker, N. (2024). The neurodiversity concept was developed collectively: An overdue correction on the origins of neurodiversity theory. *Autism, 28*, 1591–1594.

Bowlby, J. (1969). *Attachment and loss: Vol. 1. Attachment.* New York: Basic Books.

Bretherton, I. (2000). Emotional availability: An attachment perspective. *Attachment and Human Development, 2*, 233–241.

Bretherton, I., & Munholland, K. A. (1999). Internal working models in attachment relationships: A construct revisited. In J. Cassidy & P. R. Shaver (eds.), *Handbook of attachment: Theory, research, and clinical applications*. New York: The Guilford Press.

Carn, J. (undated). *Why therapist identity matters (not the blank slate).* Available from: https://www.anchoredinself.co.uk/blog/why-therapist-identity-matters-not-the-blank-slate

Carter, K. (2025). Working with my neurokin. In M. Marnau (ed.), *On being an autistic therapist*. Ross-on-Wye: PCCS Books.

Cashin, A., Buckley, T., Trollor, J. N., & Lennox, N. (2018). A scoping review of what is known of the physical health of adults with autism spectrum disorder. *Journal of Intellectual Disabilities, 22*, 96–108.

Chapman, R. (2018). *Autism, neurodiversity, and the good life: On the very possibility of autistic thriving* (Doctoral dissertation, University of Essex).

Chevallier, C., Kohls, G., Troiani, V., Brodkin, E. S., & Schultz, R. T. (2012). The social motivation theory of autism. *Trends in Cognitive Science, 16*, 231–239.

Cruwys, T., Lee, G. C., Robertson, A. M., Haslam, C., Sterling, N., Platow, M. J.,..., & Walter, Z. C. (2023). Therapists who foster social identification build stronger therapeutic working alliance and have better client outcomes. *Comprehensive Psychiatry, 124*, 152394.

de Bruijn, Y., Emmen, R. A. G., & Mesman, J. (2025). Color-evasiveness and white normativity: Examples set by parents in parent–child interactions in the Netherlands. *Cultural Diversity & Ethnic Minority Psychology, 31*(2), 333–346.

Dekker, M. (2020). From exclusion to acceptance: independent living on the autistic spectrum. In S. K. Kapp (ed.), *Autistic community and the neurodiversity movement*. Singapore: Palgrave Macmillan, pp. 41–49.

Festinger, L. (1957). *A theory of cognitive dissonance*. Evanston, IL: Stanford University Press.

Fletcher-Watson, S., Adams, J., Brook, K., Charman, T., Crane, L., Cusack, J.,..., & Pellicano, E. (2019). Making the future together: Shaping autism research through meaningful participation. *Autism, 23*(4), 943–953.

Flower, R. L., Benn, R., Bury, S., Camin, M., Muggleton, J., Richardson, E. K.,..., & Jellett, R. (2025). Defining neurodiversity affirming psychology practice for autistic adults: A Delphi study integrating psychologist and client perspectives. *Autism in Adulthood*. https://journals.sagepub.com/doi/10.1089/aut.2024.0305

Fonagy, P., Gergely, G., Jurist, E. L., & Target, M. (2002). *Affect regulation, mentalization, and the development of the self.* London: Karnac.

Fonagy, P., Steele, M., Steele, H., & Target, M. (1997). *Reflective functioning manual.* Unpublished manuscript. London: University College.

Frith, U. (1989). *Autism: Explaining the enigma.* Oxford: Blackwell.

George, C., Kaplan, N., & Main, M. (1996). *Adult attachment interview.* Unpublished manuscript. Berkeley: Department of Psychology, University of California.

George, R., & Stokes, M. A. (2018). Gender identity and sexual orientation in autism spectrum disorder. *Autism, 22*, 970–982.

Happé, F., & Frith, U. (2020). Annual research review: Looking back to look forward–changes in the concept of autism and implications for future research. *Journal of Child Psychology and Psychiatry, 61*(3), 218–232.

Harris, R. (2019). *ACT made simple: An easy-to-read primer on acceptance and commitment therapy.* New Harbinger Publications.

Hartman, D., Day, A., O'Donnell-Killen, T., Doyle, J. K., Kavanagh, M., & Azevedo, J. (2024). What does it mean to be neurodiversity affirmative? *The Psychologist.* Available from: https://www.bps.org.uk/psychologist/what-does-it-mean-be-neurodiversity-affirmative

Jones, D. R., Botha, M., & Sasson, N. J. (2025). "I'm kind of stuck in the middle. I don't know where to go": Race, autism, and intersectional stigma among Black and White autistic adults. *Autism in Adulthood.* https://doi.org/10.1177/25739581251374440

Jurist, E.L. and Meehan, K.B. (2009). Attachment, mentalization and reflective functioning. In J. H. Obegi & E. Berant (eds.), *Attachment theory and research in clinical work with adults*. New York: Guilford Press, pp. 71–93.

Kanner, L. (1943). Autistic disturbance of affective contact. *Nervous Child, 2*, 217–250.

Kras, J. F. (2009). The "ransom notes" affair: When the neurodiversity movement came of age. *Disability Studies Quarterly, 30*(1). https://dsq-sds.org/article/ojs_id/1065/

Leadbitter, K., Buckle, K. L., Ellis, C., & Dekker, M. (2021). Autistic self-advocacy and the neurodiversity movement: Implications for autism early intervention research and practice. *Frontiers in Psychology, 12*, 635690.

Lemma, A. (2003). *Introduction to the practice of psychoanalytic psychotherapy*. Chichester, West Sussex and Hoboken, NJ: John Wiley & Sons.

Lim, A., Young, R. L., & Brewer, N. (2022). Autistic adults may be erroneously perceived as deceptive and lacking credibility. *Journal of Autism and Developmental Disorders, 52*, 490–507.

Meins, E. (1997). *Security of attachment and the social development of cognition*. Psychology Press.

Milton, D. E. (2012). On the ontological status of autism: The 'double empathy problem'. *Disability & Society, 27*, 883–887.

Murray, D., Lesser, M., & Lawson, W. (2005). Attention, monotropism and the diagnostic criteria for autism. *Autism, 9*, 139–156.

Pellicano, E., Lawson, W., Hall, G., Mahony, J., Lilley, R., Heyworth, M.,…, & Yudell, M. (2022). "I knew she'd get it, and get me": Participants' perspectives of a participatory autism research project. *Autism in Adulthood, 4*(2), 120–129.

Plaisime, M. V., Jipguep-Akhtar, M. C., & Belcher, H. M. (2023). 'White People are the default': A qualitative analysis of medical trainees' perceptions of cultural competency, medical culture, and racial bias. *SSM-Qualitative Research in Health, 4*, 100312.

Premack, D., & Woodruff, G. (1978). Does the chimpanzee have a "theory of mind"? *Behavioral and Brain Sciences, 1*, 515–526.

Robertson, A. M., Cruwys, T., Quayle, A., Stevens, M., Platow, M. J., & Scholz, B. (2025). Goldilocks disclosures: A qualitative exploration of when therapist self-disclosure of lived experience is "just right". *Psychological Services, 23*(2), 375–386. https://doi.org/10.1037/ser0000959

Rogers, C. R. (1961). *On becoming a person: A therapist's view of psychotherapy*. Boston, MA: Houghton Mifflin Company.

Rong, Y., Yang, C.-J., Jin, Y., & Wang, Y. (2021). Prevalence of attention-deficit/hyperactivity disorder in individuals with autism spectrum disorder: A meta-analysis. *Research in Autism Spectrum Disorders, 83*, 101759.

Rutgers, A. H., Bakermans-Kranenburg, M. J., van IJzendoorn, M. H., & van Berckelaer-Onnes, I. A. (2004). Autism and attachment: A meta-analytic review. *Journal of Child Psychology and Psychiatry, 45*, 1123–1134.

Ryle, A., & Kerr, I. B. (2020). *Introducing cognitive analytic therapy: Principles and practice of a relational approach to mental health*. Hoboken, NJ: John Wiley & Sons.

Sasson, N. J., Faso, D. J., Nugent, J., Lovell, S., Kennedy, D. P., & Grossman, R. B. (2017). Neurotypical peers are less willing to interact with those with autism based on thin slice judgments. *Scientific Reports, 7*, 40700.

Sette, G., Coppola, G., & Cassibba, R. (2015). The transmission of attachment across generations: The state of art and new theoretical perspectives. *Scandinavian Journal of Psychology, 56*, 315–326.

Shaw, S. C., Carravallah, L., Johnson, M., O'Sullivan, J., Chown, N., Neilson, S., & Doherty, M. (2024). Barriers to healthcare and a 'triple empathy problem' may lead to adverse outcomes for autistic adults: A qualitative study. *Autism, 28*, 1746–1757.

Smith, J. D. (2015). Creative restorations: Holding a mirror to the self in brief dynamic therapy. *Psychodynamic Practice, 21*(4), 300–319.

Stark, E., Ali, D., Ayre, A., Schneider, N., Parveen, S., Marais, K.,…, & Pender, R. (2021). Coproduction with autistic adults: Reflections from the authentistic research collective. *Autism in Adulthood, 3*(2), 195–203.

Sun, L., Lukkarinen, L., Noppari, T., Nazari-Farsani, S., Putkinen, V., Seppälä, K.,…, & Nummenmaa, L. (2022). Aberrant motor contagion of emotions in psychopathy and high-functioning autism. *Cerebral Cortex, 33*(2), 374–384.

Taylor, E. L., Target, M., & Charman, T. (2008). Attachment in adults with high-functioning autism. *Attachment & Human Development, 10*(2), 143–163.

Turnock, A., Langley, K., & Jones, C. R. (2022). Understanding stigma in autism: A narrative review and theoretical model. *Autism in Adulthood,* 4(1), 76–91.

Walker, N. (2021). *Neuroqueer heresies: Notes on the neurodiversity paradigm, autistic empowerment, and postnormal possibilities.* Fort Worth, TX: Autonomous Press.

Ward, J., & Schneider, B. (2009). The reaches of heteronormativity: An introduction. *Gender & Society, 23*(4), 433–439.

Welton, R. S. (2018). Therapist anonymity: Being a blank screen in a touch screen world. *Psychiatrics News, 53*(22), 14–15.

Zurn, P. (2024). Re-citing the origins of neuroqueer. *Kennedy Institute of Ethics Journal, 34*, 333–364.

Chapter 7

Bridging two worlds

Lived experience and clinical psychology in healthcare settings

Sophie Gwinnett

Introduction

Clinical psychology has long grappled with the tension between personal subjectivity and professional neutrality. Yet what happens when we find ourselves in clinical work that so closely aligns with our own lived experience of disability? In this chapter, I explore these dual positions and how my personal health journey is inseparable from my professional identity.

Living with type 1 diabetes and later breast cancer, while also at times experiencing intense periods of health anxiety, has profoundly shaped how I understand the interplay between physical health, emotional wellbeing and the relational dynamics of care. These experiences have not only influenced how I work in physical health settings but have also provided insights that I could not have gained otherwise.

Drawing on these experiences, I share a trauma-informed and relational framework for understanding health anxiety that emerged from my own experiences of disability and therapy. Through doing so, I hope to demonstrate how lived experience of disability can meaningfully shape psychological practice, not only within the therapeutic encounter but also within the broader culture of healthcare.

By telling this story, I aim to bridge the patient/professional divide, to name some of the challenges of working in our profession while living with a disability, and to highlight the unique perspectives that such experiences can offer in doing so. This chapter contributes to the wider project of normalising and valuing open discourse about disability in psychology and of recognising lived experience as a vital source of professional wisdom.

The diagnosis

My diagnosis of type 1 diabetes came at the age of 11, a time when I was beginning to establish a sense of independence and identity. When the symptoms emerged, I instinctively knew something was wrong. At the GP surgery, my blood glucose was tested, and I was sent straight to hospital. Some of the children on the ward

DOI: 10.4324/9781003636014-8

were very unwell, which frightened me. My mum was beside herself with anguish. I knew I had to be brave; I suspect I was told that by well-meaning adults.

What had once been a carefree relationship with my body quickly shifted to one of hypervigilance and calculation. Every meal, activity, and social interaction carried with it the burden of medical decision-making. The word *control* echoed everywhere. “Good control” was the aim, but with hard work, I was told I could achieve “excellent control”. Management of the condition in 1990 was far less advanced and offered none of today’s diabetes technology. Instead, treatment involved daily injections, rigid eating regimes with careful carbohydrate counting, and regular finger-prick testing of blood glucose levels. Alongside this came education about the long-term risks of poor control: limb amputation, blindness, kidney failure, and stroke. These hovered in the background like a constant, low-level threat. At the same time, I was warned of the immediate dangers of hypoglycaemia, when blood glucose falls dangerously low.

One night in hospital, I overheard my doctor telling the team, “Sophie may have a hypo in the night, we’ll just have to wait and see”. My body filled with dread. I was convinced I would die that night. I cried silently in bed, terrified, wishing for my mum. That night nothing happened, though hundreds of hypos would follow in later years. Still, that moment marked the start of enduring vigilance, scanning my body for signs of danger.

In the months that followed, I learned how to manage my condition with determination to achieve “excellent control”. I was keen to reassure those around me so as not to exacerbate their sadness at my diagnosis, feeling responsible not only for my own wellbeing, but for loved ones too. I once heard someone say, “I guess you’ve become accustomed to it, like brushing your teeth”. That became my script: *“Oh it’s fine, it’s as normal for me as brushing my teeth!”* – the answer I offered whenever anyone asked what it was like to live with T1D. In reality, my adolescence became defined by constant monitoring and balancing. Too much or too little insulin could be life-threatening, and keeping myself alive became my daily task. T1D is a condition that requires a high level of self-management. I would see my hospital team two to three times each year, but the responsibility for keeping my blood glucose levels within a safe range sat firmly with me.

Research from Stanford University (2014) estimates that people with T1D make around 180 additional health-related decisions every day compared to non-diabetics. Hour-to-hour medical decisions can understandably lead to exhaustion and overwhelm. According to Scibilia (2022), many people living with the condition will experience “diabetes burnout” at some point in their lives, often leading to higher psychological distress and poorer diabetes outcomes (Helgeson, 2021). Research shows that acceptance, utilisation of social resources, and psychological interventions can all mitigate diabetes burnout (Helgeson, 2021; Cyranka et al., 2024; Kahkoska et al., 2025), but for me as a young person, these resources were a long way off as I felt the weight of medical responsibility, a responsibility that would profoundly shape how I came to understand myself and later, my clients.

The cost of invisibility

As I moved further into adolescence, I became acutely aware of my difference. Like most teenagers, I only wanted to fit in. The shame of having T1D gnawed away at me, while outwardly I worked hard to hide it. T1D is classed as an "unseen disability". I would hide in toilet cubicles to inject or test, to be doubly sure. The emotional cost of appearing fine often left me feeling overwhelmed and exhausted. According to Ashraf and Cheng (2024), T1D-related blame, mockery, and discrimination are common, and I worked hard to minimise or hide my condition. Like most people with T1D, I regularly found myself on the receiving end of misconceptions about the condition, such as being asked if I'd brought it upon myself by eating too much sugar or not managing my weight (Willis, 2025).

Hospital check-ups were a particular source of fear; I was terrified of being reprimanded, unsure of the relationship with my healthcare team. They were not teachers yet always evaluating me, generous with praise when my control was good, equally generous with critique when it was not. My sense of worth became entangled with diabetes control. My numbers telling a story about me – responsible or careless, compliant or resistant. Over time, avoidance behaviours began to creep into my care. I fabricated blood glucose readings, presenting carefully written but fictional logs to give the appearance of perfect control. Willis (2025) identifies this common pattern in people with diabetes, where a perceived sense of failure can cause people to avoid diabetes consultations or hide perceived "flaws" and I experienced, at times, a deep sense of shame and inadequacy when attending consultations.

In my later teens and early twenties, I grew more willing to disclose it to others, but the underlying shame persisted. By then, though, the shame had found a powerful companion: health anxiety. Years of relentless responsibility, masking, and monitoring had taken their toll. I felt consumed by worry and fear about my health. This is not unusual, research shows that young people with T1D experience anxiety and depression at two to three times the rate of their non-diabetic peers (Rechenberg et al., 2017) and the intensive, lifelong responsibility of managing diabetes can significantly impact a person's mental health, which in turn can impact diabetes outcomes (Tenreiro & Hatipoglu, 2025).

Looking back now, I can see what I could not possibly have understood at 11 years old. At the time, it seemed like I was expected simply to adjust. But through a trauma-informed lens, I now recognise what was happening beneath the surface: the sudden responsibility for my own survival, the fear of reprimand if I got it wrong, the pressure to maintain "good control", the sadness and guilt for the understandable distress this created for those around me and my need to reassure them, the embarrassment of being different, and the dread of the future complications that might lie ahead.

"Trauma" can be defined as "any overwhelming event that a person experiences, where they are powerless to deal effectively with the situation" (Waft, 2023). Looking back now, I can see that my hypervigilance, shame, anxiety, avoidance, and need for invisibility can be understood as necessary adaptations in the face of overwhelming health-related changes, trauma responses designed to keep me calm and ensure my survival at a time when I felt overwhelmed by threat and responsibility (Bloom, 1999). Such adaptations would continue to shape my personal relationship with health and, eventually, my clinical practice.

From patient to psychologist

By my late teens, I already knew I wanted to pursue a career in psychology. Looking back, I have little doubt that my experience of growing up with T1D played a defining role in that decision. As a child, my regular hospital appointments were often a source of anxiety. Yet, amidst the clinical routines, there were moments of unexpected comfort. I remember seeing a kind clinical psychologist in the waiting area. She would sit beside me for a few minutes and talk, not about my blood sugars, not about control or compliance, but about me. She asked about my hobbies, my interests, and my friends. She saw the girl behind the diagnosis. I don't recall ever having formal therapy, but I do recall the warmth of those interactions. According to Van Der Kolk (2014), the social engagement system shuts down during trauma, disconnecting people from themselves and others. Creating opportunities for relational safety is crucial in trauma healing as it fosters a sense of belonging and security. In hindsight and with this lens of trauma-informed care, I can see what those moments in the waiting room represented: a brief sanctuary of relational safety in an environment otherwise charged with responsibility, vulnerability, and the silent weight of being "the patient".

I accepted a post as an Assistant Clinical Psychologist in the very hospital where I had been diagnosed 12 years earlier. This gave me my first taste of the subtle but powerful dynamics of "othering" in healthcare. "Otherness" or "Othering" refers to the process by which a dominant group ("us") constructs out-groups ("them"), leading to potential stigmatisation and discrimination (Staszak, 2020). Within healthcare, Othering can negatively impact professional relationships and patient outcomes (Roberts & Schiavenato, 2017). Within the clinical team, I often heard frustration voiced about patients who were "non-compliant" or who struggled to manage their conditions in a prescribed way. Too often, these frustrations carried an implicit thread of blame, as though imperfect self-management somehow justified poor outcomes. It struck me how quickly patients could be reduced to their perceived failures, rather than understood in the context of their lives. Foucault (1975) described this as the "medical gaze", a process whereby healthcare professionals choose to focus only on selected biomedical factors of a patient's problem, thereby filtering out all other elements of a person's story.

At the time, I kept my own diabetes hidden. I feared that disclosure would alter how I was perceived that I would no longer be part of the "us" of the team but instead shifted into the "them" of the patient group. This tension has been well captured by Bam (2025), who describes how people with unseen disabilities often conceal their conditions to avoid anticipated stigma and being seen as "less than" or "other". My own non-disclosure reflected this same protective strategy. In my experience, hospitals are often hierarchical places of work and as a junior member of the team, I lacked confidence to challenge stereotypes or advocate for a more compassionate narrative within a power-laden system, a phenomenon termed "organisational silence" by Morrison and Milliken (2000). So, I stayed silent, I did my work diligently, sharing my own diagnosis only when strictly necessary. But privately, I carried the quiet knowledge of how it felt to sit on both sides of the consultation, and in years to come, this dual perspective would influence my professional curiosity as to how healthcare can do better.

Missed opportunities for psychological care

During my Doctorate in Clinical Psychology, I started a family. My pregnancies, medically classified as high risk due to my diabetes, introduced a new and intense layer of health anxiety. Weekly scans, relentless monitoring, and weekly medical appointments only fuelled my already well-practiced hypervigilance. I immersed myself in reading about the risks to both mother and baby with T1D and lived with an almost constant sense of dread. Despite being surrounded by healthcare professionals, my distress was never once acknowledged. The dominant medical model has long been critiqued for its focus on biomedical processes within the body, which can create reductionistic care by overlooking social and psychological factors (Engel, 1977; Fuller, 2017). Here, I was experiencing this first-hand as my hospital care focused exclusively on physical outcomes for my baby and for me, overlooking the emotional toll.

The irony is that we know from research that pregnancy in women with chronic medical conditions is associated with higher rates of peripartum anxiety and depression (Brown et al., 2018), and that these difficulties can negatively affect both maternal wellbeing and infant outcomes if left unsupported (Tripathy, 2020; Smorti et al., 2019). The weight of responsibility that I carried, managing not only my own life but that of my unborn child, was immense. My health anxiety reached its peak during this period. Thankfully, all three of my children were born without complication, but living with overwhelming health anxiety throughout pregnancy and early motherhood was profoundly difficult.

Once qualified, I specialised in physical health psychology, this time working in the very hospital where I also received my adult diabetes care. My clinical work often brought me into contact with individuals living through immense physical health challenges. I was fascinated by the work and deeply committed to my clients, often marvelling at their capacity to manage what I had so often feared in imagination.

Yet my dual role as both clinician and patient was complex. As a patient in the same hospital, I was never offered any psychological care myself despite me, at times, voicing my anxiety. These presented missed opportunities to acknowledge the psychological burden of living with a long-term condition, to normalise it, and to offer psychologically informed care. This reflects a wider systemic issue; mental health is often noticed but not acted upon in medical settings, flagged as a "problem" but not always integrated into routine care pathways. This is despite evidence supporting the validity and utility of biopsychosocial approaches in the management of chronic health conditions (Wade & Halligan, 2017).

Working across several hospital teams, I observed how each developed their own narratives about patients living with psychological distress alongside physical health conditions. I witnessed some of the teams embracing psychological input, making space for reflective practice, and consulting closely with psychology colleagues. In these environments, patients were understood more holistically, often through a trauma-informed lens which was the cornerstone of our psychology-based framework. Evidence demonstrates that earlier adverse experiences can impact later physical health (Martín-Higarza et al., 2020) and trauma-informed care, whereby all staff have a basic understanding of traumatic stress and can respond with care, collaboration, and respect, can lead to improved patient outcomes and greater professional satisfaction (Purkey et al., 2018).

Other teams, however, described anxious "heartsink" patients and responded in ways that minimised or dismissed their struggles. The absence of emotional care often compounded patients' distress, reinforcing their sense of being difficult, non-compliant, or "too much". This process can be re-traumatising for people who experienced past distressing events, inadvertently deepening the problem (Huo et al., 2023).

As time went on, the parallels between my own lived experience and the experiences of my clients became increasingly difficult to ignore. I felt a growing drive to bridge the divide between "us" and "them", to challenge the artificial separation between healthcare professionals and patients. By this stage, my own diabetes had become much more visible. I had moved away from injections and finger-prick testing and onto an insulin pump and continuous glucose monitoring, devices that are worn on the body, often openly visible on the arms. I grew more accepting of my condition, more willing to speak openly with colleagues, and when asked and when appropriate, with clients. Instead of fuelling shame, increased openness reduced it. An important lesson that would inform my future clinical work.

Breast cancer and psychologically informed care

In 2015, at the age of 35, my world shifted again. I was unexpectedly diagnosed with Stage 3 breast cancer. The diagnosis was profoundly disorientating, not only because of its seriousness, but because I was working within the very same cancer service where I would now receive treatment. Once again, I was both clinician and patient, my professional and personal worlds colliding in the most intimate of ways. However, this time there was a marked difference in the psychological approach of the medical team who cared for me, as I experienced for the first time my psychological needs being explicitly acknowledged by my medical team.

I underwent chemotherapy, radiotherapy, and a double mastectomy with reconstruction. At every stage, my medical team took time to ask about my emotional well-being alongside my physical health. This attentiveness helped me to feel understood and contained. Evidence tells us that emotional support during cancer treatment is associated with reduced distress and improved quality of life (Cillessen et al., 2019; de la Torre-Luque et al., 2016), and here, I was experiencing it first-hand.

There was a well-attended breast cancer support group locally but having worked therapeutically with many of the people who attended, I did not feel able to join. Although I didn't voice this to my breast cancer surgeon, I suspect she sensed it. Instead, she asked if I would like her to connect me with two women of a similar age who were receiving treatment with her at a different hospital. That small act of curiosity and care proved invaluable. The opportunity to form supportive peer relationships was exactly what I needed, and those women remain close friends of mine today.

Experiencing cancer within the same hospital where I worked gave me a unique vantage point. I saw clearly the power of attending to emotions as well as physical health in clinical conversations. This was mirrored in my primary care experience. I recall within a few days of diagnosis, an out-of-the-blue phone call from my GP to check in on my physical wellbeing, but more importantly, my emotional wellbeing. These calls continued every few weeks throughout my year of treatment, and I distinctly recall the sense of relational warmth and safety that they provided.

These experiences further ignited my interest in supporting medical teams to develop psychologically informed care, particularly for people experiencing health difficulties or health anxiety, people like me, whose fears and vulnerabilities are often hidden beneath the surface of "good" clinical outcomes.

Returning to the hospital environment after a year of cancer treatment also made one thing unmistakably clear: I needed a change. Carrying the identities of both patient and psychologist in that setting felt too heavy, too entangled. In 2016, I made the decision to leave my NHS role and establish my own private practice.

From personal healing to professional approach

Private practice gave me more opportunity to specialise in health anxiety and to reflect on the evolving therapeutic model that was taking shape in my mind. Around this time, having trained in EMDR (Eye Movement Desensitisation Reprocessing) to strengthen my skills in trauma work, I made the decision to engage in EMDR therapy myself, focusing on the trauma of the cancer diagnosis and treatment and the fear of recurrence. What unfolded during those sessions took me by surprise.

Although our intention was to process cancer-related memories, my therapist and I repeatedly found ourselves drawn back to much earlier material, the unresolved trauma of my diabetes diagnosis, and the many years of living in a state of hypervigilant fear. One pivotal session returned me to the hospital bed at age 11, overhearing the ward doctor telling the team that I might have a hypo event overnight. Until that moment, I had not consciously recalled the memory. But as we processed it, the terror came rushing back: the loneliness of the ward, the certainty that I would die before morning, and the desperate longing for my mother's presence and the safety of home. The intensity of those feelings was visceral, as though I were reliving them in the present.

Through EMDR, the memory began to shift and soften. I was able to integrate new, more adaptive information, that I had already lived with T1D for more than two decades without serious complications, that I had always done my best to manage it, and that this was, in fact, good enough. Something profound changed: I have not experienced a single episode of health anxiety since.

This experience clarified something that would become central to my practice: my health anxiety was never a failing or a pathology; it was a protective part of me that had evolved to keep me safe while navigating a condition that demanded constant vigilance. Viewing health anxiety as a "part" stems from a psychological approach called Internal Family Systems (IFS). Schwartz (2021) describes how we are made up of multiple parts, protectors who are simply trying to keep us safe and developed in response to other parts that carry emotions and memories from earlier times of vulnerability. These inner protectors can become stuck in their role, terrified that if they stop something terrible will happen. The hypervigilance and checking behaviours, once pathologised by a diabetes specialist as "excessive", had functioned to protect me from both physical risk and the emotional pain of being told I wasn't managing well enough. My protective health-anxious part had been working tirelessly on my behalf, albeit in a way that had become overzealous.

This personal healing gave new weight and clarity to my emerging clinical approach. In my work with clients experiencing health anxiety, I noticed a consistent pattern: repeatedly, therapy would lead us back to their earlier moments of vulnerability, times when their nervous systems felt alone, unsafe, or overwhelmed. Through trauma-informed therapeutic models such as Eye Movement Desensitisation Reprocessing (EMDR), we could access and process these memories, integrating them so that they no longer carried the same overwhelming charge. When combined with third-wave approaches such as Acceptance and Commitment Therapy, clients could both reduce the distress of past trauma and learn to relate differently to the protective parts that drove their present-day anxiety.

The guiding question that emerged for me, both personally and clinically, was this: *When in your life did this protective part understandably need to emerge?* By framing health anxiety not as a disorder to be eradicated, but as a protector that needed to be understood, softened, and integrated, clients often found a pathway to healing that was compassionate and sustainable.

A trauma-informed approach to health anxiety

These layered personal and professional experiences now underpin my trauma-informed and relational approach to health anxiety, which provides an example of how my lived experience has shaped my clinical work. It is an approach that holds the whole person in mind, attends to the roots beneath the symptoms, and offers compassionate guidance to both clients and medical teams as they navigate the complexities of this presentation.

The dominant model of health anxiety in the literature remains largely CBT-informed (Salkovskis & Warwick, 1986; Cooper et al., 2017; Kikas et al., 2024).

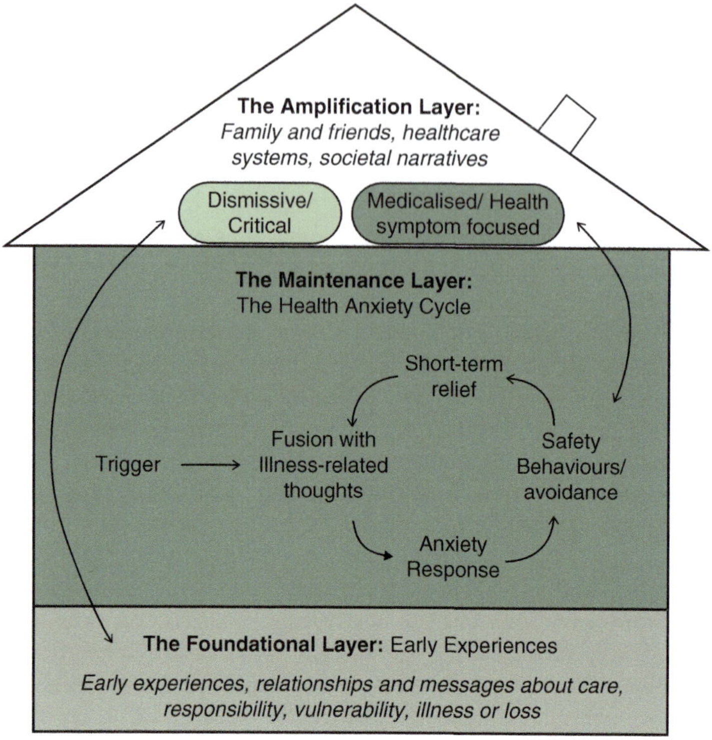

Figure 7.1 A layered approach to health anxiety: the house metaphor.

While attendance to current cognitions, emotional responses, and behaviours is undoubtedly important, there is also a very small body of research that recognises that earlier experiences of vulnerability, illness, loss, or lack of consistent caregiving can also shape health anxiety (Thorgaard et al., 2017; Wearden et al., 2006; Noyes et al., 2002). My own lived experience, and later countless therapeutic encounters with clients, led me to develop a framework for health anxiety that recognises it not as an irrational problem to be eliminated but as an adaptive survival strategy that has simply become over extended. Explained through the metaphor of a house, I now use this model in my work with clients and healthcare teams to help them to understand and work with health anxiety (see Figure 7.1).

The foundational layer recognises the impact of adverse early experiences and the later development of health anxiety. Not everyone with such a history will develop health anxiety, and not everyone with health anxiety has these experiences, but there appears to be a relationship that increases vulnerability. Like the unseen foundations of a house, these formative experiences may be out of immediate view, but their structural impact is significant.

The maintenance layer captures the processes that sustain health anxiety in the present day. Like endlessly wandering from room to room in a house, people become caught in loops of ruminating, checking, reassurance seeking, monitoring, and avoiding. While catastrophic illness-related thoughts are common, it is the degree of *fusion* with these thoughts that matters (Fergus, 2015). When thoughts are experienced as urgent, dangerous, and true, the body responds accordingly, activating anxiety that can then be misinterpreted as further evidence of illness. Safety behaviours such as googling symptoms, repeated medical appointments, or reassurance seeking from loved ones bring short-lived relief but quickly feed back into doubt. These safety behaviours offer momentary reassurance but are ultimately unsustainable. Helping clients (and the healthcare teams around them) to map these maintenance cycles can open space for new, more flexible responses.

The attic layer represents the influence of family responses, healthcare systems, and wider societal narratives. This is where health anxiety is unintentionally amplified. When people seek reassurance, dismissive responses such as *"you're just being irrational"* can evoke shame and further anxiety. These experiences may also echo earlier relational patterns. Conversely, overly medicalised responses, tests, scans, or referrals given when not clinically indicated, may offer temporary reassurance but often heighten uncertainty and reinforce the cycle. Both responses are protective in their own way, yet both can make the anxiety worse over time.

Understanding health anxiety through these three interconnected layers provides a richer, more compassionate framework. It shifts the focus from eradicating symptoms to recognising the protective intentions beneath them, and from individual blame to systemic understanding. When clients, families, and medical teams begin to view health anxiety in this way shame diminishes, compassion grows, and long-term healing becomes possible.

The role of medical teams in psychological safety

My dual identity as both patient and clinician has shaped my approach to working with healthcare teams. In supervision, training, and consultation, I have sat with brilliant, compassionate clinicians who openly admit that, when faced with health anxiety, they feel stuck, helpless, or frustrated. Most people enter healthcare with the best intentions of providing thoughtful, empathic care yet health anxiety does not only impact those who live with it, but it also affects those trying to help.

One of the most striking parallels between my experience as a patient and my work alongside medical teams is how easily even the most dedicated healthcare professionals can slip into subtle dehumanisation. For me, the memory of a diabetes doctor remarking half mockingly that I "*might have OCD*" when viewing the frequency of my glucose monitoring was searing. It was likely intended lightly, yet what I heard was "*you are too much*". What I did not receive, in that moment, was the psychological care that could have made a difference.

In the consulting room, healthcare professionals have described to me a parallel process unfolding. Patients with health anxiety often feel stuck, hopeless, and powerless. They look to their healthcare professionals for answers. Yet those clinicians, working under immense pressures of time, resources, risk, and litigation, can quickly feel the same helplessness. Understandably, this can cause frustration in clinicians (Le et al., 2022), and in response, they may default to two positions: dismissing the patient as quickly as possible (Jordan et al., 2015), or over-medicalising with repeated scans and tests that are not clinically indicated and at great cost to healthcare services (Hannah et al., 2023). Both may be understandable attempts to reduce the clinician's own anxiety, and this is where trauma-informed practice can be transformative.

In medicine, endless attention is given to infection control, patient safety, negligence, and risk. What is less often discussed is *psychological safety*: the assurance that patients can show their vulnerability, voice their fears, and still feel contained rather than humiliated. When we consider that one of the early antecedents for health anxiety is attachment insecurity (Noyes et al., 2002), it makes sense that relational warmth and safety are valuable tools in overcoming it. Without them, cycles of anxiety and shame are likely to be perpetuated. Slowing down to offer a trauma-informed, psychologically safe consultation may take only a minute longer in the consulting room, but it can save hours, resources, and patient suffering further down the line.

Practical strategies for trauma-informed consultations

"Trauma-informed care" involves organisations or systems realising the widespread impact of trauma and the signs and symptoms of such, and integrating knowledge about trauma into their policies, processes, and practices while actively resisting re-traumatising those they seek to serve (SAMHSA, 2014). Key principles include establishing safety, building trust, collaborating with service users and moving past stereotypes and biases, and being responsive to the needs of individuals served (UK Government Office for Health Improvement and Disparities, 2022).

What does this look like in practice? When working with healthcare teams, I often invite them to get curious about the person's context, to understand how patterns of health anxiety may once have been adaptive strategies that enabled survival. When we hold these narratives in mind, our clinical stance shifts. We are no longer simply intervening on thoughts or symptoms; we are bearing witness to a story that makes sense, a story of protection. I have seen how offering medical teams access to psychologically informed supervision, consultation, and reflective practice can significantly support this shift. It helps clinicians move from frustration to curiosity, and from helplessness to compassion.

Encouraging GPs and other medical staff to gently name health anxiety is an important part of this process. Instead of moving too quickly to challenge the logic of health fears, they can first validate them as understandable strategies in the aftermath of adverse earlier experiences, while also attending to tone, body language, and active listening to support relational safety and to build trust. Crucially, we can also help them address patients' understandable fear that, in naming health anxiety, their very real symptoms will not be dismissed or overlooked when they *do* fit a clinical pathway, while encouraging alternative coping strategies outside of the consultation room when they don't. Shared care plans that balance medical safety with psychological insight allow collaboration, rather than frustration, to guide the consultation.

These small but meaningful relational shifts build safety, reduce shame, and open the possibility of more adaptive ways forward, for both patients and professionals (Le et al., 2022).

The role of lived experience

As someone who has long relied on physical health services, and at times lived with significant health anxiety, I often reflect on how my career has come full circle. I now find myself offering to others, and training medical teams to provide, the very support and understanding that once felt absent in my own healthcare journey.

Thanks to social media, I am now connected to a thriving community of people living with T1D, many of whom also work in healthcare, informed by their personal experiences. What strikes me is how often we provide the very care we once needed ourselves.

As a child managing a long-term condition, I learned responsibility for my health early. This shaped the lens through which I saw myself and over time, created the capacity to sit with others in similar positions, as someone who understands what it means to live with fear and uncertainty about health.

This is why I actively encourage the involvement of people with lived experience in clinical practice. Until recently, I ran groups for people living with persistent pain. Crucially, I involved individuals who had themselves navigated this reality, not as volunteers but as paid members of staff. Their wisdom and insight were as essential to the process as any medical or professional input. According to the UK Government's Office for Health Improvement and Disparities (2022), involving service users in the development and delivery of services is a key principle of trauma-informed practice.

Of course, we must remain mindful of some of the challenges of bringing lived experience into our work; risk of stigma and discrimination, disclosure dilemmas, confidentiality concerns, and access to support, to name a few. Creating a culture of openness and compassion around lived experience within the workplace, while also providing access to supervision, peer support, consultation, and personal therapy is key (Kemp et al., 2020). As psychologists, we are fortunate that these practices are often embedded as a central aspect of our profession. Drawing on these resources and ensuring continued access in our teams and services is crucial to sustaining this work safely and effectively.

Conclusion

This chapter has sought to show that disability is not separate from clinical psychology but woven through it. My lived experiences of diabetes and cancer have shaped how I sit with clients, how I supervise colleagues, and how I train healthcare teams. My approach to health anxiety is one expression of this, a framework that understands health anxiety through a trauma-informed and relational lens, not as irrationality but as protection: an understandable survival strategy that invites curiosity and collaborative care.

Yet the significance extends beyond individual therapy. Vulnerability is never only private; it is also systemic. Too often, the emotional costs of disability go unseen or unacknowledged, and for me, this led to health anxiety. My story is one example of how care that is trauma-informed, relational, and curious can create not only medical safety, but also psychological safety.

As psychologists, our responsibility is not only to ease individual suffering but also to transform the systems and cultures in which we work. This means reducing othering, amplifying the role of lived experience, and supporting healthcare teams to meet patients not from a place of distance, but with curiosity, understanding, and relational warmth. For our profession, it means making space for lived experience as a core part of our clinical and political identity, so that psychology can more fully reflect, and better serve, those we seek to help.

References

Ashraf, M. N., & Cheng, A. Y. Y. (2024). Impact of living with stigma in persons with Type 1 Diabetes: A patient–physician perspective. *Diabetes Therapy*, *15*, 311–316. https://doi.org/10.1007/s13300-023-01528-9

Bam, A. (2025). Invisibility, stigma and workplace support: Experiences of individuals with chronic disorders. *SA Journal of Human Resource Management*, *23*, 2859. https://doi.org/10.4102/sajhrm.v23i0.2859

Bloom, S. (1999). *Trauma Theory Abbreviated.* Final Action Plan: A Coordinated Community Response to Family Violence ed. Harrisburg, PA: Office of Attorney General, Commonwealth of Pennsylvania.

Brown, H. K., Qazilbash, A., Rahim, N., Dennis, C.-L., & Vigod, S. N. (2018). Chronic medical conditions and peripartum mental illness: A systematic review and meta-analysis. *American Journal of Epidemiology*, *187*(9), 2060–2068. https://doi.org/10.1093/aje/kwy080

Cillessen, L., Johannsen, M., Speckens, A. E. M., & Zachariae, R. (2019). Mindfulness-based interventions for psychological and physical health outcomes in cancer patients and survivors: A systematic review and meta-analysis of randomized controlled trials. *Psycho-Oncology*, *28*(12). https://doi.org/10.1002/pon.5214

Cooper, K., Gregory, J. D., Walker, I., Lambe, S., & Salkovskis, P. M. (2017). Cognitive behaviour therapy for health anxiety: A systematic review and meta-analysis – Corrigendum. *Behavioural and Cognitive Psychotherapy*, *45*(6), 673–673. https://doi.org/10.1017/s1352465817000510

Cyranka, K., Klupa, T., Pilecki, M., Sarna-Palacz, D., Juryk, A., Storman, D., Dudek, D., Malecki, M. T., & Matejko, B. (2024). Diabetes distress and diabetes burnout explored in various areas of life in patients with type 1 diabetes: Effect of short-term psychological intervention. *Endocrine*, *85*. https://doi.org/10.1007/s12020-024-03760-0

de la Torre-Luque, A., Gambara, H., López, E., & Cruzado, J. A. (2016). Psychological treatments to improve quality of life in cancer contexts: A meta-analysis. *International Journal of Clinical and Health Psychology*, *16*(2), 211–219. https://doi.org/10.1016/j.ijchp.2015.07.005

Engel, G. L. (1977). The need for a new medical model: A challenge for biomedicine. *Holistic Medicine*, *4*(1), 129–136. https://doi.org/10.1126/science.847460

Fergus, T. A. (2015). I really believe I suffer from a health problem: Examining an association between cognitive fusion and healthy anxiety. *Journal of Clinical Psychology*, *71*(9), 920–934. https://doi.org/10.1002/jclp.22194

Foucault, M. (1975). *The Birth of the Clinic*. Vintage Books.

Fuller, J. (2017). The new medical model: A renewed challenge for biomedicine. *Canadian Medical Association Journal*, *189*(17), E640–E641. https://doi.org/10.1503/cmaj.160627

Hannah, K., Marie, K., Olaf, H., et al. (2023). The global economic burden of health anxiety/hypochondriasis- a systematic review. *BMC Public Health*, *23*, 2237. https://doi.org/10.1186/s12889-023-17159-5

Helgeson, V. S. (2021). Diabetes burnout among emerging adults with type 1 diabetes: A mixed methods investigation. *Journal of Behavioral Medicine*, *44*(3). https://doi.org/10.1007/s10865-020-00198-3

Huo, Y., Couzner, L., Windsor, T., Laver, K., Dissanayaka, N. N., & Cations, M. (2023). Barriers and enablers for the implementation of trauma-informed care in healthcare settings: A systematic review. *Implementation Science Communications*, *4*(1), 49. https://doi.org/10.1186/s43058-023-00428-0

Jordan, K. D., Williams, P. G., & Smith, T. W. (2015). Interpersonal distinctions among hypochondriacal trait components: Styles, goals, vulnerabilities, and perceptions of health care providers. *Journal of Social and Clinical Psychology*, *34*(6), 459–475. https://doi.org/10.1521/jscp.2015.34.6.459

Kahkoska, A., Ercolino, G., Ortega, J., Fruik, A., Young, L., & Freeman, N. (2025). Primed for precision: A review of the evidence for heterogeneous treatment effects in diabetes distress treatments among adults with type 1 diabetes and recommendations for future research. *Current Diabetes Reports*, *25*(1). https://doi.org/10.1007/s11892-025-01594-2

Kemp, N., Scior, K., Clements, H., & Mackenzie-White, K. (2020). *British Psychological Society: Supporting and Valuing Lived Experience of Mental Health Difficulties in Clinical Psychology Training*. https://cms.bps.org.uk/sites/default/files/2022-07/Lived%20experience%20of%20mental%20health%20difficulties%20in%20clinical%20psychology%20training.pdf

Kikas, K., Werner-Seidler, A., Upton, E., & Newby, J. (2024). Illness anxiety disorder: A review of the current research and future directions. *Current Psychiatry Reports*, *26*(7). https://doi.org/10.1007/s11920-024-01507-2

Le, T. L., Mylopoulos, M., Bearss, E., Geist, R., & Maunder, R. (2022). Multiple symptoms and health anxiety in primary care: A qualitative study of tensions and collaboration between patients and family physicians. *BMJ Open*, *12*(4), e050716. https://doi.org/10.1136/bmjopen-2021-050716

Martín-Higarza, Y., Fontanil, Y., Méndez, M. D., & Ezama, E. (2020). The direct and indirect influences of adverse childhood experiences on physical health: A cross-sectional study. *International Journal of Environmental Research and Public Health*, *17*(22), 8507. https://doi.org/10.3390/ijerph17228507

Morrison, E. W., & Milliken, F. J. (2000). Organizational silence: A barrier to change and development in a pluralistic world. *Academy of Management Review*, *25*(4), 706–725. https://doi.org/10.5465/amr.2000.3707697

Noyes, R., Stuart, S., Langbehn, D. R., Happel, R. L., Longley, S. L., & Yagla, S. J. (2002). Childhood antecedents of hypochondriasis. *Psychosomatics*, *43*(4), 282–289. https://doi.org/10.1176/appi.psy.43.4.282

Office for Health Improvement & Disparities. (2022, November 2). *Working Definition of Trauma-Informed Practice*. GOV.uk; Office for Health Improvement & Disparities. https://www.gov.uk/government/publications/working-definition-of-trauma-informed-practice/working-definition-of-trauma-informed-practice

Purkey, E., Patel, R., & Phillips, S. P. (2018). Trauma-informed care: Better care for everyone. *Canadian Family Physician, 64*(3), 170–172. https://www.cfp.ca/content/64/3/170.short

Rechenberg, K., Whittemore, R., & Grey, M. (2017). Anxiety in youth with type 1 diabetes. *Journal of Pediatric Nursing, 32*(32), 64–71. https://doi.org/10.1016/j.pedn.2016.08.007

Roberts, M. L. A., & Schiavenato, M. (2017). Othering in the nursing context: A concept analysis. *Nursing Open, 4*(3), 174–181. https://doi.org/10.1002/nop2.82

Salkovskis, P. M., & Warwick, H. M. C. (1986). Morbid preoccupations, health anxiety and reassurance: A cognitive-behavioural approach to hypochondriasis. *Behaviour Research and Therapy, 24*(5), 597–602. https://doi.org/10.1016/0005-7967(86)90041-0

SAMHSA. (2014). *Trauma-Informed Care in Behavioral Health Services KAP KEYS FOR CLINICIANS KAP Keys Based on TIP 57*. https://library.samhsa.gov/sites/default/files/sma15-4420.pdf

Schwartz, R. C. (2021). *No Bad Parts: Healing Trauma and Restoring Wholeness with the Internal Family Systems Model*. Boulder, CO: Sounds True.

Scibilia, R. (2022, May). *Ascensia | Diabetes and Coronavirus Series (Article 1): Maintaining Mental Wellbeing during COVID-19*. Ascensia.com. https://www.ascensia.com/press/living-with-diabetes-burnout/

Smorti, M., Ponti, L., & Tani, F. (2019). The effect of maternal depression and anxiety on labour and the well-being of the newborn. *Journal of Obstetrics and Gynaecology: The Journal of the Institute of Obstetrics and Gynaecology, 39*(4), 492–497. https://doi.org/10.1080/01443615.2018.1536697

Stanford Medicine. (2014, May). *New Research Shows How to Keep Diabetics Safer during Sleep*. News Center. https://med.stanford.edu/news/insights/2014/05/new-research-keeps-diabetics-safer-during-sleep.html

Staszak, J.-F. (2020). Other/otherness. *International Encyclopedia of Human Geography, 10*, 25–31. https://doi.org/10.1016/b978-0-08-102295-5.10204-5

Tenreiro, K., & Hatipoglu, B. (2025). Mind matters: Mental health and diabetes management. *The Journal of Clinical Endocrinology & Metabolism, 110*(Supplement_2), S131–S136. https://doi.org/10.1210/clinem/dgae607

Thorgaard, M. V., Frostholm, L., & Rask, C. U. (2017). Childhood and family factors in the development of health anxiety: A systematic review. *Children's Health Care, 47*(2), 198–238. https://doi.org/10.1080/02739615.2017.1318390

Tripathy, P. (2020). A public health approach to perinatal mental health: Improving health and wellbeing of mothers and babies. *Journal of Gynaecology Obstetrics and Human Reproduction, 49*(6), 101747. https://doi.org/10.1016/j.jogoh.2020.101747

Van Der Kolk, B. (2014). *The Body Keeps the Score: Brain, Mind, and Body in the Healing of Trauma by Bessel van der Kolk, MD | Key Takeaways, Analysis & Review*. Idreambooks Inc.

Wade, D. T., & Halligan, P. W. (2017). The biopsychosocial model of illness: A model whose time has come. *Clinical Rehabilitation, 31*(8), 995–1004. https://doi.org/10.1177/0269215517709890

Waft, Y. (2023). *Coping with Trauma: Surviving and Thriving in the Face of Overwhelming Events.* Sequoia Books.

Wearden, A., Perryman, K., & Ward, V. (2006). Adult attachment, reassurance seeking and hypochondriacal concerns in college students. *Journal of Health Psychology, 11*(6), 877–886. https://doi.org/10.1177/1359105306069086

Willis, T. (2025). *I've Been Really Bad.* Know Diabetes. https://www.knowdiabetes.org.uk/blog/shame/

Chapter 8

Recognizing the value of one's expertise and experience

A forensic psychologist's journey with both physical and psychological disability

Veronica Solaris

Introduction

Aaron T. Beck's cognitive therapy, which later evolved into cognitive behavioral therapy (CBT), has given rise to a growing body of evidence-based approaches, including acceptance and commitment therapy (ACT), mindfulness-based interventions, and the positive psychology movement (Clark, 2014; Frostadottir & Dorjee, 2019; Harris, 2023; Leyland, 2012; Padesky & Mooney, 2012). These approaches are grounded in the premise that bias beliefs, and appraisals play a central role in the development and maintenance of psychological distress and disorders (Clark, 2014; Frostadottir & Dorjee, 2019; Harris, 2023). CBT models propose through collaborative therapeutic relationships, cognitive reconstruction techniques, and the exploration of maladaptive schemas—defined as enduring mental representations or problematic core beliefs—can reduce distress, alleviate symptoms contributing to psychopathology, and enhance overall well-being (Clark, 2014; Harris, 2023; Leyland, 2012). Furthermore, treatment strategies and cognitive restructuring tools that cultivate cognitive flexibility, gratitude, acceptance, and challenging negative thought patterns, support the development of personal strengths and positive psychological qualities including resilience, self-compassion, and effective problem-solving (Clark, 2014; Frostadottir & Dorjee, 2019; Harris, 2023; Leyland, 2012; Padesky & Mooney, 2012).

Empirically supported CBT principles are reflected not only in research but also in lived experience and professional clinical practice. My professional journey as a psychologist with disabilities illustrates how perceived limitations can be transformed into capabilities and adaptive psychological qualities, serving as a practical application of CBT-based strategies with clients experiencing mental disorders. Confronting and overcoming both visible and invisible injuries following a head trauma cultivated resilience and redirected the trajectory of my life toward purposeful healing. The integration of personal and professional CBT tools within forensic populations has enhanced clinical effectiveness, reduced recidivism, improved anger management, and supported clients in discovering their own capacity for transformation (Wilson et al., 2005).

Both personal experiences and clinical expertise create an intersection that informs the therapeutic presence I bring into the setting. A psychologist with a

DOI: 10.4324/9781003636014-9

disability enters the therapeutic practice not only with a visible difference such as an altered gait that quietly communicates adaptability and perseverance—but also with a lifelong repertoire of coping strategies, insight, and resilience. These experiences closely align with the goals of CBT, including fostering cognitive flexibility, reframing underlying beliefs that maintain psychological distress. In this way, the therapist's lived experience functions much like that of a seasoned expert, whose depth of expertise transforms seemingly simple interventions into meaningful and effective outcomes.

It is evident that CBT therapy models demonstrate a high degree of effectiveness in helping individuals develop positive psychological qualities and adaptive attributes to cope with life challenges (Fava & Ruini, 2003; Mooney & Padesky, 2002; Padesky, 2006). Consistent with this body of research, the application of CBT-based techniques—including sustained gratitude journaling that integrates self-compassion and the systematic examination of dysfunctional thoughts—has been associated with increased resilience, reductions in depressive and anxiety symptoms, and decreased negative rumination (Clark, 2014; Frostadottir & Dorjee, 2019; Harris, 2023; Leyland, 2012; Padesky & Mooney, 2012). These experiences allow me to draw upon a lifetime of accumulated skills in cognitive flexibility and the use of appropriate accommodations to role-model effective coping, validate client experiences, and support the therapeutic process of collaborative empiricism (Clark, 2014). Through the process, both clinical expertise and shared lived experiences are incorporated into the exploration and resolution of clients' difficulties. By demonstrating how limitations can be addressed and overcome, I aim to enhance clients' self-awareness, resilience, and confidence in managing their mental health by collaboratively structuring realistic treatment goals and normalizing change.

For the past two years, I have worn a large black brace on my left leg to prevent knee hyperextension. Although this is a relatively recent development, clients in our initial sessions almost invariably glance at the brace with concern and ask, "How did you injure your knee?" To them, it appears as though I have recently undergone knee surgery, as braces are commonly associated with post-surgical recovery. I have continued to wear the brace for months, and now years. What clients often do not realize is that their well-intentioned question touches on a much longer journey that began with a childhood injury sustained on a school playground.

To preserve early therapeutic trust and avoid diverting the focus of treatment, I respond briefly and intentionally: "It's an old injury. I can tell you more about it later." From experience, I have learned that "later" involves providing concrete examples of how I apply ACT principles in practice. This includes exploring clients' recurring themes of struggle with curiosity, normalizing their experiences, and bringing awareness to unhelpful, distorted, or negatively biased thinking patterns. When these patterns are gently examined and challenged, clients often develop greater self-compassion and more adaptive, positive self-talk (Harris, 2023).

This growing body of evidence within the positive psychology movement demonstrates that intentionally focusing on gratitude and positive emotional experiences—rather than negativity—is strongly associated with improved psychological well-being

(McCullough et al., 2004). McCullough et al. (2004) found that the regular practice of gratitude promotes improved moods and enduring affective traits. Despite the ongoing limitations associated with disability, modeling a shift from deficit-focused thinking to strength-based practices appears to foster emotional resilience and adaptive coping.

At the age of 12, my ambitions of becoming a firefighter disappeared when an ill-fitted schoolyard swing propelled me headfirst onto asphalt. The resulting traumatic brain injury had not only profound personal consequences but also challenged nationwide reforms in playground safety policy. As a result of the accident, I sustained extensive injuries and remained in a coma for a month. Upon regaining consciousness, I overheard my paediatrician deliver a devastating prognosis to my parent: "She will never walk, drive a car, attend college, hold a job, or live independently." In that moment, I lost not only my physical capabilities but also the identity I had once known as an athlete. Rebuilding my life from that point forward, I was forced to relearn all basic motor functions, proper speech, and cognitive strategies for learning. Despite residual muscle spasticity and left-sided weakness, I eventually regained the ability to walk—but with a noticeable gait abnormality and limited mobility.

More traumatic than the physical impairments were the psychological tolls of my experience—particularly the rare and terrifying phenomenon of being lucid during my month-long comatose state. Unbeknownst to the medical staff, I retained an altered consciousness and awareness while being entirely unable to speak, move, or respond. As a result, I endured numerous life-saving interventions with full cognitive awareness, yet without the ability to communicate my distress or pain. This left deep emotional scars and lasting wounds. Upon awakening, I not only confronted the profound grief of losing my physical identity and my full mental capacity, but I also began to grapple with chronic, unexplained pain, depressive symptoms, severe anxiety, and complex post-traumatic stress disorder from the series of events I experienced when I was supposed to be unconscious in a coma. The invisible wounds, in many ways, proved even more persistent and debilitating than the visible ones.

For the next 15 years, I experienced intense psychological symptoms—including anxious distress, depressive grief, and vivid, intrusive recollections of trauma—stemming from the numerous medical procedures I endured while presumed unconscious. I unknowingly carried these unexamined memories, rooted in the terrifying experience of being immobile and voiceless, suspended in a state between wakefulness and sleep. In that space, I had no control or autonomy—only the capacity to drift between wakefulness and sleep. Even after emerging from the coma, I remained psychologically confined by its effects, plagued by learned helplessness, persistent nightmares, distressing flashbacks of painful medical interventions, and dissociative episodes. This psychological suffering, compounded by an ever-present, unrelenting physical pain, became an invisible burden that followed me through adolescence and early adulthood.

By the age of 12, I had experienced a profound loss of independence because of newly acquired disabilities, along with the loss of the life I once knew, the aspirations I had envisioned, and my sense of self. The use of CBT and ACT journaling prompts to process painful memories, reconnect with my core sense of self, and reframe my identity as both *able* and *valuable* facilitated meaningful psychological change. Through mindfulness and self-compassionate dialogue, I challenged entrenched negative narratives and maladaptive themes, leading to increased cognitive flexibility, greater acceptance of limitations, and a renewed focus on personal strengths. Consistent with this experience, ACT-based practices that emphasize reshaping core beliefs and personal narratives and engaging in regular gratitude practices have been shown to support emotional regulation and reduce psychological distress (Frostadottir & Dorjee, 2019; Harris, 2023; Padesky & Mooney, 2012).

Many individuals in my life who have witnessed my journey remind me that I have overcome extraordinary challenges that many individuals never face in a lifetime. I was shattered—physically, emotionally, and spiritually—thrust into a state of profound emotional despair. Struggling with tremendous grief and robbed of my strengths, instead of staying in despair, this propelled me to shift drastically to rely on and build up my only other virtue in my superpower, my mind—I examined carefully my thinking patterns keeping my negative emotions and symptoms of distress alive.

At times, I share with clients that at the age of 12—while barely able to move—I began to intuitively apply a foundational CBT strategy by transforming negative schemas and harsh self-judgments into value-driven action that gradually reshaped my core beliefs. In the face of adversity, strength-based CBT approaches that emphasize identifying and cultivating personal strengths have been shown to bolster resilience and enhance problem-solving across both positive and negative life events (Harris, 2023; Padesky & Mooney, 2012).

Overwhelmed by psychological and physical symptoms, I often told myself, "I can't do anything. I've lost everything." Gradually, I shifted that narrative toward language aligned with purposeful action: "Let's see what I can do with what I still have—my mind." Viktor Frankl (2006) wrote, "*When we are no longer able to change a situation, we are challenged to change ourselves*." It was in the face of adversity and reframing that I learned to adapt my perspective and cultivate resilience and hope.

A client who knew the source of my disability once asked me, "How did you do it? What inside of you helped you overcome everything?" I responded simply: *"It started with one thing I valued—my mind."* Although it felt as though everything else had been taken from me, my capacity to change how I understood my situation became the force that sustained me through ongoing challenges. I frequently use this example of cognitive awareness and reframing to help clients recognize their own internal resources and their capacity to challenge maladaptive thought patterns.

This lived experience reflects the cognitive restructuring processes central to CBT theory. A core premise of cognitive restructuring involves modifying problematic schematic content by questioning the automatic acceptance of negative, schema-congruent interpretations and encouraging consideration of more adaptive, schema-incongruent information, thereby supporting a more balanced evaluation of experience (Clark, 2014). Assisting clients in generating alternative perspectives, evaluating problems from multiple angles, and considering potential outcomes equips them with tools to develop more adaptive schemas and achieve meaningful symptom reduction (Clark, 2014).

As described in Scarlet's Superhero Therapy (2016)—a guidebook grounded in ACT, trauma, and crisis holds the potential to transform vulnerabilities into strengths. Through my own practice of intensive journaling, initially guided by early coping strategies and later framed by CBT and ACT principles, I learned to process internal experiences, confront avoidance patterns, cultivate acceptance, and develop cognitive-diffusion strategies for managing symptoms (Harris, 2023; Scarlet, 2016).

The most transformative insight I gained and impart to my clients is that even in the aftermath of catastrophic loss and despair, individuals can still find peace, meaning, and authentic happiness by cognitive structuring and reframing perceived weaknesses as sources of strength. My physical disability and lived experience of psychological suffering, combined with years of clinical practice, have become akin to an engineer's hammer—knowing precisely where and how to apply it. That metaphor reflects the CBT process of therapeutic collaboration, in which therapist and client work together to identify distorted thoughts and subject them to logical examination and empirical hypothesis testing, thereby realigning thinking with reality (Clark, 1995, p. 155). This collaborative helps clients develop the skills to restore vitality and reclaim meaningful lives.

My first professional role involved working with both victims and offenders of domestic violence to better understand the thoughts and emotions underlying criminal behavior. Others often assumed that facilitating domestic violence groups for offenders while having a visible mobility disability placed me at heightened risk—that walking with a cane somehow made me vulnerable. People questioned how I could sit in a room with 12 male perpetrators and teach anger regulation, nonviolent problem-solving, and healthier communication patterns.

What was often overlooked was that my physical presence conveyed a different kind of authority—one grounded not in physical strength, but in emotional intelligence, lived experience, and compassion. I did not fear them because there was a mutual respect. Combined with application of ACT and CBT, these approaches allowed me to foster resilience and emotional regulation by helping participants de-escalate cognitive distortions and challenge maladaptive patterns of thinking, informed by structured assessment and intervention strategies for anger (Clark, 2014; Harris, 2023).

When I began my first doctoral practicum at an adult drug rehabilitation center in Oakland, a supervisor explained that her decision to hire me to work with men on parole and probation with extensive criminal histories in a substance recovery program was not based solely on my academic credentials. She pointed to the way I walked—explaining that my body carried an unspoken message of pain and resilience—"She knows suffering," she said. "Maybe she'll understand mine." The unspoken suffering that was relayed could resonate with criminal populations who carried layers of trauma and unfair disadvantage. It signaled that I went through a difficult journey and did the internal work to overcome it. Establishing rapport with overly guarded men became a strength by incorporating self-revelation of my struggle through helping them formulate a realistic cognitive plan for their recovery. My disability did not convey weakness, but rather a silent narrative of increased emotional toughness. It communicated that I had lived through hardship and emerged stronger—an implicit message of being an expert problem-solver and possessing adaptive insight. My disability conveyed that I was like the engineer, an experiential expert—equipped with not only clinical knowledge but lived wisdom.

I have many situations where my walking and presence served as a non-verbal narrative of perseverance and survival. During my doctoral program, I volunteered in an in-house prison program. This restorative justice programming for incarcerated individuals to partake in programming for crime prevention, healing, and accountability. What I discovered instead was how significant an impression I made on the men inside. I served as an example before them not as an impartial facilitator, but as someone who knew how to rebuild herself after loss and despair.

I took part in a day-long workshop with about 60–70 inmates discussing the impact of domestic violence and prevention practices. At the end of the programming, among various counsellors, they asked me to deliver the closing speech. I suspected that it was not because of my clinical background but rather because my disability bared an unspoken message of transformation and integrity. They must have seen in me that resilience and determination were within reach. My physical disability appeared to imply credibility of overcoming loss and having a disadvantage, empowered because of it, and not limited by it. I had to give them an example of how change comes with challenging our thinking.

Out loud, I shared this proverb, "The man with the greatest wealth is not the one who has the most, but the one who needs the least" (Arabic, n.d.). Afterward, many of the men shook my hand because they resonated with the simple words which affirmed similar journeys through radical loss, trauma, and recovery, not through minimization, but through empowerment. They were resonating with the meaning which symbolized being left with nothing and finding hope that something stronger could come of it. It was an example of powerful self-talk that guided recovery through finding freedom by shifting and redirecting their beliefs.

Exposure to a high-security correctional environment through intentional flooding to address a core fear of perceived threat represented a clinically significant turning point, demonstrating that direct confrontation of fear can reduce avoidance and promote the adaptive management of feared internal experiences.

A close family member who witnessed my life-long journey of adversity, once said, "Most people are more disabled than you are." Her words captured an insightful truth: my life had become a series of experiments—testing reality and negative hypotheses, no longer using fear as an excuse. This is a perspective I now share with clients who struggle with fear-based avoidance. While my physical limitations imposed real constraints, they could not justify emotional avoidance in the pursuit of meaningful goals. As reflected in ACT, my value-driven commitment- to prove to others and to myself that I was capable, guided my efforts toward success-focused schemas (Harris, 2023). In many ways, my disability dismantled the excuses I might otherwise have used to hold myself back. Ironically, the disability became the facilitator of courage and that anything was possible. That day I realized that I arrived despite it and because of it and it mattered that I was there.

Early on, I had to evaluate and deliberately set aside my excuses and internalized narratives that amplified fear. All along, my disability challenged and dismantled beliefs that I could not accomplish my goals. In truth, I never viewed myself as incapable; rather, it was the assumptions of others that imposed limiting interpretations on my abilities. Ultimately, others' opinions did not determine what I believed I could accomplish. Instead, I intentionally employed cognitive restructuring strategies, choosing not to view the world through the lens of perceived limitations but through an awareness of what remained within my control. This involved challenging cognitive distortions such as all-or-nothing thinking and decatastrophizing by utilizing realistic appraisals of available options (Clark, 2014). I consistently viewed myself as capable of achieving my aspirations. Where others perceived limitations, I experienced determination, grounded in authenticity and a commitment to carving my own path to success.

For the first time in my academic and professional journey, the disability became front and center- not as a source of empowerment, but as a perceived liability. It had never been a barrier. I later learned, through a trusted source, that my use of a cane was possibly seen as a safety concern. I was indirectly asked whether I would consider using a wheelchair—an option that I considered disempowering and inappropriate because they labeled my core sense of self as unstable.

After coming so far in my career, it was crushing to be dismissed based on how I walked. It was the first time I encountered such professional rejection, not eliminated because a lack of competence, but because of a physical aspect of myself. The experience activated deep feelings of injustice that I could no longer work within the prison setting. And because the message was delivered informally and with no official protocol or explanation, there was no remedy or support.

Although others may have used disability as an excuse, I refused to allow it to become my own. Rather than remaining stuck, I embraced my capacity for reinvention by—often inadvertently—drawing on ACT and CBT strategies to re-envision my future. Through intentional shifts in thinking and behavior, I redirected my efforts toward behavioral activation (BA) aligned with my goals, ultimately focusing on becoming a forensic expert. BA is an evidence-based approach that serves to alter existing (mal) adaptive coping strategies by strengthening exposure to positive reinforcement in our environments. This serves to increase motivation and promote a sense of control (McCauley et al., 2016).

I made a conscious decision not to dwell on comparing myself to others in ways that framed me as disadvantaged. By maintaining optimistic and hope, I was able to reframe my core beliefs—viewing myself as capable rather than defined by physical barriers. Here, I employed a growth-mindset to my disability in that I developed more resilience and persistence in the face of adversity and was learning new adaptive ways of working with my goals (Zhao et al., 2017). Although I couldn't work directly within the prison setting, I redirected my focus toward other deeply meaningful values, examining the impact of prison conditions as the subject of my dissertation.

My doctoral dissertation reflected an intersection between my clinical work with individuals involved in the criminal justice system and my research on the psychological symptoms associated with solitary confinement. I connected these findings to my own experience of isolation while in a coma, a period that echoed the psychological disability I carried afterward. I had not anticipated that the trauma of being trapped within my own mind would so closely parallel and motivate my study of the effects of conditions of imprisonment. This journey, combined with navigating my professional role as a forensic psychologist with disabilities, deepened both my scholarly understanding and my lived insight into the field.

Disclosure of the disability has served as a CBT therapeutic tool that has promoted client self-awareness and emotional growth

Throughout my professional journey, I have improved my clinical skills while navigating the impact of my physical disability. This unique perspective has strengthened my ability to ethically redirect self-disclosure, always with the patient's recovery and therapeutic goals in mind. Rapport building is critical to the therapeutic alliance. Having worked with multicultural forensic populations—men, women, and adolescents cycling through court-mandated treatment and incarceration, severe trauma, and substance use—I learned that approaching them often required adherence to an unspoken rule: trust must be earned, and it begins with the clinician's willingness to share something personal first. Many of these individuals had endured life-long struggles with disrupted trust and difficulties sharing intimate details, often flooded with shame and guilt. The observable nature of my walking gait frequently triggered marked curiosity in clients, which appeared to occupy significant emotional and cognitive space during the sessions and influenced interpersonal dynamics. It shifted the focus away from the clients' recovery and often may have been a defense mechanism to redirect exploring difficult topics.

Although therapeutic self-disclosure tends to undermine the premise of CBT evidence-based strategies, it's a powerful tool toward building trust and rapport. For example, Goldfried et al. (2003) highlighted how while CBT places importance on intersession change, self-disclosure within the therapeutic space can enhance the client-therapist relationship and what is more, support client change.

Before sharing any personal experiences, I consistently evaluate two key factors to ensure ethical and professional practice. First, I consider whether the information is being shared for the therapeutic benefit of the client rather than for my own needs—specifically, whether the disclosure supports the client's therapeutic growth. I aim to identify the intent and potential therapeutic gain promptly. Second,

I assess the client's cognitive capacity, the severity of mental illness, and the intensity of trauma history to determine whether these variables might complicate or distort the interpretation of the information shared.

By sharing a few personal details revolving around the disability, I create moments of mutual vulnerability that invite clients to share more openly. This form of therapeutic reciprocity facilitated safety and authenticity that promoted deeper participation in treatment. It has been an unspoken quid pro quo, "something for something," where the vulnerability stimulated a deeper engagement in the therapeutic process. I have learned to respond thoughtfully to each client's unique reactions to my self-disclosures by attending closely to their feedback and shifts in affect. When I sense resistance or discomfort, I intentionally redirect the focus back to the client, guiding them to identify negative thought patterns and bolster strengths in ways that are appropriate to the client's specific context and needs.

Often, the difference in the power dynamic between the doctor and patient not only impacts sharing information but also may play a role in the reason why individuals fear coming to therapy in the first place. Ethical considerations suggest balancing fostering a more egalitarian relationship while not creating a burden for the client by inadvertently having them care for the therapist (Zur & Wolz, 2022).

When I began working for a psychiatric hospital's outpatient center which consisted of running various psychoeducational and CBT-oriented groups which taught basic life skills, anxiety management, and emotional regulation strategies for individuals with developmental challenges. I kept having experiences where I was often abruptly confronted with inappropriate questions during groups, such as, "What happened to you?" "What's wrong with you?" These inquiries reflected not only the curiosity of the clients but also the impaired socialization and disinhibited nature of the psychiatric patients. Initially, I was caught off guard. The experiences reminded me of similar moments in public where random people would bluntly ask, "What's the matter with you?"—questions that always felt intrusive and difficult to respond to. However, in a clinical setting, these experiences were more challenging and intricately layered with an impact on the patient's functioning. Patients often asked these questions without any established therapeutic relationship.

The therapeutic relationship in CBT, as with other models, is arguably an integral part of therapy (Okamoto et al., 2019), and its ingredients include authenticity, empathy, and positive alliance (Norcross & Wampold, 2011). Not having this established relationship made the inquiries disruptive, random, and awkward. Furthermore, in these situations, I had to stop, separate myself many times, and realize that it wasn't about me, but related to the overall symptomology they came with, a small part that impacted their functioning.

I brought these situations to clinical supervision where I learned to reframe the experience not as disruptive, but as a therapeutic tool of modeling and rapport building. Through this lens of curiosity and compassion, I adapted my self-disclosure based on each client's readiness and psychological presentation. When it was appropriate, I redirected the moment using CBT Socratic questioning and guided discovery tools to evaluate the validity of their dysfunctional assumptions by having them ask themselves, "How do people usually react when you ask that type of question?" (Clark, 2014; Fenn & Byrne, 2013). This gentle approach allowed me to reinforce social etiquette and boundaries without shaming the patient. It also highlighted keeping the focus on relationship-building, emotional regulation, and educating them with insight for cultural norms.

Padesky (1993) described guided discovery, a central concept in CBT, as a collaborative process that assists clients in identifying and examining underlying assumptions that shape their thoughts, emotions, and behaviors. Using Socratic questioning, clients are encouraged to explore alternative perspectives, evaluate the accuracy of unhelpful beliefs, and generate more balanced interpretations of their experiences (Padesky, 1993). This approach supports clients in discovering solutions independently rather than being directed toward conclusions, thereby strengthening insight, autonomy, and adaptive coping in a safe environment (Fenn & Byrne, 2013).

Another challenge I have with a visible mobility impairment is the complex message it often communicates, one of an unspoken blends of misperceived fragility alongside strength, vulnerability, and a resonating compassion.

When I worked at the adult drug rehabilitation center, I worked with several vulnerable individuals. There was one moment of mutual authenticity and shared humanity, where an unreachable individual crossed paths with a therapist with a physical disability. By allowing him to see my physical vulnerability, combined with mutual compassion and his emotional openness in that moment, I was able to access his self-awareness. I used flexible perspective taking to help him look at his current behavior and consider alternative thoughts when I asked, "What do you have to do differently? Here's an opportunity to shift gears and focus on a different direction." In that moment, I incorporated ACT BA and choice point evaluation to highlight his goals and move him toward the life and person he wanted to be (Harris, 2023). Although his future remained uncertain, the moment served as a reminder that empathy and mutual compassion can break through hardened walls (OpenAI, 2025).

Potential risks of perceived vulnerability and self-disclosure

While working in the psychiatric hospital, I encountered a complex and at times unsafe intersection between my disability, the use of compassion to foster rapport, and my perceived nonthreatening presence. I cultivated a space of mutual compassion as he asked about my experiences living with a disability. I listened with empathy, creating a safe therapeutic space that allowed him to reflect and process his struggles.

In what felt like a moment shaped by comfort, trust, and safety built through our therapeutic rapport, the client disclosed that he felt too vulnerable. In that brief instant, the security of the therapeutic bond intersected with the inherent clinical risk of the treatment setting. This experience illustrates the complexity of working within dual professional roles as a psychologist—fostering an empathic and trusting therapeutic connection while simultaneously maintaining appropriate professional boundaries and a nonthreatening clinical presence.

This experience heightened my awareness of the delicate balance between physical presence, therapeutic engagement, and safety, particularly when working with vulnerable individuals, forensic populations, and high-risk settings. By offering compassion and empathic Socratic questioning to help clients shift attention away from rigid or distress-focused thinking and explore alternative perspectives (Fenn & Byrne, 2013), I learned to support disclosure while remaining attentive to clinical risk and environmental context.

During my postdoctoral placement working with chronic pain patients, I began to integrate CBT more systematically into treatment. This approach allowed me to structure interventions and treatment plans that incorporated mind-body strategies, such as progressive muscle relaxation, identification of cognitive distortions that maintain pain, and cultivation of acceptance and commitment to self-management. The integration of these mind–body approaches was associated with improvements in pain-related outcomes and overall functioning (Hassed, 2013).

Fine-tuning the self-disclosure of my disability to empower client's resiliency and self-advocacy

I continued to carefully practice self-disclosure during my post-doctoral training working under a forensic psychologist and Qualified Medical examiner for individuals injured at work. These patients often demonstrated limited progress with physical recovery post-surgery, pain management, and alleviation due to the complex sequelae of the emotional symptoms and unresolved grief and loss due to the catastrophic injuries. Happening during the Covid pandemic, I began incorporating telehealth into my clinical practice for the first time. In this format, clients were unable to see my physical disability. Many of these clients were struggling with the despair of career-ending injuries, loss of professional identity, and, in many cases, the onset of physical disability where I had to assist them in reshaping the journey of their recovery. I selectively disclosed my own disability to help clients reframe and reconstruct their recovery narratives in ways that supported the restoration of meaning and purpose in their lives. Using Cognitive Processing Therapy (CPT), an adaptation of CBT, we carefully examined rigid maladaptive thinking patterns, or "stuck points" that maintained trauma symptoms and worked to restructure them. I also incorporated Rational Emotive Behavior Therapy (REBT) ABC model (Antecedents-Beliefs-Consequence) to help clients identify the relationship between thoughts to emotions and behaviors (Ellis, 1992).

Using ABC diagrams, I helped clients become aware of the connections between (A) *activating or catastrophic events*, (B) the *thoughts* associated with those events, and (C) the resulting emotional response, such as grief. Together, we examined negative thought patterns that elevated "manufactured" emotions by attempting to change the past through cognitions (e.g., "I'll never be happy again unless I can walk.") (Resick et al., 2024). We then explored acceptance and identified healthier self-talk that incorporated self-compassion and alternative ways for them to express what was meaningful to them.

Drawing on core principles of ACT theory, we identified ways in which the individual's sense of self could continue through acts of remembrance and value-consistent living. This process involved clarifying values, defusing unhelpful thinking patterns, and supporting participation in meaningful goals and ADLs through creative and adaptive strategies that moved clients toward their chosen paths (Harris, 2023).

To build rapport, establish credibility, and normalize resilience in the face of hardship, I frequently incorporated personal examples from my own disability and recovery journey. I gave specific examples of adapting strategically by looking at different ways of accomplishing goals, identifying more options, or using the internet as a knowledge resource for problem solving. I shared strategies such as pacing and relearning ADLs, demonstrating how gradual adjustments could support clients in restoring their functioning. For instance, when working with a client with a severe knee injury, I suggested a simple adaptation: using a stool in the kitchen for BA. This practical modification not only made the task simple and accessible but also reinforced the idea that recovery often involves using CPT by challenging stuck thoughts and negative automatic thoughts to promote creative problem-solving. One of the main goals of CPT is cognitive flexibility by helping clients challenge their rigid thinking patterns to help them get out of feeling helpless (Resick et al., 2024).

This experience deepened my understanding of how personal adversity, when used with intention, can serve as a therapeutic tool. My disability not only allowed me to empathize more fully with clients' struggles but also helped me foster a sense of empowerment—showing them that while loss and change are inevitable, resilience and self-advocacy can reshape the future path. I guided them in transforming their anxieties about medical procedures and treatments into practical questions, weighing pros and cons, and advocating for themselves in a compensation system that often felt unsupportive and rushed.

Work-related injuries often led to persistent negative thoughts, fueling anxiety and depression, reflected in high scores on the Pain Catastrophizing Scale (PCS). Many clients struggled with conditions such as Somatic Symptom Disorder, depression, and PTSD, with little physical improvement due to dysfunctional thinking. To address this, I highlighted common PCS thoughts (e.g., "The pain is awful, and I feel overwhelmed") and used the ABC model to help clients connect thoughts, emotions, and behaviors. I reinforced these concepts by sharing my own recovery experiences, demonstrating the power of cognitive change—like sharing how my psychological distress delayed my physical recovery.

I often share my experience of undergoing two nearly identical foot surgeries to illustrate the impact of cognition on recovery. The first recovery was relatively smooth, requiring only brief use of pain medication and allowing me to walk independently within three months. The second surgery, however, was significantly more painful and required nearly double the medication and recovery time. The critical difference was not the procedure itself, but my psychological state following the second surgery—persistent negativity and sadness appeared to slow the healing process.

This experience highlights a core principle of CBT: thoughts and emotional states can either exacerbate or alleviate physical and psychological recovery. Shifting toward gratitude and more adaptive thinking can foster resilience, improve emotional regulation, enhance pain management, support physical recovery, and facilitate meaning-making. Sharing how my lived experience as a psychologist with a disability has evolved into experiential expertise allows me to model the application of foundational CBT and ACT principles, ultimately demonstrating how vulnerability can be transformed into therapeutic strength.

I often share this experience with clients as an example of recognizing and appreciating an unspoken accomplishment—one that reflects competence, clinical strength, and resilience in the face of physical limitations. In doing so, I model gratitude-based cognitive reappraisal by reframing an initially challenging situation into an outcome that can be genuinely appreciated.

References

Arabic proverb. (n.d.). *The man with the greatest wealth is not the one who has the most, but the one who needs the least*. Traditional proverb.

Clark, D. A. (1995). Perceived limitations of standard cognitive therapy: A consideration of efforts to revise Beck's theory and therapy. *Journal of Cognitive Psychotherapy*, 9(3), 153–172.

Clark, D. A. (2014). Cognitive behavioral therapy: A historical overview. In S. G. Hofmann (Ed.), *The Wiley handbook of cognitive behavioral therapy* (Vol. 1, D. J. A. Dozois, Ed., pp. 1–22). John Wiley & Sons.

Ellis, A. (1992). The revised ABC's of rational-emotive therapy (RET). *Journal Rational-Emotive & Cognitive-Behavior Therapy*, 9, 139–172.

Fava, G.A., & Ruini, C. (2003). Development and characteristics of a well-being enhancing psychotherapeutic strategy: Wellbeing therapy. *Journal of Behavior Therapy and Experimental Psychiatry*, 34, 45–63.

Fenn, K., & Byrne, M. (2013). The key principles of cognitive behavioural therapy. *InnovAiT*, 6(9), 579–585. https://doi.org/10.1177/1755738012471029

Frankl, V. E. (2006). *Man's search for meaning*. Beacon Press. (Original work published 1946).

Frostadottir, A. D., & Dorjee, D. (2019). Effects of mindfulness-based cognitive therapy (MBCT) and compassion focused therapy (CFT) on symptom change, mindfulness, self-compassion, and rumination in clients with depression, anxiety, and stress. *Frontiers in Psychology*, 10, Article 1099, 1–11.

Goldfried, M. R., Burckell, L. A., & Eubanks-Carter, C. (2003 May). Therapist self-disclosure in cognitive-behavior therapy. *Journal of Clinical Psychology*, 59(5), 555–568. https://doi.org/10.1002/jclp.10159. PMID: 12696131.

Harris, R. (2023). Using ACT with core beliefs, narratives, and schemas: Useful tips for ACT practitioners. *The Happiness Trap*. https://thehappinesstrap.com

Hassed, C. (2013). Mind–body therapies: Use in chronic pain management. *Australian Family Physician*, 42(1–2), 112–116.

Leyland, M. (2012). Gratitude diaries as part of the CBT toolkit: Do they ameliorate depression, negative thinking and hopelessness, and increase gratitude? (Doctoral dissertation, Coventry University).

McCauley, E., Gudmundsen, G., Schloredt, K., Martell, C., Rhew, I., Hubley, S., et al. (2016). The adolescent behavioral activation program: Adapting behavioral activation as a treatment for depression in adolescence. *Journal of Clinical Child & Adolescent Psychology*, 45, 291–304. https://doi.org/10.1080/15374416.2014.979933

McCullough, M. E., Tsang, J.-A., & Emmons, R. A. (2004). Gratitude in intermediate affective terrain: Links of grateful moods with individual differences and daily emotional experience. *Journal of Personality and Social Psychology*, 86(2), 295–309.

Mooney, K.A., & Padesky, C.A. (2001). Creative developments in cognitive therapy. *One-day workshop presented at the World Congress of Behavioral and Cognitive Therapies*, Vancouver, Canada.

Norcross, J. C., & Wampold, B. E. (2011). Evidence-based therapy relationships: Research conclusions and clinical practices. In J. C. Norcross (Ed.), *Psychotherapy relationships that work: Evidence-based responsiveness* (pp. 423–430). Oxford University Press. https://doi.org/10.1093/acprof:oso/9780199737208.003.0021

Okamoto, A., Dattillio, F. M., Dobson, K. S., & Kazantzis, N. (2019). The therapeutic relationship in cognitive-behavioral therapy: Essential features and common challenges. *Practice Innovations*, 4(2), 112–123. https://doi.org/10.1037/pri0000088

OpenAI. (2026). ChatGPT (GPT-5.5) [Large language model]. https://chatgpt.com

Padesky, C. (1993). Socratic questioning: changing minds or guiding discovery? *Keynote address delivered at European Association for Behavioural and Cognitive Psychotherapies Conference*, London.

Padesky, C. A. (2006). The next phase: Building positive qualities with cognitive therapy. *Invited address presented at the International Congress of Cognitive Psychotherapy*, Göteborg, Sweden.

Padesky, C. A., & Mooney, K. A. (2012). Strengths-based cognitive–behavioural therapy: A four-step model to build resilience. *Clinical Psychology & Psychotherapy*, 19(4), 283–290. https://doi.org/10.1002/cpp.1795

Resick, P. A., Monson, C. M., & Chard, K. M. (2024). *Cognitive processing therapy for PTSD: A comprehensive therapist manual*. The Guilford Press.

Scarlet, J. (2016). *Superhero therapy*. New Harbinger Publications.

Wilson, D. B., Bouffard, L. A., & MacKenzie, D. L. (2005). A quantitative review of structured, group-oriented cognitive–behavioral programs for offenders. *Criminal Justice and Behavior*, 32(2), 172–204.

Zhao, F., Zhang, Z.-H., Bi, L., Xiao-Shuang, W., Wang, W.-J., Li, Y.-F., et al. (2017). The association between life events and internet addiction among Chinese vocational school students: The mediating role of depression. *Computers in Human Behavior*, 70, 30–38. https://doi.org/10.1016/j.chb.2016.12.057

Zur, O., & Wolz, B. (2022). *What films can teach psychotherapists about therapist self disclosure in psychotherapy* [Review of what films can teach psychotherapists about therapist self-disclosure in psychotherapy]. Zur Institute.

Chapter 9

Using the Acceptance and Commitment Therapy Matrix to explore behaviours related to a complex physical health diagnosis

Dawn Johnson

Introduction

Storytelling is one of the most fundamental skills that humans engage in. For millennia, we have used verbal sounds to pass information to others, to share wisdom, sound warnings, provide consistency to our shared values and ideas, and to educate future generations on surviving in an often-hostile environment. Fables and nursery rhymes are good examples of life lessons that are passed down through generations via a rehearsed narrative.

The words we use to tell the stories of our lives matter. How we understand those words, and the importance and power we give to them matters. In short, the power is in the words. The meanings we make from words influence our thoughts, feelings, and behaviours and shape our responses to stimuli. Everything is about relating, and the consequences of that relating (Barnes-Holmes & McEnteggart, 2020).

This chapter is largely about my own storytelling venture. My 'disability' is a recent diagnosis, albeit something I have lived with for my entire life. The storytelling in this chapter is about how I am making sense of what my condition means for me, and how the words I use to describe and define myself are a significant and important part of the process of making sense of something that feels new to me, and yet all rather familiar. This chapter draws on the philosophy and science of acceptance and commitment therapy (ACT). While the commonly cited Hexaflex model of ACT (Hayes et al., 2006) provides a helpful overview of the core concepts of the ACT model, it is a rather basic summary of a very complex amalgamation of philosophical perspectives and the science of language. To delve into some of the deeper concepts of ACT, I will draw on the science of language – relational frame theory (RFT) and briefly on the underlying philosophical stance of functional contextualism. I will illustrate these theoretical concepts and how they apply to my personal experience of getting a diagnosis of a chronic health condition later in life, and how I have used my knowledge of ACT and contextual behavioural sciences to adapt to working as a psychologist with a 'disability' by using the ACT Matrix (Polk & Schoendorff, 2014; Polk et al., 2016).

Whenever I have read books about people with an illness (largely because I have been looking for some kind of answer that would help me to unlock the magic

DOI: 10.4324/9781003636014-10

secret!), I have wanted to know what their specific issue was, so much so that I have scoured the book to find out what their illness was and then, with that itch scratched, have returned to the first few chapters and settled in for the ride. With that in mind, I will first give some information about my personal health condition, then reflect on what it means for me to have a 'disability' using the ACT matrix.

Ehlers-Danlos Syndrome

Ehlers-Danlos Syndromes (EDS) are a group of 13 separate genetic conditions, each affecting the body's connective tissue (Ehlers-Danlos Support UK, 2017). Of the four types of animal tissue (epithelial tissue, muscle tissue, nervous tissue, and connective tissue), connective tissue is the most abundant and diverse (Nezwek & Varacallo, 2022), with an estimated 30%–40% of the body being made up of this tissue type. It lies between other tissues and organs, separating the organs, while also holding the body together. For people with EDS, the connective tissue is often fragile and stretchy, which has wide implications for injury, health issues, and quality of life.

While 12 of the conditions are identifiable via genetic testing, the hypermobile type (hEDS) is not, despite there being observations of genetic links passed down the familial line. Research is progressing in this area, and there may be a time in the not-too-distant future when hEDS is more easily identifiable from a traditional medical model testing perspective (Alsiri & Palmer, 2023; Ritelli et al., 2024).

I have hEDS. This is the most common form of EDS, although the prevalence is unknown due to difficulties with diagnosis, notably misdiagnosis and underdiagnosis of people living with the condition. It is possible to have hypermobility spectrum disorder (HSD) without having EDS. It is also possible to have a different form of EDS, and there may be no symptoms of hypermobility, so sometimes the overlapping language of these labels can feel confusing. Sometimes, HSD alone can present for someone as more severe than hEDS, so there is little consistency in the severity of the impact based solely on the diagnostic label attached.

Upon encountering hEDS, my assumption was that the main impact of the condition is hypermobile joints, meaning they move to a greater range than most. This had certainly been true for me for all my life, and in my childhood and younger adulthood caused little to no day-to-day concern. However, it is common for pain related to hypermobile joints to increase with age, and this has also been my experience. However, flexibility in joints is by far the only impact of hEDS; in fact, for me, it is the least bothersome part of the condition, due to the complexity and severity of other aspects of the diagnosis, which cause day-to-day and long-term difficulties. Due to connective tissue being such an abundant tissue in the body, the symptoms are vastly more complex and far-reaching than simply joint hyperextension (see Ehlers-Danlos Support UK [n.d.] for a list of possible comorbidities, although this is not a comprehensive list of what people with hEDS can experience). Until I received a diagnosis and educated myself about this condition, I had no idea that I had been managing so many complications in life that most other people simply do not have to contend with.

Diagnosis later in life

My journey to getting a diagnosis of hEDS has been incredibly long and more of a random meandering through a range of professionals' doors that I thought would be helpful for individual presenting symptoms. It was via the least expected professional that I was suddenly seen in a more holistic manner, and my four decades of symptoms started to be pieced together as one whole jigsaw puzzle. For decades, I had been treated (or frequently, *not* treated) for individual symptoms despite many of them being recurring and worsening, rather than them being seen in the context of my previous medical history. Many EDS support groups have adopted the symbol of a zebra. This association is inspired by the medical phrase, 'when you hear hoofbeats, think horses, not zebras'. The intended lesson here is that medical professionals should consider the simplest solution first. The zebra is therefore an accurate representation of the difficulties posed by EDS, since taking the simplest approach of managing presenting symptoms in silo never catches the complexity of the holistic impact of EDS on a person's life. The idea that something more complex or rare was happening for me was completely overlooked. The possibility of hEDS was raised with my general medical practitioner (GP), who informed me they had never heard of EDS (any of the types). I was referred to rheumatology; however, this referral was rejected as there is no formal EDS pathway in the NHS. The same GP therefore ended up being the person to give me a diagnosis based on a Beighton Score assessment (a nine-point system used to measure joint hypermobility; see Malek et al., 2021). I have since paid privately to have other conditions ruled out, as hEDS is only supposed to be a given after excluding all other medical possibilities (which was refused by my GP). Despite my somewhat unorthodox assessment process, I was finally given a diagnostic label that explained a lifelong presentation.

Sense-making of my history using the ACT matrix

Getting a diagnosis later in life was an important contextual factor that impacted how I felt about my condition. The ACT Matrix is an assessment and formulation tool that also nicely captures the six core components of the ACT model and an understanding of the relational frames that are keeping people stuck in their patterns of behaviour (see Johnson & Bennett, 2023 for an illustration of the overlay of these). Briefly, Box 1 represents values, Box 2 represents the internal experiences we often get caught up with and respond to as if they are facts, Box 3 epitomises experiential avoidance of Box 2 content, Box 4 outlines the committed action people could choose to take in line with their values, and the centre circle denotes self-as-context which is our ability to adopt the perspective of being a non-judgemental 'observer' of our lives (i.e. both internal and external experiences in relation to a life event). The acceptance part of the Hexaflex is captured in the interplay between Boxes 1 and 2, whereby people learn to understand that Box 2 content is merely the price you pay for caring so deeply about the content of Box 1. Awareness of the present moment comes from attending to the Matrix and tuning

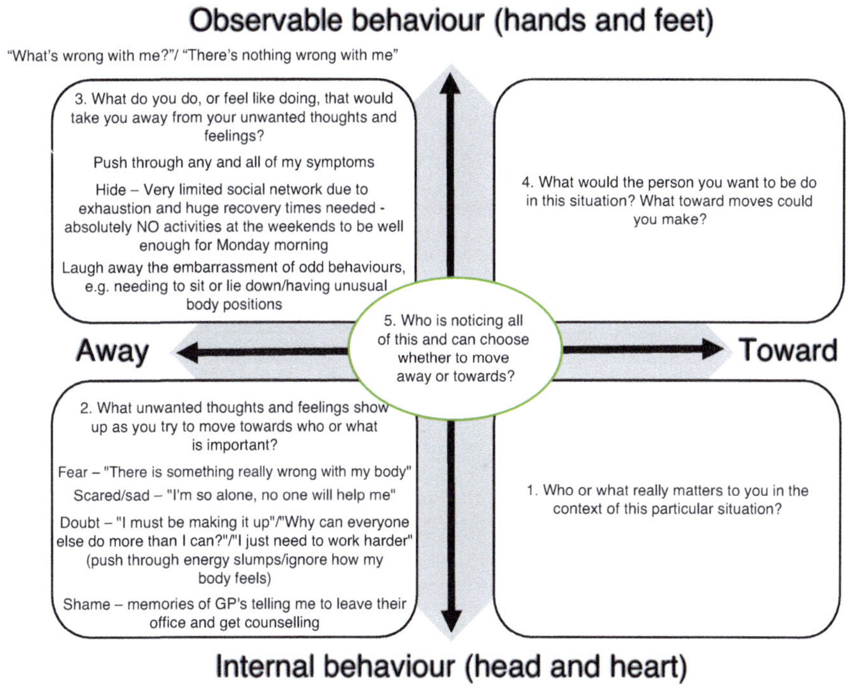

Figure 9.1 'What's wrong with me? Matrix', adapted from Polk & Schoendorff (2014).

into the content of it, as well as tuning into each moment of lived experience via the self-as-context centre circle.

The Matrix is helpful in identifying behaviours that are in line with our values (often referred to as towards moves) and those that take us away from our unwanted internal experiences (away moves). Some of these patterns of my behaviour will be explored below in relation to my own health condition and the narratives I held about myself at the time of getting my diagnosis (Figure 9.1), and since I have utilised the skills of ACT and RFT to add in new behavioural repertoires (Figure 9.2).

Figure 9.1 illustrates that after four decades of invalidation from medical professionals of my presenting symptoms, I was stuck in a pattern of noticing unwanted internal experiences, and working incredibly hard to push them away, for example, by 'proving' to myself and others that I was indeed 'OK' by 'pushing through all of my symptoms'.

Without even reading the words on the above Matrix, it is clear to see that three sections of the five are empty. This feels like a helpful representation of how things were at the time of getting my diagnosis. I was stuck in the maintenance cycle of moving away from what was causing me distress and discomfort, and in doing so, I was reinforcing the narratives in Box 2 (e.g. unwanted internal experiences), leading to more of the same responsive behaviours that felt 'logical' and contextually helpful in Box 3 (e.g. behaviours that function to reduce the impact of Box 2

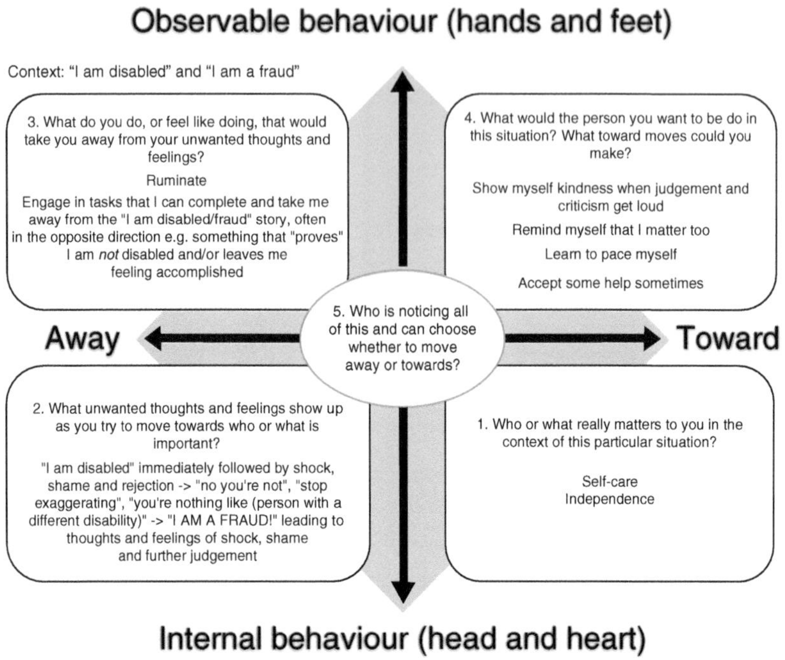

Figure 9.2 'I am a fraud Matrix', adapted from Polk & Schoendorff (2014).

content). Around and around, I was cycling in a series of behaviours that took me away from my unwanted internal experiences (away moves), without any awareness that this was my pattern of behaviour.

Once hEDS had been raised, I had thought that getting a diagnosis would feel like a validating process. It was not. It hurt. The revelation of getting a diagnosis of something life-long later in life was a hard emotional wave to ride. I had anticipated that the diagnosis would either feel emotionally neutral or somewhat relieving, perhaps a nod of validation of my decades of visiting health professionals with a pattern of chronic pain, injury, and fatigue. Instead, it landed hard and heavy, and I struggled with the loss of hope that 'if I just…', I could find a magic answer to make the long list of symptoms disappear. I felt a loss of the life I had hoped for, the life I might have if I could just get to a point of being reliably healthy and well. And then I was told that I might never have this, not for want of trying, but because there is a problem with the tissue that holds my body together. Thus, inevitably and unpredictably, my joints will spontaneously move, my tissue will tear, and my body will let me down repeatedly, resulting in yet more injury and pain. During the times I had sought medical help, I had assumed I was facing a discreet problem for which there would be a solution, and when the right treatment was implemented, I would then be 'well'. My diagnosis confirmed that this would never be the pattern of events, hence turning to ACT to give me the skills to manage the life-long condition.

The above Matrix helps to illustrate what ACT can bring to someone in my position. I felt stuck, sad, alone, helpless and hopeless of future change. My diagnosis was, after all, life-long, and there is no cure or even a treatment/support pathway I could utilise. So, what could I do now? Well, looking again at the above Matrix makes it clear that there was a huge amount I could do. It provided me with hope, not of a health change, but instead of me becoming a more empowered noticer and chooser in my own life. That was hard, because it meant a degree of acceptance was also needed, and who wants to accept ill health? ACT is not a magic pill, or a 'miracle solution'. It takes time and effort. I had to develop new skills, and I had never had to practice these before, so they were (and still are) terrifying at times, and exhausting to manage. They are, however, incredibly helpful in living a different life to the 'away moves cycle' I was stuck in.

In the above Matrix, Boxes 1, 4, and 5 are empty. This was where my work was, and this is what ACT could offer to my life. I could learn what values would need to be front and centre for me to start living the life I wanted (Box 1). I could start to embody them, in big and small ways every day (Box 4), and I could tune in to seeing the whole of my Matrix by taking the perspective represented in the centre circle (5). By adding these things into my Matrix, I have learned that life will be a constant cycle of skilful monitoring of symptoms, plotting my current health against an estimated calculation of what an activity will 'cost' me, either in terms of energy or possible injury, and guesstimating whether every single task in my day is worth doing or not. It is tiresome, it is beyond restrictive, and this speaks mostly to the practical management of my condition, not to the deeper issue of what all this means for my identity and sense of 'self', which is much more psychologically bewildering.

The stories we tell ourselves

For most of my life, I felt I had a clear narrative about my 'self'. I should note here that the self is a complex concept that is beyond the scope of this chapter (see Bennett [2017] and McHugh et al. [2019] for a more comprehensive exploration of this topic). From a basic RFT perspective, narrative statements about the self can be experienced as if they are objectively true (McHugh et al., 2019). When using 'I am…' statements, we are placing our 'self' in a frame of coordination with another stimulus, that to us can feel highly coherent. For example, let us consider the statement, 'I am female'. For me, I derive this quickly (there is low derivation), I do not have any sense of doubt (it is inflexible), it is complex (based on my understanding of gender issues and my view of what that means for me), and it is coherent with how I view myself in the world. For these reasons, this 'I am' statement makes sense to me and thus causes me no distress.

Language learning in the human brain sets us up to derive relational networks. Once we have acquired the skill of doing this, it is impossible to *not* do it. We can relate any arbitrary stimulus to another. However, while this is developmentally adaptive, it can also lead to significant suffering. For example, if I did not feel like I was female – this would lead to high derivation (i.e. hard to make the link between 'me' and 'female') and low coherence with my sense of myself in the world. Simply hearing myself referred to as female could lead to obvious distress. Distress can also occur when we add in an assessment or judgement of these derivations (e.g. 'I am stupid for feeling like this').

In relation to my health condition, one of the most distressing relational frames for me is, 'I am disabled'. I will look at this in more detail through an RFT lens as it has shown itself to be one of the hardest relations to make any sense of. I simply cannot comprehend the frame of coordination between 'Dawn' and 'disability'. Let us first explore what we mean by 'disability'. This definition matters because fusion and inflexibility with what a disability is contribute to my difficulty with accepting the coordination between 'I' and 'disabled'.

Deciding what disability is or is not is achieved via socially constructed narratives. If we fit the social narrative of what is generally accepted to be disabled, that frame of co-ordination is easier to make. My own understanding of what a disability is feels quite 'old fashioned' and out of date, and it is from this perspective that I judge myself so harshly. Akin to domestic abuse historically being understood only as physical violence and now being agreed to include controlling and coercive behaviours, as well as sexual violence (Domestic Abuse Act, 2021), our social narratives about disability have been updated and modified to reflect the growing needs of those without obvious physical differences (Office for Disability Issues, 2013). A narrow definition of the notion of a disability includes things like limb differences, the use of a wheelchair or walking aides, or observable difficulties in mobility. A more updated understanding of disability includes conditions construed as 'hidden' (Office for Disability Issues, 2013). That means that the historical cues referred to above are absent, despite a person having some additional needs, whether those be physical or cognitive.

hEDS could fit either definition of disability, depending on severity and how the diagnosis presents for any given person. So far, for me, it would be classed as a hidden disability, as although it is inconsistent in its presentation, it *is* substantial and long-term, which are the criteria that the UK government uses to define disability (Office for Disability Issues, 2013). At times in my life, a combination of luck and good self-management means I appear well enough not to be described as 'disabled' and outwardly I would present as 'fine'. At other times, there are certainly more significant needs where I would feel more legitimate in, for example, using a disabled toilet, even though outwardly no-one would notice anything different about my presentation. However, this has not been an easy psychological transition to make from my previous narrative of, 'there is nothing wrong with me'. Thankfully, the world is changing and evolving to become a more inclusive place, with some disabled toilet doors now having signs stating, 'not all disabilities are obvious', encouraging a more inclusive and compassionate perspective. These changes help to update our societal views of what a disability is and what behavioural repertoires people with a disability may display.

My self-story

Understanding the above, in addition to receiving a diagnosis later in life, it makes sense to me that I struggle with the coordination relation between 'I' and 'disabled'. One of the most painful judgements this leads to my mind making about me is the persistent thought, 'I am a fraud'. What I mean by that is that I, relate myself and 'fraud' in a frame of coordination. To put it another way, it would be just as accurate in my mind to put an equal sign between 'I' and 'fraud'. This thought is evoked by attempts to make meaning of 'I am disabled'. The distress is caused by my rigid understanding of what it is to have a disability, that I assess myself to be in a frame of opposition to what I view the rigid and old fashioned perspective of 'disability' to be, and that therefore, whenever I do anything that is aligned with the narrative of *having* a disability, or *being* disabled, my mind concludes that I am being fraudulent. It is this negative and critical appraisal of my 'self' that causes distress (McHugh et al., 2019).

'I am a fraud' wanders around my mind with differing levels of volume and tone, some more easy to distance myself from than others. It has shown up a lot throughout writing this book chapter. When it has sounded quieter or softer, it has felt possible to welcome it in to sit beside me as words get typed onto a page. However, when it has sounded louder and angrier, it has sometimes resulted in a lot of procrastination, as a way of removing myself from the discomfort of the thought. These 'away moves' are well-rehearsed, and sometimes well-disguised as towards moves. One of the difficulties is that it is not simply a case of 'I' and 'fraud' being in a frame of coordination; there are multiple relational frames occurring, and many of them cause me some level of distress. RFT offers me a helpful theory to start to do some sense making of my experiences. It also provides a route into understanding which ACT techniques might be of service to me.

Managing hEDS and my self-story using ACT

The ACT Matrix below helps to capture some of the relational frames that keep me stuck in an away cycle, as well as each of the four quadrants, identifying patterns of behaviour. Some of these will be explored below in relation to my own health condition and the narratives I hold about myself.

It is helpful to start the Matrix wherever there is data, and what I noticed about completing my Matrix is that there was abundant data for Box 2 – the internal thoughts, feelings, and sensations that show up in response to me receiving a chronic health diagnosis. The content shown above is an illustrative sample of the multitude of my unwanted internal experiences. What became evident as I completed the information in Box 3 was the desperate desire to push away all internal discomfort, and thus easily engage in numerous away moves as a means of 'proving' that my diagnosis does not really have a significant impact on my independence. The Matrix was a helpful illustration that I was stuck in a maintenance cycle of away moves, with my behavioural responses serving to strengthen the struggle with the content of Box 2, thus, prompting me to engage in further away moves to prove my worth.

What became evident was the absence of any connection with the content of the boxes on the right-hand side of the Matrix. In fact, it took great effort to begin to populate these boxes. Up to a point that my health would no longer allow it, I had clung tightly to my values of love, care, kindness, and connection to others. I would willingly put others first. However, in the face of a worsening health situation, I could no longer pursue only these values. Part of my journey with hEDS, RFT, and ACT has therefore been to learn to prioritise other values, and to bring to the forefront some that had been less rehearsed. I am still learning to add my name to the list of people that matter. The two main values included in Box 1 of the Matrix are 'self-care' (both because I must and want to take care of myself) and 'independence'. These have led to me experimenting with new behaviours that are different, almost counter-intuitive, expressions of my values. For example, to maintain my independence and not end up *more* disabled by hEDS, I have had to learn to pace myself carefully and ask for help long before I would ideally want to. The irony is that when I do not seek help, I lose my independence much more quickly due to the inevitable increase in symptoms that occurs in the context of poor self-care. Using the Matrix in this way has helped me to better support my management of hEDS.

In terms of addressing the distress evoked by the judgement and self-criticism of the left-hand side of the Matrix, RFT is helpful in clarifying the nature of the relations. Often, Boxes 1 and 2 are held in a frame of opposition. For example, I *would* live my values if only the difficult things in Box 2 did not stop me. One of the first relations we can aim to change via the process of acceptance is that Boxes 1 and 2 are not in opposition but rather, in coordination. In my example, this means learning that the distressing thoughts 'I am disabled' and 'I am a fraud' *only* show up because I care so much about my value of independence. I want to behaviourally embody this value with complete integrity, thus any help needed must mean I am *not* independent, which lands as very challenging. Instead of this thought being seen as the enemy, it can be possible to see 'I am a fraud' with acceptance that our pain and values are inextricably linked. We simply cannot have one without the other.

Another unhelpful relational frame identified when I first completed the Matrix is that there was a frame of causation between Boxes 2 and 3, like a logical response that was almost inevitable. RFT helps identify that I could also build a frame of causation between Boxes 2 and 4. What this means in practice is that we can learn additional 'if___, then___' relations. Our established behaviours are often coordinated with our moods, thus making it logical that when I notice difficult internal stimuli, I would work hard at avoidance to minimise the impact of the emotional content, generating the maintenance cycle between Boxes 2 and 3. However, by also building a frame of causation between Boxes 2 and 4, it is possible to begin to respond to Box 2 stimuli with Box 4 behaviours. Thus, experiencing psychological discomfort moves from being the automatic cue to avoid, to being the cue to mindfully choose between avoidant and value-driven responses. For me, this includes an increase in compassion and kindness by reminding myself that I matter and need kindness when criticism shows up. It also includes learning to ask for help when I need it, not seeing that as 'weak', but rather as something that boosts my independence in the long-term and takes me in a more helpful direction in life.

The power of language – a brief introduction to the science of relational frame theory

In terms of contextual behaviourism, RFT is often described as the science and ACT as the art. ACT has some well-known strategies to use with clients, and memorable metaphors can be recycled without real psychological precision, albeit often still helpful to affect some behaviour change in therapeutic work with clients. RFT, however, explains the relational networks that are at play and contribute to us as humans staying stuck in behavioural patterns because language is so impactful to our thoughts, feelings, and behaviours (Hayes et al., 2001). It is like looking under the bonnet of a car and seeing a mechanical fault. You may know what the problem is, but simply noticing it does not provide the intervention needed to get the car back on the road. Since it shares roots with ACT, RFT can provide more precise theoretically driven interventions.

Stories have always been an accessible way of communicating ideas between large numbers of people. As humans evolved and began living in larger groups, eventually forming cities, visual marks were created which became representations of verbal content. This written form of language was a superpower to human development, in that it allowed information to be shared much more widely amongst people who perhaps would not otherwise ordinarily meet, whether that be because of differences in social class, status, education, or geography. Language, both verbal and written, changes how humans experience the world. Without it, we would never have been able to cooperate to the level that we have or achieved the enormous societal complexity that is evident today, in comparison to our hunter-gatherer ancestors (Harari, 2014).

RFT postulates that we learn to relate stimuli to one another, allowing us to further learn that a verbal sound can refer to an object or concept that may or may not be seen (or even 'real' in an ontological sense). RFT refers to this relational learning as 'arbitrarily applicable relational responding', known as 'AARRing' (see Barnes-Holmes et al. [2020] for information on the hyper-dimensional multi-level [HDML] and a comprehensive explanation of the five developmental levels of AARRing).

The HDML identifies four behavioural dimensions, described in turn. These are important as they provide a precise understanding of why some behaviour change is effective more quickly than at other times. The Matrix in Figure 9.2 for example may look like it contains all the (brief) information that I would need to then implement change, and 'ta-dah!', I would feel better, behave differently, hold a more positive perspective of myself and ultimately experience less struggle with my chronic health condition/disability. However, that rarely is the case. Using a Matrix to draw out patterns and identify maintenance cycles is only part of the process of change. Another key part of effecting change is to undermine the languaging we use for ourselves. The four behavioural dimensions of the HDML model help us to assess the stuckness of each.

The first dimension is *coherence*. The higher the coherence someone has with a story about themselves, or the way the world around them works, the harder it is to challenge or weaken. For me, I had absolutely zero coherence with disability, and 100% coherence with 'fine', 'well', 'able' type labels. The coherence I had with a label that may then be more honouring of my lived experiences therefore felt utterly jarring and incredibly *incoherent* and hard to accept as I had been denied an explanation of my condition for 40 years.

The second behavioural dimension is *complexity*. We can tell highly complex stories about ourselves such as, 'I am broken, and also fine, I am lazy, despite working really hard, I am always tired but I sleep too much'. We can also have stories about ourselves that have low complexity 'I am broken'; however, therapeutically, both are hard to weaken since the other behavioural dimensions are still at play. For example, if one finds their story of 'I am broken' to be completely coherent with their life experiences, then the fact that it only contains one description makes it no easier to therapeutically change.

The third dimension is *derivation*. This refers to how quickly we derive relations between stimuli. Driving a car is a great example of the process of moving from high derivation (takes longer to derive relations) to low derivation (we derive relations almost instantaneously). When we first sit in the driving seat, we are faced with many tasks to do all at once. It takes practice for the tasks to become easier, until we are so rehearsed at them that we just do them automatically. With an experienced driver, there is low derivation between multiple tasks such as changing gear, checking mirrors, indicating, turning wiper blades on/off, etc. The same is true of the cognitive links that we make. The more rehearsed they are, the quicker the link happens. By the age of 40, the links I made had low derivation, meaning I made them instantly, without consideration or space to assess if they were helpful or not. Thoughts such as 'I am broken' or 'there is something wrong with me' felt normal and natural and left me feeling hopeless and helpless. The speed of the derivations really matters to the impact it has as we need a little space between thought and action to be able to make a new behavioural choice.

The final behavioural dimension described in the HDML model is *flexibility*. This pertains to how fixed a particular view is, or whether there is flexibility in the understanding of a connection between stimuli. The lower the flexibility, the harder the connection is to change. In my example above, there was no flexibility. I was stuck, I was broken, I was doomed.

The impact of medical gaslighting

Prior to my diagnosis, I had understood I had experienced medical gaslighting. The diagnosis and what I have since learned about the condition emphasises the extent to which my symptoms had been overlooked and minimised. Medical gaslighting is not simply the absence of a diagnosis; it has been repeated experiences of medical professionals telling me the exact opposite of how my body feels, downplaying symptoms, not offering exploratory tests that may have helped find answers, and at times blaming me for my injuries or experiences. My medical records are sprinkled with 'TATT' meaning 'tired all the time', from as early as my teenage years. However, it feels like this is about as honouring as it got. I have had GPs tell me to 'leave their office', 'go for counselling', 'there are labels for people like you', and 'no you do not', after telling them a long list of symptoms I was experiencing in my body. This level of gaslighting is discombobulating and utterly confusing. On a day-to-day basis, I was historically working full-time, and when GPs and other medical professionals would tell me things like the above, I would genuinely question my symptoms, my pain levels, and my injuries. Surely, they could not all be wrong? Surely, I could not be the only correct voice? The behavioural dimensions of the HDML help to understand the significant impact of such medical gaslighting. It is not simply that after being told 1000 times, 'there is nothing wrong with you' I suddenly believe someone when they announce there is in fact something very wrong with me. Behaviour change does not happen like that, and we know that because of our understanding of how brains relate information (Törneke, 2010).

My journey to getting a diagnosis of hEDS has clearly not been easy, or particularly supportive. The contextual factors of getting a diagnosis later in life alongside many decades of medical gaslighting have had an impact on how I have been able to make sense of this diagnosis, and how easy (or rather, how difficult) it has been to learn to manage my health issues differently, now I have more knowledge and understanding about why they occur.

How I have adapted as a psychologist living with a disability

In terms of the practicalities of doing the job of a clinical psychologist, my health issues have resulted in me making several tweaks to my job. I work solely in private practice, and while this decision had been made in advance of me receiving a diagnosis, I am now very aware that I would not be reliably well enough to undertake the regular hours that would be required in a contracted service. I am always very mindful of my unpredictable energy levels and hEDS symptoms so must manage my diary carefully to ensure I am not too exhausted to function well. This is true on a day-to-day basis in terms of how many clients I see and other tasks, both personal and professional, that I undertake. This is also very important for other events in my calendar, such as running training events or organising and attending conferences. When I know I have larger, more tiring, commitments in my diary, I will ensure that all other commitments are postponed, reduced, or managed, to make sufficient time for me to rest and recover after exertion in line with the literature about post-exertional malaise (Hartle et al., 2021).

As ever, the practical and the emotional are two different factors. I think it is common for many psychologists to judge themselves about supporting others when their own lives are not 'perfect'. This may be related to chaos in family networks, or debt, housing, and health issues. Whatever it is we can beat ourselves up with a sentence akin to, 'how can I support other people when I cannot even…'. I have had to manage my own version of that, not only in relation to the practicalities of managing my health diagnosis, but also the psychological impact of that for me. I did not feel grounded or cohesive in my sense of self. I felt like my world had turned upside-down, and I judged myself for not being a good enough psychologist to be able to manage the internal storm I felt I was in. So, I used the model I so often draw upon. I used my RFT and ACT knowledge and skills to get eyes on what was happening for me, and why I felt so unstable and emotionally dysregulated. The Matrix helped me to formulate this via an ACT and RFT lens. I could make sense of the impact of medical gaslighting and how it had significantly shaped the narratives I held about myself regarding my health and wellness (or lack thereof at times). I am still on this journey, partly because it is a life-long condition and partly because it still feels very new. I am learning to reach out and be less of an island because connection with safe and trusted people is grounding, and it also helps me make the value-driven life choice of maintaining my independence through seeking support when I need it. I am learning to listen more to my body, and what it is asking for, and I am still learning that it is OK to give it what it needs when I can.

It would feel remiss of me not to mention 'mental health'. At the start of this chapter, when I defined EDS, I also stated that it is known to have several possible comorbidities, with 'anxiety' being listed as one of them. As a contextualist, I often find the diagnostic terminology of mental health labels unhelpful. This languaging around our emotional world is merely a shorthand which aims to explain that I get these yucky feelings inside of my body, the nature of which is shared by others in a similar way. This is what we mean by 'anxiety'. Without wishing to protest too much, I push against the idea that 'anxiety' is labelled as a separate 'disorder' or a condition that people 'have'. Instead, it seems logical, and completely normal to me, that I, and thousands of people living with additional health issues requiring careful management, would experience unpleasant internal thoughts and sensations. Yes, I absolutely could use the shorthand descriptor 'anxiety' to describe my feelings when I am asked to do something challenging like present at a conference. I am immediately flooded with thoughts such as, 'Can I travel the day before?', 'Will I feel OK on the day?', 'Will I have injured myself and have to cancel?'. The feelings are visceral and palpable. And yet, I think they are contextually very appropriate and not at all indicative of a 'mental health problem'. The philosophical stance of the ACT model has helped me as a human, and as a psychologist, both in respect of my own life experiences, but also in how I hold my clients. The philosophical stance of ACT holds that people get stuck within a set of contextual factors and rehearsed behavioural patterns that make sense to them (Blackledge, 2015), despite perhaps being outdated and now unhelpful, as mine were to me. My own experience of using RFT and ACT means I feel confident in supporting others by using the same.

Conclusion

This chapter has explored the use of RFT in understanding the narratives at play in relation to my health condition. ACT was the psychological model used to explore and explain the intervention strategies that have been, and continue to be of service, in relation to me accepting and defusing from the stimuli that keep me feeling stuck. One conclusion that can therefore be drawn from this chapter is that, according to RFT, my mind works perfectly! There is nothing amiss with my mind deriving relations, and the natural consequences of that for me as a verbal organism mean that some of those derivations evoke distress because of the meaning made from them.

The universal science of language for humans means that there is no division of 'them' and 'us'. We are all subject to the same patterns above; thus, there is a more compassionate perspective to the sometimes-exaggerated expectation that being a psychologist brings. Of course, I still struggle. Being a psychologist does not immunise me from this. And so, I do what I ask of my clients, and courageously lean into the distress, noticing what is showing up for me. I use the skills of psychological flexibility (Hayes et al., 1999) to increase compassion for myself, ensuring I am on the list of people that matter. I tune in, realising what my towards or away moves could be in any specific moment, and I choose with awareness which of those I may wish to take at that time. I appreciate that the cost of avoidance is that it takes me away from my values, while also knowing that it is a valid choice at times.

Sometimes I find it helpful to remind myself that I am just Dawn. I contain multitudes. In essence, this is the view from the centre of the Matrix, seeing my 'self' as a context for my experiences. I can zoom out of the detail of any single experience, such as a distressing thought, and realise that the person is always bigger than their content. Humans are not defined by any one of their personal characteristics, past behaviours, beliefs, life experiences, or health issues. Framing this hierarchical relation between person and content can help us to feel like our feet are a little more planted on the floor and our heads are held a little higher. Zooming into the detail of one's life can absolutely be helpful, for example doing lots of learning and research about my condition has required me to be very zoomed in to one aspect of my life for prolonged periods. However, it is our ability to flexibly zoom in and out as necessary that is crucial. Most importantly, using RFT to help make sense of the relevant relational networks is key to understanding distress, and using ACT skills to effect change and find a more compassionate response is an approach I find so helpful to my own life, and the lives of those I work with.

References

Alsiri, N., & Palmer, S. (2023). Biomechanical changes in the gastrocnemius medius-Achilles tendon complex in people with hypermobility spectrum disorders: a cross-sectional compression sonoelastography study. *Frontiers in Medicine (Lausanne), 10*. https://doi.org/10.3389/fmed.2023.1062808

Barnes-Holmes, D., Barnes-Holmes, Y., & McEnteggart, C. (2020). Updating RFT (more field than frame) and its implications for process-based therapy. *The Psychological Record, 70*, 605–624.

Barnes-Holmes, Y., & McEnteggart, C. (2020). *Process-based behavior therapy week 1: introduction to process-based behavior therapy, behavior analysis and functional analysis, and the concepts of updated RFT.* [Course notes]. Dublin: Perspectives Ireland.

Bennett, R. (2017). From esteem to acceptance: contemporary perspectives on the self. *Psychotherapy Section Review, 59*, 8–15.

Blackledge, J.T. (2015). *Cognitive defusion in practice.* Oakland, CA: Context Press.

Domestic Abuse Act. (2021). Retrieved 19/12/25 from: https://www.gov.uk/government/publications/domestic-abuse-act-2021

Ehlers-Danlos Support UK. (2017). *What is EDS?* Retrieved 09/09/2025 from: https://www.ehlers-danlos.org/what-is-eds/

Ehlers-Danlos Support UK. (n.d.). *Conditions linked to EDS.* Retrieved 12/09/2025 from: https://www.ehlers-danlos.org/what-is-eds/information-on-eds/conditions-linked-to-eds/

Harari, Y.N. (2014). *Sapiens: a brief history of humankind.* London: Harvill Secker.

Hartle, M., Bateman, L., & Vernon, S.D. (2021). Dissecting the nature of post-exertional malaise. *Fatigue: Biomedicine, Health & Behavior, 9*(1), 33–44. https://doi.org/10.1080/21641846.2021.1905415

Hayes, S.C., Barnes-Holmes, D., & Roche, B. (2001). *Relational frame theory: a post-skinnerian account of human language and cognition.* New York: Plenum/Kluwer.

Hayes, S.C., Luoma, J., Bond, F.W., Masuda, A., & Lillis, J. (2006). Acceptance and commitment therapy: model, processes and outcomes. *Behaviour Research and Therapy, 44*(1), 1–25.

Hayes, S.C., Strosahl, K.D., & Wilson, K.G. (1999). *Acceptance and commitment therapy: an experiential approach to behavior change.* New York: Guilford Press.

Johnson, D., & Bennett, R. (2023). *Acceptance and commitment therapy: responses to frequently asked questions.* London: Routledge.

Malek, S., Reinhold, E.J., & Pearce, G. S. (2021). The Beighton Score as a measure of generalised joint hypermobility. *Rheumatology International, 41*(10), 1707–1716. https://doi.org/10.1007/s00296-021-04832-4

McHugh, L., Stewart, I., & Almada, P. (2019). *A contextual behavioural guide to the self.* Oakland, CA: Context Press.

Nezwek, T.A., & Varacallo, M.A. (2022). *Physiology, connective tissue.* In: StatPearls [Internet]. Treasure Island (FL): StatPearls Publishing. Retrieved 06/09/2025 from: https://www.ncbi.nlm.nih.gov/books/NBK542226/

Office for Disability Issues. (2013). *Disability: Equality Act 2010 – guidance on matters to be taken into account in determining questions relating to the definition of disability.* Retrieved 12/09/2025 from: https://www.gov.uk/government/publications/equality-act-guidance/disability-equality-act-2010-guidance-on-matters-to-be-taken-into-account-in-determining-questions-relating-to-the-definition-of-disability-html#section-b-substantial

Polk, K.L., & Schoendorff, B. (Eds.). (2014). *The ACT matrix: a new approach to building psychological flexibility across settings and populations.* Oakland, CA: New Harbinger.

Polk, K.L., Schoendorff, B., Webster, M., & Olaz, F.O. (2016). *The essential guide to the ACT matrix: a step-by-step approach to using the ACT matrix model in clinical practice.* Oakland, CA: Context Press.

Ritelli, M., Chiarelli, N., Cinquina, V., Bertini, V., Piantoni, S., Caproli, A., Pina, S.E.L.D., Franceschini, F., Zarattini, G., Gandy, W., Venturini, M., Zoppi, N., & Colombi, M. (2024). Bridging the diagnostic gap for hypermobile Ehlers-Danlos Syndrome and hypermobility spectrum disorders: evidence of a common extracellular matrix fragmentation pattern in patient plasma as a potential biomarker. *American Journal of Medical Genetics Part A*, *197*(1). https://doi.org/10.1002/ajmg.a.63857

Törneke, N. (2010). *Learning RFT: an introduction to relational frame theory and its clinical application.* Oakland, CA: New Harbinger.

Chapter 10

The invisible struggle

Reflecting on living with dyslexia, navigating shame, and cultivating self-compassion

Debra Ford

Introduction

The words on the page began to blur together yet again. I was a trainee clinical psychologist, and it was not due to overindulgence in the student lifestyle. No, it was because my brain was working in overdrive to try to decode the jumble of words and process what I was reading. I had read the first sentence of the research paper several times, but nothing registered. In my study group, I was expected to succinctly summarise the paper.

My chest tightened, my heart raced, I was feeling hotter, and that familiar voice appeared, "You can't even read, you do not belong here." From a compassion-focused therapy (CFT; Gilbert, 2010) perspective, this was my threat system in full activation. My body responded as though I was in real danger; heart racing, tense muscles, mind searching for escape routes. However, the threat was not physical; it was a fear of being exposed, of not being good enough, of shame. My threat system had always been efficient, maybe even overly so. This is what happens when dyslexia meets high expectations like this.

At the time, my instinct was to fight the feeling or hide it. I would double-check my work obsessively, speak only when I was sure my words were perfect, or bury myself in preparation so no one would see my mistakes. It looked like diligence from the outside; it felt like a matter of survival on the inside.

For years, this was how dyslexia presented itself to me. It was not just in practical struggles like reading, spelling, and processing information, but also in waves of self-criticism and the fear of judgement that accompanied them. The challenge was about the way I related to those difficulties. I lived with a vigilant inner critic, always ready to point out mistakes before anyone else could. It kept me safe in some ways, but it also made me wary and exhausted from constant hypervigilance and over-preparation. CFT explains this inner critic as a negative internal voice, stemming from early childhood, that governs with harshness to shield against perceived failure and rejection, yet leaves one mired in shame and self-criticism.

At the time, my understanding of a soothing system, or a compassionate self that could respond to myself with the same warmth and compassion I offered my clients, was limited. My world was organised around threat and drive. I would

DOI: 10.4324/9781003636014-11

avoid mistakes at all costs and push myself to compensate. It took time and a CFT to realise there was another way to relate to myself.

Living with dyslexia has shaped my experiences as both a trainee and practising clinical psychologist in ways that were often hidden, frustrating, and challenging. In this chapter, I share my story and explore how viewing these experiences through the lens of CFT has helped me understand and relate to myself more kindly and impact my role as an aspiring and qualified Clinical Psychologist. My lived experience now informs how I work with clients who carry similar invisible struggles. It has made me more attuned to the subtle forms of shame and avoidance that clients bring and has strengthened my belief that compassion is not an "add-on" but a core therapeutic process.

Dyslexia and its invisible impact

Specific Learning Difficulties affect the way information is learned and processed. There are several Specific Learning Difficulties, including Dyscalculia, Dyslexia, Dyspraxia, and Attention Deficit Hyperactivity Disorder. Dyslexia is one of the most common Specific Learning Difficulties and is thought to affect 4%–8% of the population (NHS Choices, n.d). People with dyslexia, also known as developmental dyslexia, present with average to above-average intelligence (Shaywitz, 2003). Dyslexia can also be acquired, for example, following a brain injury (Cogo-Moreira et al., 2012). People with dyslexia think and learn differently from others (Shaywitz, 2003), and not everyone experiences dyslexia in the same way. However, dyslexia can be described as "a learning difficulty that primarily affects the skills involved in accurate and fluent word reading and spelling" (Dyslexia Action, n.d.). Dyslexia occurs regardless of intellectual ability, and its main features include difficulties with phonological awareness, verbal processing speed, and verbal memory. Associated problems can include difficulties with motor coordination, mental calculation, concentration, time perception, and organisation (Dyslexia Action, n.d.). As dyslexia is a disability that is not immediately obvious to others, it can be described as a hidden, invisible, or non-visible disability (Cabinet Office, n.d.).

Research into non-visible disabilities consistently highlights the psychological burden that arises not only from the functional difficulties themselves, but from the social and emotional challenges of living with a hidden difference. Individuals with non-visible disabilities frequently describe the effort of "passing" as non-disabled, or concealing their struggles, which has been shown to predict lower self-esteem and poorer mental health outcomes (Nalavany, et al, 2013). The invisibility of such conditions often creates ongoing dilemmas around disclosure, leaving individuals vulnerable to experiences of shame, stigma, and self-criticism (Fitzgerald & Paterson, 2007).

More recent research emphasises that concealment is not a neutral act, but one associated with significant emotional costs. For example, Nalavany et al. (2013) found that adults with dyslexia who concealed their difficulties reported lower self-esteem and reduced psychological wellbeing, notably when family support was lacking. These findings align with broader literature on internalised ableism, which describes the process by which negative societal views of disability are absorbed and turned inward, reinforcing self-blame, self-doubt, and heightened vulnerability to mental health difficulties (Campbell, 2009).

Much of the research investigating the psychological outcomes of dyslexia has focused on studies involving children. Several studies have demonstrated that children with dyslexia experience behavioural and emotional difficulties (Narimani et al., 2009; Snowling et al., 2007), lower self-esteem (Alexander-Passe, 2006; Humphrey & Mullins, 2002; Rosenthal, 1973; Terras et al., 2009), and higher levels of anxiety (Haddadian et al., 2012; Narimani et al., 2009; Koulopoulou, 2010; Skulová, 1978) as compared with their peers.

Studies focusing on children with dyslexia have identified several key factors that are thought to influence psychological outcomes, such as self-esteem and anxiety. Parental attitudes towards their child's dyslexia are thought to directly impact the child's self-esteem, with lower self-esteem being seen in children whose parents have negative attitudes towards their difficulties (Rosenthal, 1973; Terras et al., 2009). Lower self-esteem is also demonstrated in children who do not feel supported by their parents, teachers, or peers (Singer, 2008). Furthermore, Glazzard (2010) recommends that an early diagnosis of dyslexia is beneficial for a child's self-image, having found that a positive early diagnosis contributed to self-esteem. Additionally, coping style has been demonstrated to affect anxiety, with children using emotion-focused and avoidance coping, experiencing higher levels of anxiety (Alexander-Passe, 2006; Tsovili, 2004). In summary, these studies have identified coping style, parental support, and age at diagnosis to be predictive of psychological outcomes in children with dyslexia.

Although fewer studies have investigated the psychological outcomes of dyslexia in adults, similar findings have been demonstrated (Carroll & Iles, 2006; Nelson et al., 2015; Ghisi et al., 2016; Nelson & Liebel, 2018; Coates et al., 2025). For example, Carroll and Iles (2006) found that dyslexic students in higher education showed higher levels of academic and social anxiety when compared with students without learning difficulties. Riddick et al. (1999) found that dyslexic university students exhibited significantly lower self-esteem compared to a control group. The dyslexic students also reported feeling more anxious and less competent in their university work. Stigma, shame, and concerns regarding disclosure are commonly reported among students with dyslexia. Many individuals choose not to disclose their difficulties due to apprehension about negative judgement, which can contribute to identity confusion and heightened emotional distress (Morris & Turnbull, 2006; Evans, 2014; Newlands et al., 2015; Alexander, 2023; Hamilton-Clark, 2024). Perfectionistic tendencies are also frequently observed within this population. Students may strive to present themselves as faultless to peers and educators, a pattern that can exacerbate stress and promote maladaptive coping behaviours (Stoeber & Rountree, 2021). Furthermore, low self-esteem and diminished self-confidence are prevalent, particularly among those diagnosed with dyslexia later in life. This suggests that delayed identification of dyslexia may intensify experiences of inadequacy and self-doubt (Nalavany & Carawan, 2012; Ghisi et al., 2016; Brunswick & Bargary, 2022; Hamilton-Clark, 2024).

Again, there have been a limited number of studies examining factors that influence psychological outcomes in adults with dyslexia. Bazen et al. (2023) found that perceived negative consequences of dyslexia were significantly associated with environmental factors, such as institutional support and self-perceived literacy skills, rather than with objective measures of reading and writing ability. More recently, Niolaki et al. (2025) demonstrated that self-compassion in adults with dyslexia mediates the relationship between self-esteem, self-efficacy, and anxiety, suggesting that internal self-regulation resources may play a key role in psychological wellbeing. Stark and Johnson (2025) demonstrated the importance of early diagnosis to help shape positive outcomes for people with dyslexia. Nalavany and Carawan (2012) found that perceived family support can influence self-esteem in adults with dyslexia, particularly during early adulthood. This emerging body of evidence underlines that psychological outcomes are not solely determined by literacy deficits but are strongly mediated by socio-emotional and environmental factors.

Taken together, these studies suggest that the experience of living with a non-visible disability, such as dyslexia, is closely linked with a heightened sense of shame, anxiety, depression, and diminished self-worth. From a CFT perspective, these outcomes can be understood as the result of prolonged activation of the threat system, fuelled by self-criticism and fears of exposure, and highlight the importance of cultivating compassionate self-relating as a buffer against these challenges.

For me, these research findings resonate on a personal level. My journey as a clinical psychologist with dyslexia has been shaped not only by the practical challenges of reading, writing, and information processing, but also by the hidden nature of the condition. Like many others with non-visible disabilities, I have often faced the dilemma of whether to disclose my dyslexia or remain silent, each choice carrying its own risks. At times, the effort of concealing my difficulties has fed into feelings of shame and self-criticism, mirroring the research findings on the emotional toll of "passing" as non-disabled. Understanding these experiences through the lens of CFT has helped me see them not as personal flaws, but as predictable outcomes of living in an ableist culture that prizes speed, efficiency, and perfection. This shift in perspective has been vital in learning to respond to my own struggles with greater warmth and self-compassion.

Understanding dyslexia through a compassion-focused therapy lens

CFT offers a useful framework for making sense of the psychological challenges associated with dyslexia and other non-visible disabilities. According to CFT, our minds have evolved with multiple affect regulation systems: a threat system, focused on detecting danger and self-protection; a drive system, geared towards striving and achievement; and a soothing system, which allows us to feel safe, connected, and cared for (Gilbert, 2010). When living with dyslexia, particularly in a society that often equates intelligence with literacy skills and speed of processing, the threat and drive systems can become chronically over-activated. In contrast, the drive system may fuel perfectionism and overcompensation in an effort to appear "good enough."

In my own experience, these dynamics have played a central role. I often found myself caught between my drive system, pushing me to prove my competence, and my threat system, warning me that I might be "found out," with little support from the soothing system that could provide balance and safety. Research on shame and concealment in invisible disabilities helps explain why these patterns can feel so entrenched: the act of hiding difference keeps the threat system activated, and the absence of open acknowledgement makes it challenging to access supportive social responses (Nalavany et al., 2012; Ysasi et al., 2018). From a CFT perspective, the key therapeutic task is therefore to cultivate compassion, both from others and within oneself, to regulate threat and drive, and to foster a kinder, more balanced way of relating to difficulty (Gilbert, 2009).

A central idea in CFT is that self-criticism often functions as a threat-based strategy. When I made mistakes or my difficulties became more apparent, my inner critic could emerge as a way to anticipate judgement from others and protect me from rejection. This became a familiar cycle where I would often respond to errors in spelling, a slow reading speed, or difficulties with written tasks by turning the criticism on myself before anyone else had a chance. At the time, this felt protective, as though being harsh with myself might reduce the risk of others thinking less of me. However, from a CFT perspective, this cycle of self-criticism entrenches the dominance of the threat system, leaving little space for learning, growth, or kindness. Ultimately, by fostering compassion, CFT offers a pathway to shift these patterns and create an environment that supports both acceptance and positive change.

Early experiences through a CFT framework

Research suggests that individuals with non-visible learning differences, such as dyslexia, often develop complex patterns of threat anticipation, self-criticism, and compensatory effort long before formal assessment of diagnosis (Nalavany & Carawan, 2012; Nalavany et al., 2013, 2023). My own experiences reflect this broader pattern. Although I was not formally diagnosed with dyslexia until my Master's degree, I had long sensed that something was "different" in the way I processed written and spoken information. Throughout school, everyday classroom practices, such as reading aloud and at the same speed as others, often triggered a familiar mix of apprehension and self-consciousness. Even though I was performing well academically, there was a persistent mismatch between my overall academic abilities and the difficulties I encountered when reading or spelling was required. Whenever I had to read aloud, the fear of stumbling over words or losing my place was ever-present. Listening to others read aloud with ease, my heart would be pounding as my turn approached. Peers and teachers sometimes responded with humour at my mistakes, and I learned early that it was safer to laugh along than reveal the humiliation underneath.

From a CFT perspective, these experiences can be understood as repeated activation of the threat system. Specifically, the social threat has evolved to monitor cues of rejection (Gilbert, 2005, 2010). For a young person with a non-visible disability, such as dyslexia, the classroom can become a setting where mistakes feel dangerous and not merely inconvenient, carrying heightened emotional significance. In my case, my body and mind perceived the possibility of social exposure, ridicule, and judgement as real dangers. Even routine academic tasks elicited physiological arousal, narrowing attention, and amplifying self-focused threat monitoring. This reaction was often followed by the use of safety behaviours, for example, laughing along with peers to mask embarrassment, avoiding reading aloud, or closely monitoring others to anticipate expectations. These behaviours reduced immediate social risk but reinforced an internal narrative of vulnerability and exposure.

In this context, my drive system became highly engaged. I developed meticulous strategies to avoid errors, such as pre-reading material, scanning for difficult words, rehearsing silently, and over-preparing for even routine classroom activities. These behaviours were adaptive in their own way, reducing the likelihood of public mistakes and offering a sense of control. However, they were also time-consuming, often limiting my ability to fully engage in lessons. They reflected what CFT describes as threat-based drive; a pattern in which achievement behaviours are motivated less by personal interest or growth and more by an attempt to reduce shame, avoid exposure, and maintain social acceptance. This form of coping is common among individuals with late-identified dyslexia, who often invest significant energy in masking or compensating for difficulties that others cannot see (Nalavany et al., 2013).

In contrast, my soothing system largely remained underdeveloped. The care-focused emotional regulation system that supports feelings of safety, acceptance, and self-reassurance. As my difficulties were invisible and undiagnosed, there was little opportunity to experience validation or gentle reassurance from teachers, peers, or even myself. I internalised the belief that I had to handle my struggles on my own, forming a pattern of self-reliance that protected me from immediate criticism but made me vulnerable to shame and self-criticism. These experiences reflect research on non-visible disabilities, which indicates that late diagnosis and the need to conceal difficulties often exacerbate feelings of shame, self-criticism, and low self-esteem (Nalavany et al., 2013). The absence of a diagnosis and the invisibility of dyslexia during my formative years meant that my struggles were largely ignored, raising the psychological burden and creating a pattern of hyper-vigilance and overcompensation that continued into later life.

Reflecting on these formative experiences highlights the complex relationship between threat, drive, and soothing systems. The threat system responded to the fear of exposure and ridicule, the drive system pushed me to overcompensate and work harder than my peers, and the soothing system remained underdeveloped. Understanding this dynamic through a CFT framework has been pivotal in reframing my early experiences. Reframing that my experiences were not evidence of inadequacy, but as understandable responses to an environment that lacked awareness, attunement, and support for non-visible learning differences. These dynamics shaped not only my coping strategies at that time but also my early understanding of difference, self-worth, and the hidden emotional effects of dyslexia, a pattern that would persist into university and clinical training.

Academic and early professional life through a CFT lens

Both research and my personal experiences indicate that individuals with dyslexia often encounter increasing cognitive and social demands in higher education. For me, as academic demands increased through undergraduate and postgraduate study, the harder it became to conceal my dyslexia, and the psychological load became more pronounced. Tasks that were inherently incongruent with dyslexia such as reading, processing, and synthesising large volumes of information, organising time, and structuring written work consistently triggered my threat system activation. This, as is common with dyslexia, led to heightened anxiety, hypervigilance to potential mistakes, and fear of negative evaluation (Gilbert, 2010). Assignments often felt paralysing, resulting in avoidance or withdrawal. Inevitably, this led to last-minute work, making it even more challenging to produce the quality I knew I was capable of. In CFT terms, this pattern reflects prolonged threat system arousal in the absence of adequate soothing, which intensifies self-criticism and undermines self-confidence (Gilbert, 2009; Vidal & Soldevilla., 2023). The resulting hypervigilance and anxiety often felt paralysing, sometimes leading to shut down or avoidance, particularly with challenging assignments or essays.

Examinations posed similar challenges. Reading and understanding questions, spelling correctly, structuring answers, and including all relevant content under strict time limits created intense cognitive and emotional load. Pages quickly became chaotic with arrows, corrections, and rewritten words, yet there was never enough time to complete the tasks to the standard I desired. The combination of high expectations, cognitive overload, and constant pressure left me fatigued, anxious, and acutely aware of my differences.

From a broader neurophysiological perspective, these emotional and cognitive reactions can also be understood through the lens of polyvagal theory (Porges, 2001, 2009). Activation of the threat system engages sympathetic branch of the autonomic nervous system, driving fight or flight responses. This could manifest as overpreparation, hypervigilance, or avoidance. In extreme stress, dorsal vagal shutdown can occur, manifesting in dissociation, numbness, or disengagement under overwhelming threat. In my experience, the dorsal vagal response was apparent when essay tasks or exams felt insurmountable as my body and mind simply "shut down," despite conscious awareness of the work that needed to be done. Repeated activation of these circuits reduced access to the ventral vagal system, a branch of the parasympathetic nervous system, which supports calm, social engagement, and self-soothing (Porges, 2001).

Polyvagal theory can be seen to align with the CFT three-system model. In this conceptual framing, the threat system corresponds to the sympathetic and dorsal vagal arousal, the drive system reflects effortful, goal-directed coping under threat, and the soothing system represents ventral vagal activation, supporting self-compassion and social connectedness. This framing highlights how perspectives from polyvagal theory may complement CFT's three-systems model (Gilbert, 2010; Porges, 2007). Dyslexic-related experiences often impair access to soothing, leaving individuals highly susceptible to self-criticism, shame, and avoidance. In my case, meticulous pre-reading, over-preparation, and rehearsing were adaptive attempts to maintain competence and social safety, but they also reinforced the cycle of threat-driven effort and limited self-soothing.

Research supports this pattern in non-visible disabilities. Individuals with late or hidden diagnoses often experience prolonged threat activation, increased shame, and negative self-evaluation, which can inhibit help-seeking and exacerbate psychological distress (Nalavany et al., 2013). From both polyvagal and CFT perspectives, the combination of hypervigilance, heightened threat, and insufficient soothing explains why academic tasks can feel overwhelming and why exhaustion, shutdown, or last-minute work is a common experience.

This prolonged activation of the threat system, combined with limited access to the soothing system, can strengthen self-criticism, avoidance, and internalised shame, making it more difficult to get support or advocate for oneself. This aligns closely with my experience as despite suspecting dyslexia from a young age, I did not seek formal assessment until completing my Master's degree. Even then, the shame and fear of negative judgement prevented me from sharing my diagnosis with peers and supervisors. Knowing others with dyslexia, who were open about their diagnosis, elicited genuine admiration and compassion towards them, yet I still continued to feel self-critical and embarrassed. This reflected the CFT concept of an underdeveloped soothing system, where the capacity to provide oneself with reassurance and care is limited (Gilbert, 2010).

Seeking a formal diagnosis represented an early but significant act of self-compassion, providing external validation for the difficulties I had long experienced and allowing the possibility of practical support. In CFT terms, this step marked the emergence of compassionate self-activation, in which I began to engage the soothing system to respond to my own struggles rather than relying solely on threat-driven drive behaviours. This gradually led to a shift from self-blame to a more balanced self-perspective, recognising that compassion could be a valuable tool for managing the challenges of dyslexia, both academically and personally.

Despite these gains, entering the professional environment as an assistant psychologist reactivated old patterns. Despite finally having a formal diagnosis, an irrefutable explanation for my difficulties, the familiar lack of self-assurance resurfaced. The threat system was immediately engaged by the power dynamic inherent in supervision and professional assessment. I vividly recall a supervisor providing feedback on a report and gently mentioning several "dyslexic style" errors. From a CFT perspective, such feedback could be a cue for compassionate engagement, yet my threat system and hypervigilance filtered it through the lens of criticism. I dismissed the comment, attributing errors to an oversight rather than recognising it as a safe prompt for disclosure. My drive system remained oriented towards overcompensation, while my soothing system only intermittently engaged. This illustrated the continued tension between self-protective effort and self-reassuring compassion in professional contexts.

In summary, the interplay of threat, drive, and soothing systems provides a valuable framework for understanding the cognitive, emotional, and behavioural patterns I exhibited during late undergraduate study, postgraduate training, and early professional life. Autobiographical experiences of over-preparation, avoidance, and hypervigilance can thus be reframed not as evidence of personal inadequacy, but as predictable responses to persistent threat activation in the context of an underdeveloped soothing system. Integrating this CFT perspective highlights both the challenges associated with non-visible disabilities and the potential for developing compassionate self-regulation strategies to support learning, wellbeing, and professional functioning.

Clinical training and beyond: facing dyslexia in clinical practice

Applying for any job with a non-visible disability can cause considerable anxiety (Santuzzi et al., 2014). Important considerations arise regarding whether to acknowledge this on the application or withhold it. This dilemma was no different for many psychology doctoral applicants with non-visible disabilities. The training courses are fiercely competitive, and as little as one point on an application can make a huge difference. I was acutely aware of this when applying and knew that even one deduction for spelling or grammar could be the difference between getting an interview or not. After much deliberation, I checked the "disability" box for the first time since my diagnosis. I felt a wave of ambivalence: part of me wanted to add a caveat, convinced that others were more deserving or had more "visible" disabilities. Yet another part of me recognised the practical reality that acknowledging my dyslexia could ensure that minor grammatical errors were considered in context. The small act of disclosure represented a tentative activation of the soothing system, enabling me to act in my own interest with self-kindness and pragmatism. For the first time, I was experimenting with responding to my needs instead of allowing self-criticism and shame to control my decisions.

CFT understands acceptance and recognition of disability as part of developing a compassionate mind that can turn towards suffering with courage, wisdom, and care rather than shame or attack. In this context, acknowledging my disability was not passive resignation. It was an informed, realistic recognition of my needs that legitimised seeking support and reasonable adjustments. The soothing system is central to this process. It is associated with feelings of safety, warmth, and connectedness, and is activated when people relate to themselves with kindness, reassurance, and a sense of common humanity. When someone chooses to disclose a non-visible disability in a way that honours their needs, they are drawing on the soothing system to counteract threat-based fears of judgement or inadequacy, allowing themselves to be protected and supported rather than driven by perfectionism or self-criticism.

Clinical training was the first time I genuinely began to relate to myself with greater compassion, rather than pushing through difficulties in silence. Ticking the disability box opened up a whole new world of support and marked an important shift from "just coping" to actively acknowledging and responding to my needs. In practical terms, the support I received focused on mitigating the learning needs associated with dyslexia, such as access to a proofreader, specialist software, extra time, and a separate exam room. While these adjustments were invaluable, the support remained almost entirely practical, with little attention paid to the emotional impact of living and training with a non-visible disability. This mirrors Carroll and Iles (2006) observation that most universities often prioritise academic or functional accommodations over psychological support. They proposed that emotional wellbeing should be assessed for dyslexic students in higher education. On reflection, the absence of psychological support is surprising in a clinical psychology training programme. The practical aids addressed my learning needs, yet a psychological gap remained unfulfilled, highlighting the necessity of holistic accommodations that encompass both practical and emotional support. Although additional psychological support would likely have been available on request, research suggests that students with dyslexia find disclosure difficult (Morris & Turnbull, 2006, 2007; Evans, 2014). This highlights the importance of university doctoral training staff proactively initiating conversations around the potential psychological impact of non-visible disabilities, rather than relying solely on students to advocate for themselves, in order to provide truly holistic support.

Looking back through a CFT lens, the adjustments and support I received during clinical training symbolised more than practical accommodations. They represented an external form of compassion, with others recognising and validating struggles that had long been hidden. This external compassion provided a scaffold for cultivating the compassionate self, enabling the internalisation of care and gradually strengthening the soothing system while down-regulating threat-driven responses (Gilbert, 2009, 2014). From a polyvagal perspective, such validation can cue the ventral vagal system, supporting feelings of safety, connection, and engagement in learning and professional tasks (Porges, 2007).

Despite this support, the lasting influence of shame, shaped by previous experiences and societal expectations, remained prominent. Some supervisors exhibited little understanding of dyslexia-related challenges. Observing or overhearing critical remarks about colleagues' grammatical mistakes, and experiencing dismissal when gently suggesting dyslexia as a factor, heightened threat-system activation and intensified self-criticism and hypervigilance. These experiences illustrate ableist societal structures. Certain norms and expectations that privilege certain cognitive abilities can reinforce internalised shame and push the drive system into overdrive. This can lead to excessive efforts to conceal difficulties and overcompensate (Campbell, 2009; Coates McDowall et al., 2025; Morris & Turnbull, 2007).

Over time, interactions with compassionate supervisors during training and qualified practice provided opportunities to "test the waters" regarding disclosure. Even tentative disclosure was initially anxiety-provoking, as the threat system remained alert to potential judgement and scrutiny. However, the absence of negative consequences and the presence of support gradually allowed the soothing system to engage, permitting the development of self-compassion and more adaptive coping. Moments such as reflecting on a client with similar experiences of shame and masking highlighted a core principle of CFT. The difficulty of directing compassion inward, especially when the self has been shaped by prolonged internalised criticism. Reflecting on this in supervision provided me with a space to recognise the dialogue between the critical, shaming voice and the emerging self-compassionate voice. It was a small change, but it planted a seed. From then on, I started to notice how often my threat response kicked in when I made a mistake or struggled to process information quickly. Gradually, I experimented with offering myself the same care and patience I gave to my clients.

I have long practised progressive muscle relaxation, finding comfort in the rhythm of tensing and releasing muscles, which allowed my body to release some of its habitual tension. Looking back, this was likely my earliest form of self-soothing, even though I initially approached it as a simple stress-management technique. From a CFT perspective, such practices can support activation of the soothing system, counteract chronic threat system arousal, and foster physiological and emotional regulation (Gilbert, 2009, 2014). Research on relaxation techniques indicates that they reduce sympathetic nervous system activation, lower cortisol levels, and improve heart rate variability, supporting both mental and physical wellbeing (Varvogli & Darviri, 2011; Porges, 2007). Additionally, progressive muscle relaxation enhances interoceptive awareness, which is central to mind-body integration and the development of self-compassion (Mehling et al., 2011). By deliberately attending to sensations of tension and release, I gradually learned to notice stress signals earlier and respond with patience and care, a skill that is also transferable to clinical practice when supporting clients to regulate anxiety or self-critical thought patterns.

Initially, my compassionate practices were limited. I took slow breaths before speaking in meetings, and before working late into the night, paused to ask myself, "What would be the kindest thing to do right now?" I labelled this practise as my "Compassion Pause," a moment to ground myself. I practised compassionate breathing, slowing my breath to cue my soothing system and signal to my body that it was safe. Aligning with CFT principles of activating the soothing system to downregulate threat and promote emotional balance (Gilbert, 2009). I also experimented with compassionate imagery, envisioning a kinder, reassuring self who could face difficulties without avoidance. Research in CFT suggests that imagery techniques can enhance self-compassion, reduce self-criticism, and improve emotion regulation by strengthening neural pathways associated with safety and affiliation (Rockliff et al., 2008;

Matos et al., 2017). In my therapy practice, I've noticed how clients, much like myself, benefit from connecting the threat-based system to practical applications. For example, clients can benefit from visualisation exercises that help them view their inner critic as a fearful part needing comfort rather than confrontation. This perspective shift enables them to cultivate self-compassion, resulting in a notable reduction in distress. Making this connection concrete not only enhances the therapeutic alliance but also empowers clients to respond with greater kindness to their personal challenges.

These practices were particularly useful in managing dyslexia-related stress, such as the anxiety triggered by exams, written assignments, or potential judgement from peers and supervisors. When my inner critic said, "*You'll never get this report done on time*," I would imagine that compassionate self-responding: "*Yes, this is hard. But we'll take it step by step*." I would visualise a supportive self, guiding me through the task step by step, rather than becoming overwhelmed and catastrophising potential mistakes. This imagined self-compassion not only reduced physiological arousal but also helped me sustain focus and persevere through cognitive challenges. Gradually, these skills started to show up at work. I could admit in a meeting, "*I just need a few minutes to process that*" without shame showing on my face. When facilitating training sessions, without embarrassment, I inform participants that due to my dyslexia, there may be some "unconventional" spelling. I recovered more quickly after stumbling over words during a presentation. Although my threat system was still there, it no longer had sole control of the wheel. Over time, these techniques allowed me to respond to stress with increased patience and kindness towards myself, illustrating how CFT interventions can be applied for both personal development and for informing supportive clinical practice with clients.

Present day: navigating dyslexia with compassion

Even now, dyslexia still impacts my professional life. Writing reports continues to take approximately twice as long as my colleagues, highlighting the ongoing impact on my efficiency. Presentations still bring that familiar flutter of fear about "getting it wrong." And, working in neuropsychology, I find the irony in the fact that some of the cognitive assessments I conduct can feel like challenges themselves, followed, of course, by the inevitable mountain of report writing. But my relationship with these difficulties has changed.

Where I once pushed myself forward out of fear and shame, I now try to face these challenges with compassionate motivation, doing the work because it matters to me, not because I am desperately trying to escape self-criticism. Compassion has not erased the difficulties, but it has given me more stability and courage. I can face what feels overwhelming without being overwhelmed by it. In CFT terms, I'm still learning to keep my three emotion regulation systems in balance. Some days, threat still takes the lead. Other days, my soothing system remains steady and strong. And most often, it's a messy blend of all three. And that is okay, as it's a lifelong practice.

Through compassion, I have learned to embrace dyslexia as a fundamental part of who I am. The biggest challenge was never the spelling errors or the slower pace of writing, but how I related to dyslexia; the shame I carried and the relentless effort to hide it. With compassion, that weight has lessened. I now openly and regularly share my dyslexia. Not only does this feel gentler to me, but I've also found that people are generally understanding and willing to accommodate dyslexia-related mistakes. In clinical practice, I have observed that, when clinically appropriate, briefly disclosing my dyslexia can often help reduce the evaluative pressure clients often feel during cognitive assessments. Although only anecdotal, such disclosure appears to promote engagement by creating a slightly less threatening interpersonal environment. From a CFT perspective, this small act of transparency can help to reduce clients' sense of being scrutinised and support a more collaborative stance. In these moments, disclosure can help to normalise clients' worries, soften self-criticism, and foster a shared sense of humanity. All of which are key mechanisms through which compassion can emerge in clinical work.

Living with dyslexia has given me a firsthand understanding of shame, what it feels like to believe you are "less than," and the exhausting hypervigilance needed to avoid mistakes. These reactions are not only personal but shaped by wider societal narratives. Ableist assumptions often position literacy, speed, and accuracy as markers of intelligence or competence, leading to difficulties related to dyslexia being easily misinterpreted as personal shortcomings rather than reflections of structural bias (Campbell, 2009; Dolmage, 2017). CFT provided me with a framework to recognise these experiences for what they are, to name them, and to approach them differently. Most importantly, it reminded me that compassion isn't only for others; it must also include ourselves if we want to thrive in our work and lives.

Now, I feel passionate about empowering other psychologists with non-visible disabilities to step out of hiding if they wish to, and to accept the support available without shame. Visibility can be an act of compassion, both for ourselves and for others who may be struggling in silence. For me, compassion has transformed dyslexia from something I once masked and feared into a part of me that I can embrace, work with, and even use to help others feel less alone.

References

Alexander, D. A. (2023). The dyslexic academic: Uncovering the challenges faced as neurodiverse in academia and establishing a research agenda. *Disability and Society, 39*(11), 3036–3041.

Alexander-Passe, N. (2006). How dyslexic teenagers cope: An investigation of self-esteem, coping, and depression. *Dyslexia, 12*(4), 256–275. https://doi.org/10.1002/dys.318

Bazen, L., de Bree, E. H., van den Boer, M., & de Jong, P. F. (2023). Perceived negative consequences of dyslexia: The influence of person and environmental factors. *Annals of Dyslexia, 73*(2), 214–234.

Brunswick, N., & Bargary, S. (2022). Self-concept, creativity and developmental dyslexia in university students: Effects of age of assessment. *Dyslexia: The Journal of the British Dyslexia Association, 28*(3), 293–308. https://doi.org/10.1002/dys.1711

Cabinet Office. (n.d.). *Disability unit.* GOV.UK. https://www.gov.uk/government/organisations/disability-unit
Campbell, F. K. (2009). *Contours of ableism: The production of disability and abledness.* Palgrave Macmillan.
Carroll, J. M., & Iles, J. E. (2006). An assessment of anxiety levels in dyslexic students in higher education. *British Journal of Educational Psychology, 76*(3), 651–662. https://doi.org/10.1348/000709905X66233
Coates McDowall, H., Rimfeld, K., & Krishnan, S. (2025). Cognitive reappraisal reduces academic anxiety in university students with dyslexia. *Mind, Brain, and Education, 19*(1), 18–31.
Cogo-Moreira, H., Andriolo, R. B., Yazigi, L., Ploubidis, G. B., Brandão de Ávila, C. R., & Mari, J. J. (2012). Music education for improving reading skills in children and adolescents with dyslexia. *Cochrane Database of Systematic Reviews*, 2012(8), Art. https://doi.org/10.1002/14651858.CD009133.pub2
Dolmage, J. (2017). *Academic ableism: Disability and higher education.* University of Michigan Press.
Dyslexia Action. (n.d.). *Support for dyslexia.* https://www.dyslexiaaction.org.uk/Pages/Display.aspx?IDPost=d081fda4-71b3-44e1-81bf-2a55c7958377
Evans, W. (2014). 'I am not a dyslexic person I'm a person with dyslexia': Identity constructions of dyslexia among students in nurse education. *Journal of Advanced Nursing, 70*(2), 360–372.
Fitzgerald, H., & Paterson, K. (2007). The hidden disability dilemma for the inclusion of disabled people in sport. *Quest, 59*(4), 416–430. https://doi.org/10.1080/00336297.2007.10483557
Ghisi, M., Bottesi, G., Re, A. M., Cerea, S., & Mammarella, I. C. (2016). Socioemotional features and resilience in Italian university students with and without dyslexia. *Frontiers in Psychology, 7*, 478.
Gilbert, P. (2005). *Compassion: Conceptualisations, research and use in psychotherapy.* Routledge.
Gilbert, P. (2009). *The compassionate mind: A new approach to life's challenges.* London: Constable & Robinson.
Gilbert, P. (2010). *Compassion focused therapy: Distinctive features*. London: Routledge.
Gilbert, P. (2014). The origins and nature of compassion focused therapy. *British Journal of Clinical Psychology, 53*(1), 6–41.
Glazzard, J. (2010). The impact of dyslexia on pupils' self-esteem. *Support for Learning, 25*(2), 63–69. https://doi.org/10.1111/j.1467-9604.2010.01442.x
Griffiths, C., Norwich, B., & Burden, R. (2004). Dyslexia and psychological well-being in adults: An exploratory study. *Dyslexia, 10*(1), 1–23. https://doi.org/10.1002/dys.261
Haddadian, F., Alipour, V., Majidi, A., & Malekei, H. (2012). The effectiveness of self-instruction technique on improvement of reading performance and reduction of anxiety in primary school students with dyslexia. *Procedia – Social and Behavioral Sciences, 46*, 5366–5370. https://doi.org/10.1016/j.sbspro.2012.06.447
Hamilton-Clark, C. H. (2024). Dyslexia concealment in higher education: Exploring students' disclosure decisions in the face of UK universities' approach to dyslexia. *Journal of Research in Special Educational Needs, 24*(4), 922–935. https://doi.org/10.1111/1471-3802.12683
Humphrey, N., & Mullins, P. M. (2002). Self-concept and self-esteem in developmental dyslexia. *Journal of Research in Special Educational Needs, 2*(1), 1–13. https://doi.org/10.1111/j.1471-3802.2002.00163.x

Koulopoulou, A. (2010). Anxiety and depression symptoms in children – Comorbidity with learning disabilities. *European Psychiatry, 25*(Supplement 1), 432.

Morris, D., & Turnbull, P. (2006). Clinical experiences of students with dyslexia. *Journal of Advanced Nursing, 54*(2), 238–247. https://doi.org/10.1016/s0924-9338(10)70427-2

Matos, M., Duarte, C., Duarte, J., Pinto-Gouveia, J., Petrocchi, N., Basran, J., & Gilbert, P. (2017). Psychological and physiological effects of compassionate mind training: A pilot randomised controlled study. *Mindfulness, 8*(6), 1699–1712.

Mehling, W. E., Wrubel, J., Daubenmier, J. J., Price, C. J., Kerr, C. E., Silow, T., Gopisetty, V., & Stewart, A. L. (2011). Body awareness: A phenomenological inquiry into the common ground of mind-body therapies. *Philosophy, Ethics, and Humanities in Medicine, 6*(1).

Morris, D. K., & Turnbull, P. A. (2007). The disclosure of dyslexia in clinical practice: Experiences of student nurses in the United Kingdom. *Nurse Education Today, 27*(1), 35–42. https://doi.org/10.1016/j.nedt.2006.01.017

Nalavany, B. A., & Carawan, L. W. (2012). Perceived family support and self-esteem: The mediational role of emotional experience in adults with dyslexia. *Dyslexia, 18*(1), 54–74. https://doi.org/10.1002/dys.1435

Nalavany, B. A., Carawan, L. W., & Rennick, R. A. (2013). Adults with dyslexia, an invisible disability: The mediational role of concealment on perceived family support and self-esteem. *British Journal of Social Work, 41*(5), 568–586. https://doi.org/10.1093/bjsw/bcr016

Nalavany, B. A., Kennedy, R., Lee, M. H., Carawan, L. W., & Knight, S. M. (2023). Insights from a web-based survey into the psychosocial experiences of adults with dyslexia: Findings from a final comment question. *Dyslexia, 29*(4), 441–458.

Narimani, M., Sadeghieh Ahari, S., Homeily, N., & Siapoosh, H. (2009). A comparison of emotional intelligence and behaviour problems in dyslexic and non-dyslexic boys. *Journal of Applied Sciences, 9*(7), 1388–1392. https://doi.org/10.3923/jas.2009.1388.1392

Nelson, J. M., Lindstrom, W., & Foels, P. A. (2015). Test anxiety among college students with specific reading disability (dyslexia): Nonverbal ability and working memory as predictors. *Journal of Learning Disabilities, 48*(4), 422–432.

Nelson, J. M., & Liebel, S. W. (2018). Socially desirable responding and college students with dyslexia: Implications for the assessment of anxiety and depression. *Dyslexia, 24*(1), 44–58.

Newlands, F., Shrewsbury, D., & Robson, J. (2015). Foundation doctors and dyslexia: A qualitative study of their experiences and coping strategies. *Postgraduate Medical Journal, 91*(1073), 121–126. https://doi.org/10.1136/postgradmedj-2014-132573

NHS Choices. (n.d.). *Dyslexia.* https://www.nhs.uk/conditions/dyslexia/pages/introduction.aspx

Niolaki, G., Negoita, A. I., Terzopoulos, A., & Masterson, J. (2025). The role of self-compassion in adults with dyslexia. *Annals of Dyslexia, 75*(2), 339–361. https://doi.org/10.1007/s11881-025-00327-0

Porges, S. W. (2001). The polyvagal theory: Phylogenetic substrates of a social nervous system. *International Journal of Psychophysiology, 42*(2), 123–146. https://doi.org/10.1016/S0167-8760(01)00162-3

Porges, S. W. (2007). The polyvagal perspective. *Biological Psychology, 74*(2), 116–143. https://doi.org/10.1016/j.biopsycho.2006.06.009

Porges, S. W. (2009). The polyvagal theory: New insights into adaptive reactions of the autonomic nervous system. *Cleveland Clinic Journal of Medicine, 76*(2), 86–90.

Riddick, B., Sterling, C., Farmer, M., & Morgan, S. (1999). Self-esteem and anxiety in the educational histories of adult dyslexic students. *Dyslexia, 5*(4), 227–248. https://doi.org/10.1002/(SICI)1099-0909(199912)5:4<227::AID-DYS146 >3.0.CO;2-6

Rockliff, H., Gilbert, P., McEwan, K., Lightman, S., & Glover, D. (2008). A pilot exploration of heart rate variability and salivary cortisol responses to compassion-focused imagery. *Clinical Neuropsychiatry, 5*(3), 132–139.

Rosenthal, J. (1973). Self-esteem in dyslexic children. *Academic Therapy, 9*(1), 27–39. https://doi.org/10.1177/105345127300900104

Santuzzi, A. M., Waltz, P. R., Finkelstein, L. M., & Rupp, D. E. (2014). Invisible disabilities: Unique challenges for employees and organizations. *Industrial and Organizational Psychology, 7*(2), 253–256. https://doi.org/10.1111/iops.12134

Shaywitz, S. (2003). *Overcoming dyslexia: A new and complete science-based program for reading problems at any level.* Knopf.

Singer, E. (2008). The strategies adopted by Dutch children with dyslexia to maintain their self-esteem when teased at school. *Journal of Learning Disabilities, 41*(5), 411–423. https://doi.org/10.1177/0022219405038005040l

Skulová, M. (1978). Anxiety disorders of personal adjustment in children with specific developmental dyslexia. *Psychológia a Patopsychológia Dieťaťa, 13*(4), 315–326.

Snowling, M. J., Muter, V., & Carroll, J. (2007). Children at family risk of dyslexia: A follow-up in early adolescence. *Journal of Child Psychology and Psychiatry, 48*(6), 609–618. https://doi.org/10.1111/j.1469-7610.2006.01725.x

Stark, Z., & Johnson, A. P. (2025). Understanding the experience of adults with dyslexia: A quantitative and qualitative analysis. *Annals of Dyslexia.* Advance online publication. https://doi.org/10.1007/s11881-025-00336-z

Stoeber, J., & Rountree, M. L. (2021). Perfectionism, self-stigma, and coping in students with dyslexia: The central role of perfectionistic self-presentation. *Dyslexia: The Journal of the British Dyslexia Association, 27*(1), 62–78. https://doi.org/10.1002/dys.1672

Terras, M. M., Thompson, L. C., & Minnis, H. (2009). Dyslexia and psycho-social functioning: An exploratory study of the role of self-esteem and understanding. *Dyslexia, 15*(4), 304–327. https://doi.org/10.1002/dys.376

Tsovili, T. D. (2004). The relationship between language teachers' attitudes and the state-trait anxiety of adolescents with dyslexia. *Journal of Research in Reading, 27*(1), 69–86.

Varvogli, L., & Darviri, C. (2011). Stress management techniques: Evidence-based procedures that reduce stress and promote health. *Health Science Journal, 5*(2), 74–89.

Vidal, J., & Soldevilla, J. M. (2023). Effect of compassion-focused therapy on self-criticism and self-soothing: A meta-analysis. *British Journal of Clinical Psychology, 62*(1), 70–81. https://doi.org/10.1111/bjc.12394

Ysasi, N. A., Becton, A. B., & Chen, R. K. (2018). Stigmatizing effects of visible versus invisible disabilities. *Journal of Disability Studies, 24*(4), 22–29.

Chapter 11

In the Kingdom of the Blind, the one-eyed man is ...disabled

A social constructionist personal and professional journey

Stephanie Jones

The social construction of disability

I was born with a genetic condition that meant interventions, such as eye surgery and wearing glasses, could not correct my vision to the 20/20 acuity that is 'typical' for most people. I was made aware from a very young age that my sight was poor in comparison with other people and frequently heard myself described using language that felt both inaccurate ('she can't see') and shaming ('her eyes are bad'). I found this really difficult to comprehend because to me, what I could see was normal; it was all I had ever known, and it never changed. I remember hearing about how I was expected to struggle in life and how I might not 'cope' in different situations. As my self-awareness grew, I began to notice that I did struggle at times, but mainly with things that I was expected to do in a way that conformed to some mainstream expectation. I never struggled with things I did by myself in my own particular way, and I was often able to capitalise on my strengths, such as having a good memory, to compensate for my shortcomings. My struggles were tied to an expectation to conform, and alternative ways of coping seemed to be marginalised. I started to wonder why certain differences seemed to be viewed through a negative lens while other variations appeared to be accepted. I started to question who decides what 'struggling', 'coping', and 'normal' look like? Even as a child, I began to feel as if my 'disability' was contrived by the people and environment around me and often wondered, 'Would I know that I had a "disability" if no-one had ever told me?'. I did not yet know it, but I was becoming a Social Constructionist.

The Social Constructionist philosophy suggests that all knowledge and meaning are created by members of society interacting with each other and with their environment. In the most extreme sense, social constructionists believe that there is no objective reality or if there is, it cannot be accurately observed as it is always filtered through each individual's unique viewpoint and experience (Berger & Luckmann, 1966). When I was accepted onto a Professional Doctorate in Clinical Psychology course that prided itself on its Systemic and Social Constructions ethos, I was formally introduced to the ideas that, growing up, I had not developed the language to formulate and express. The Social Constructionist perspective suggests that our

DOI: 10.4324/9781003636014-12

experience of the world is co-constructed in the language we use to describe and represent it and in so doing, the attitudes and meanings we create (Burr, 2015). This co-creation takes place within the context of the time and culture in which we live and is usually heavily influenced by the dominant or more powerful groups in society. This philosophy has been applied to debates about race, culture, gender, and differences in ability (e.g. Loewenstein, 1994, Haslanger, 2000, Siebers, 2001, Roth et al., 2023). As you might imagine, for me, listening to the lectures and reading the literature referenced within them was like hearing the thoughts I had been having my whole life given back to me in a coherent, reasoned, and evidenced format. Learning about the Social Constructionist philosophy and its language and ideas gave shape to the things I had always felt but never fully understood. I was finally in a place where my lived experience was given a mirror in which I could finally see myself clearly.

The Social Constructionist viewpoint proposes that a person's experience of what society defines as a 'disability' is shaped by their environment and social context, which can make life easier or more difficult depending on whether it is designed with your particular characteristics in mind (Stone, 2013). It is not difficult to find examples of this idea all around us. Most societies are designed with the majority in mind, whatever type of attributes and abilities the majority might have. Even when someone has an additional or unusual attribute that might appear to give them a superior ability, such as being very tall or having an especially good memory, they rarely benefit as the environment and society is best suited to the majority, who do not possess these qualities. Pedestrian areas, for example, often feature steps, yet roads never do. This is because pedestrian areas are designed primarily for people who can walk and roads are designed for people using wheels. A Social Constructionist would argue that the limitations that a wheelchair or while cane user might experience when faced with steps are not due to an inherent deficit in the person but arise because of how the environment is constructed. You don't have to have experienced the impact of physical difference to get a sense of what it is like to live in an environment that was not designed with you in mind. Just think about the last time you visited a place where you didn't speak the language. You can't read the signs or understand the announcements, and you might have to guess what's in the food and accept directions in the form of hand gestures. You can probably get by, but you can't operate as fluidly as you do in your home environment, where the majority of people are just like you.

In the Kingdom of the Blind

When I was growing up, by way of encouragement my father would tell me 'In the Kingdom [land] of the Blind, the one-eyed man is King'. The phrase is a common idiom of Latin origin (Erasmus, 1500), understood to mean that in a place where there is no ability, someone with limited ability is superior and can dominate. The idiom paints a picture of a society in which the general population were all at some point sighted, have lost their vision, and have failed to adapt, such that the presence of a one-eyed man would be beneficial to them all. In fact, his sight, albeit monocular, would place him at such an incredible advantage over everyone else that he would instantly become their ruler and protector. However, this quote relies on a number of faulty assumptions, which are captured brilliantly by the author and sociologist, H. G. Wells in his short story entitled 'Country of the blind' (Wells, 1904). In this story, Wells invites us to imagine a place where no-one has ever had sight; a place where everything has been designed for and by the blind. As the story unfolds, we learn that, far from being revered, a hapless one-eyed explorer's ability to see quickly becomes a hindrance to him and an annoyance to his hosts. The story makes me think about how my experience of the world might have been different if the environment had been designed by people like me. I also relate to the plight of the one-eyed man, who in the blind Kingdom is othered rather than embraced.

Imagine a place where no-one has ever had sight. How might that be different? To begin with, we can assume that everything there is designed for and by people without sight. You might find that signage is all in another language, such as braille. Or perhaps there are no signs and every direction and indicator make an audible announcement or sound. Transport is likely to be automated. This might all seem like fantasy and in Wells' era was the stuff of science fiction, but driverless trains are already commonplace in our society, and as technology becomes increasingly sophisticated, self-driving cars are already in production. Most households now contain voice-activated smart devices and 'seeing' devices, such as AI glasses, have become available on the high street. Social Constructionist theory recognises that these developments reflect changing cultural norms that are influenced by how society defines convenience and productivity. For visually impaired people, these advancements have the added benefit of reshaping the environment to be more inclusive and reaffirm that disability exists in the interaction between individuals and society (Oliveira et al., 2022). These devices are inclusive by design rather than accessible as an afterthought. In the Kingdom of the Blind, more time and resources might have been devoted to developing these technologies in preference to other things they have needed less over the years, resulting in even more advancement than in a sighted kingdom.

Humans might have evolved and adapted differently without sight over a long period of time, similar to some species in the animal Kingdom. The people of the blind kingdom would likely have become more reliant on their other senses, and those senses might have become better developed over time. It is a common misconception that if someone loses their sight, they are immediately compensated by their other senses, such as touch, smell, and hearing, becoming more acute. In reality, people who lose their sight become more reliant on their other senses and pay closer attention to them, developing greater skill in utilising them over time. I have certainly relied on my memory and hearing to compensate for the limitations of my vision, and those abilities have become more developed as a result. While some of this development happened naturally in childhood, as an adult experiencing deterioration in my vision, I have certainly had to work hard to further develop the skill of using my other senses to good effect.

Neuroplasticity, where areas of the brain can adapt to take over the function of other areas, can occur over long periods of time through a process of learning and experience. Studies using magnetic resonance imaging (MRI) have shown that over a long period of time, as the visual cortex shrinks due to lack of input, the auditory cortex can expand giving rise to more capacity for the brain to recognise and process sounds (Rauschecker, 1995, Elbert et al., 2002). Humans in Wells' blind kingdom might have evolved to use methods such as echo-location or sensing air-pressure on their skin for navigation. The use of a white cane is a form of echo-location where the environment is sensed by tapping on objects that return different sounds, which a person can interpret and recognise. People have been trained to use echo-location to navigate obstacles by generating sounds, such as clicks or claps, and listening for their reflections (Thaler et al., 2011).

So, where does all this leave our one-eyed man? A Social Constructionist would suggest that in the land of the blind, the one-eyed man would be as disabled as a blind person is in a sighted world. When the dominant narrative is flipped, his ability to see does not make him superior. In our sighted world, we view sightedness as the norm and blindness as a lack, but in Wells' story, the hierarchy is reversed; the blind community is 'able' according to their own norms, and the man with sight is the deviant 'other'. Society is designed for and by the majority and, in that society, the majority can't see! He would likely be marginalised, not by an objective inferiority but because his difference does not align with the social framework of that society.

Visibility, authenticity, and bravery

In relatively recent times, a number of key laws have been passed in the UK to help reduce discrimination and unfair treatment of disabled people in employment and education. These include the Disability Discrimination Act (1995) and the Equality Act (2010). Before 1995, a person could be openly ridiculed, treated unfairly, or rejected from places of work and education on the basis of physical difference or disability. This would often manifest in the underestimation of a person's abilities and resilience, based entirely on a description, such as 'blind' without even setting eyes on the person. Although these Acts have provided a foundation for a more inclusive society, fear of negative attitudes still has a significant impact on whether individuals with disabilities choose to disclose them (Roulstone, 2009, Mastrella et al., 2026). While social constructionism provides critical tools for challenging these barriers, systemic change remains slow. My experiences of a mainstream education before these protections were even considered led to an internalised stigma and sense of shame that has strongly influenced my decisions around disclosure as an adult. In his fictional account, Wells draws our attention to the importance of perspective and idea that the needs of the majority are generally the ones that are prioritised or viewed as valid, even when the needs of the minority are essentially the same.

I recall countless examples from my school years in the 1980s and 1990s that illustrated the lack of awareness of inclusive educational principles that was common at the time. One particular teacher, for example whose writing on the blackboard was particularly small, responded to my request to write larger by saying 'No, I can't. That's just the way I write'. My teachers were aware of my visual impairment, and many were sympathetic, but most were reluctant to make the kind of low-effort, high-impact adjustments, like writing larger, that would not only have benefitted me but might also support others with undiagnosed needs. From a social constructionist perspective, this resistance to disrupting the 'norm' reflects the way educational practices are shaped by shared beliefs about what is 'normal', 'acceptable' or 'fair'. Resistance to disrupting the 'norm' firmly situated the problem within me rather than recognising the inflexibility of the system that refused to adapt. It always took a lot of courage to overcome the self-consciousness of asking, only to be shot down, leaving me feeling embarrassed and regretful. Looking back, the social meaning attached to being 'different' had already been constructed around me; I learned that needing something outside the norm was framed as an inconvenience rather than an expected part of human variation. So, not having the words to express how the teacher's response made me feel, I responded with a form of silent protest by making my own handwriting smaller and smaller until the teacher finally had to admit that she couldn't read my exercise books. I hoped that I had offered her a valuable insight into my struggle and that we might both be able to adapt for one another. However, I was simply punished until I made my writing large enough for the teacher to read, while hers remained unchanged. Through a social constructionist lens, this reinforces how power shapes what counts as normal and whose practices are allowed to remain unquestioned. The teacher's authority enabled her to maintain her own norm as the default while positioning my difference as a disruption requiring correction. Experiences like these increased my sense of hopelessness and strengthened my reluctance to request adaptations. I learned that my perspective would be marginalised and invalidated if it challenged the socially constructed narrative that blamed the individual for not fitting the system.

Looking back, it is very noticeable that when I was offered or sometimes forced to accept adaptations, such as magnifying equipment, they were generally focused on how I could adapt myself to an unremitting environment. They were very often based on a one-size-fits-all approach, and any benefits were often outweighed by the impact the adaptation would have on my peer relationships and developing sense of self. On some occasions for example, I was seated very close to the blackboard but far away from all of my classmates, whose desks remained in rows behind me. This well-intentioned seating arrangement communicated a powerful message that I was different and separate from the group. The process by which individuals or groups are positioned as different or inferior to a dominant norm is known as 'Othering' and frequently leads to marginalisation (Spivak, 1988). Being 'othered' from my peers felt embarrassing and shameful and resulted in me resisting accommodations altogether to avoid being singled out, even if those accommodations would have helped me learn. I became driven to outperform my peers and do anything I could to prove that I am more than just my disability. Although it felt empowering, this self-denial led to self-limiting behaviours, such as holding myself to impossibly high standards and distancing myself from other disabled people. These attempts to protect myself from further othering ultimately isolated me from those who might have helped normalise my lived experience and support the idea that adaptation is a collective, rather than an individual, responsibility (Shakespeare, 2014).

Things have changed significantly since the 1980s and 1990s, and I'm delighted to say that my more recent educational experiences have been a good deal more inclusive. With presentations and handouts made available electronically for all, the visually impaired student now has autonomy to manipulate lecture materials to suit their individual needs, enlarging fonts, inverting colours, using screen-readers and audio-description software, without any additional support. This is a great example of how a change in the way something is done for the majority can have a significant positive impact on the experience of the minority with little additional effort. Inclusivity of this kind goes a long way to reducing the societal stigma that I internalised growing up.

During my early teenage years and perhaps a little before, I began to experiment with developing a 'non-disabled' identity and trying it on for size. I had reached the age where there were some places I could go where I had the advantage of interacting with people who had not been forewarned that my sight was poor and therefore could not have formed any preconceptions about my abilities. I soon noticed that in these situations, where I was able to craft an identity free from the shackles of my 'disability', I felt more equal to others, and my perspective was validated. Social Constructionist theory supports the idea that when people didn't rely on pre-existing social narratives or stereotypes of what it means to be 'disabled', they interacted with me based on my behaviour, rather than assumptions, allowing a more equal and authentic interaction to take place (Berger & Luckmann, 1966). When I struggled with something, I experienced empathy from people who assumed I was just like them, rather than having those struggles becoming self-fulfilling indicators of 'disability' viewed through a biased lens. I also discovered that when I disclosed my visual impairment or if people noticed its impact after knowing me for a while, it had little impact on their expectations of me, their willingness to accommodate me or their respect for me as a person. Through these interactions, my sense of self as capable and equal was affirmed, and I could more freely perform a non-stigmatised identity (Shakespeare, 2009).

Cognitive behavioural therapy (CBT) offers a powerful framework for understanding how presenting a non-disabled identity to avoid stigma can lead to the development of negative core beliefs and a conflicted sense of self in the longer term (Pugh & Vetere, 2009). My choice to avoid social stigma by 'passing' as non-disabled can be conceptualised as a coping strategy with potentially harmful long-term effects, such as reinforcing the idea that 'I need to hide who I really am to be accepted', which over time likely contributed to the development of an 'I am not good enough' negative core belief. By the time I left school at the age of 16, I had formed a very strongly held belief that 'disability' was undesirable and that accepting the label 'disabled' was to regard myself and be regarded as less worthy. Leaving school and moving on to college, university, and employment as well as participating in hobbies and pastimes independently meant that I had the opportunity to choose to disclose my visual impairment. From this liminal space, I was able to minimise or erase parts of myself and manipulate my own narrative to support a non-disabled identity.

CBT suggests that individuals with a Defectiveness or Shame schema often engage in overcompensation strategies, such as setting increasingly high standards or pushing themselves relentlessly to achieve. I was quite prepared to earn lower grades during my education in return for rejecting the adjustments and allowances that would have been available for disabled students. I have climbed mountains (literally), learned to drive (off-road), fly, sail, and have travelled the world, often independently or in the company of people who genuinely did not know that my eyesight was quite poor in comparison with theirs. Ironically, these strategies maintain the schema by reinforcing the idea that worth is contingent on performance and making any setback or failure feel like confirmation of the core belief (Young et al., 2003). Even more frustratingly, despite my efforts, I continued to struggle against the assumption that when I did something noteworthy or rescued myself from a tight spot, someone 'must have helped'. These reactions reflect deeply rooted ableist beliefs that disabled individuals are inherently dependent and that competence must come from external support rather than internal capacity (Campbell, 2009).

I have trodden a much more challenging path in life than I could have done in the service of what I mistakenly thought of as 'equality'. For many years, I felt proud of the way I had hidden and downplayed my disability. I had even pictured myself standing before an audience talking about how I had fooled the world into thinking I was ordinary when in fact I had been guiltily hiding this big secret. I reflect on this attitude and behaviour now as both selfish and cowardly, not to mention enormously disrespectful to the millions of brave people who have lived openly with their differences in a disabling society, which they have fought hard to improve for someone like me who has only recently shrugged off the cloak of invisibility. In hindsight, my pursuit of equality was grounded in a flawed idea that connected equality with sameness, rather than recognising and accommodating difference. True equality acknowledges structural barriers and values diverse ways of navigating the world (Campbell, 2009). In attempting to conform to ableist norms to be seen as 'equal', I was unconsciously reinforcing the very systems that excluded me.

In recent years, with the help of social media, I have connected with people who have taken ownership of their disability and have broken down barriers in a way that I never thought possible. These people are not only raising awareness of the difficulties we face in a disabling environment but also challenging stereotypes and negative beliefs by showing what they can achieve and how doing things differently does not equate to doing them less well. My earlier desire to conceal my disability in response to dominant narratives is accurately described by Goffman's (1963) theory as management of a spoiled identity. His theory of stigma explains how individuals adapt their behaviour in response to perceived social devaluation.

In my case, the pride I took in being able to pass as non-disabled was, in hindsight, rooted in internalised stigma, reflecting the deeply ingrained belief that to be disabled was to be seen as 'less than'. The activists and creators I've engaged with online draw attention not just to personal struggles, but to the systems and structures that perpetuate inequality. By publicly embracing their disability and demanding change, they effectively reframe disability as a site of knowledge, agency, and cultural pride, rather than limitation. Social media has become a powerful tool for reconstructing the meaning of disability by allowing disabled people to shape their own narratives and challenge dominant assumptions. From a Social Constructionist viewpoint, it is through this collective discourse that social realities are changed. These experiences have enabled me to begin reconstructing my own identity, not as someone who has overcome disability by hiding it, but as someone who has something to offer precisely because of the insight that disability brings.

Evolving attitudes and language

Traditional models have viewed disability as a medical problem, employing language that focuses on deficits within the person and emphasising individual impairment as the source of disability. The disability rights movement of the 1970s and 1980s gave disabled people a platform to challenge the negative attitudes and assumptions that had been prominent in our society for hundreds of years (DeJong, 1983). They demanded recognition and the right to participate fully in a society free from discrimination. This movement catalysed a radical shift away from the medical model towards acknowledging that societal barriers and attitudes can be the true disabling factors. British sociologist and disability rights activist Michael Oliver (1990a, 1990b) argued that disability should be understood not as an individual tragedy but as a form of social oppression. This perspective was informed by the Union of the Physically Impaired Against Segregation (UPIAS), which defined disability as 'the disadvantage or restriction of activity caused by a contemporary social organization which takes little or no account of people who have physical impairments' (Union of the Physically Impaired Against Segregation [UPIAS], 1976). The Social Model of disability emerged in the 1990s and gained traction in the early twenty-first century (Oliver, 1990a, 1990b, 1996). The Social Model suggests that people with differences in ability are 'disabled' by the society in which they live. Coming across this model for the first time was transformative for me. It helped me make sense of why I often felt out of place in systems that weren't designed with people like me in mind; not because I was inherently incapable, but because the structures around me made participation more difficult. This model has redefined disability as a socially constructed phenomenon, and this reframing has empowered disabled individuals to shift the focus from personal limitation to systemic change (Oliver, 1990a, 1990b). Rather than asking how to fix the person, the model asks how to make society more inclusive. This paradigm shift has profoundly influenced policy and attitudes in the UK. In education for example, there has been a move towards inclusive schooling, where students with disabilities learn alongside their peers and in the workplace, employers now have a legal and ethical obligation to provide reasonable accommodations (Nind & Wearmouth, 2006). However, the rhetoric of inclusion hasn't always matched the reality. In recent years, public awareness campaigns and media representation have begun to reflect this more inclusive mindset, highlighting ability rather than limitation, but social change is still a work in progress.

With this shift in approach has come a significant transformation in the language used to describe disability, reflecting a growing recognition of disabled people as active agents of their own lives rather than passive recipients of care. Historically, the terminology used to describe visual impairment emphasised deficit, dependency, and pity. Terms like 'handicapped' were commonly used to describe various disabilities, and the negative connotations these terms carried contributed to stigmatisation and social exclusion (Barnes & Mercer, 2010). The word 'blind' has historically been used as a blanket term, ignoring the rich variation in visual ability that characterises the spectrum of visual impairment. Misconceptions that vision loss looks a certain way have frequently led to misunderstanding and resentment towards individuals who identify as blind but see anything more than total darkness.

As a child, I recall feeling a swell of anxiety whenever I heard someone describe me as 'blind' or state that 'she can't see' as I learned to anticipate the inevitable backlash from people who must have felt misled when it became obvious to them that I could see. Visual impairment, like most other disabilities, exists on a spectrum and globally, there are at least 2.2 billion people with some form of visual impairment (World Health Organization [WHO], 2023). The use of definite articles such as 'the blind' groups these 2.2 billion people into one homogenous category, denying them individuality and agency (Oliver, 1996). Fortunately, in the early twenty-first century, as part of a wider shift towards promoting language that emphasises empowerment, capability and respect of disabled people, the term 'blind' was officially replaced with 'Severely Sight Impaired' in an effort to provide a more accurate and less stigmatising description of individuals with significant vision loss. These terms acknowledge that around 85% of people who are registered as Severely Sight Impaired in the UK have some usable vision (Royal National Institute of Blind People [RNIB], 2024). Some individuals can perceive light, colour, and shape but may not be able to see details, while others might have tunnel vision, patchy vision, impaired depth perception, or have sight that fluctuates in response to another health condition. So, when you next see a person walking with a white cane and notice they can use the screen on their phone or recognise a face, remember that does not mean they can see everything clearly.

I had always felt a visceral aversion to the word 'disability', as for me the term represented stigma and misrepresentation of my abilities. Much of this resistance was connected with the sense that this label was given not claimed and that it was not representative of my identity. This tension between imposed labels and self-defined identity is central to Social Constructionism, which theorises that labels and identities are not neutral descriptors but instruments of power. Being assigned a label shapes how others see you and how you are expected to behave

(Goffman, 1963). During my 1920s, when I worked in I.T., I really started to notice and object to the use of the term 'disabled'. In I.T. and engineering, 'disabled' refers to the state of a feature, function, or component that has been turned off or rendered inactive. A greyed-out button or a printer powered off is usually labelled 'disabled' in the user interface. In this binary world, things can only be 'enabled' or 'disabled', meaning that they are either fully functional or completely inactive. I recall connecting with a sense of anger that such a description could ever be applied to a person. I wanted to be 'enabled'.

When disability advocacy pushed for person-first language and terms such as 'person with a disability' became popular, I reluctantly claimed 'person with a visual impairment' for myself (Snow, 2007). The social model of disability, which distinguishes between impairment and disability, has played a pivotal role in the linguistic transformations we are witnessing in society today (Shakespeare, 2014). People with various physical and mental health conditions have started to reclaim the language that was once used to other them. In the world of visual impairment, people can be heard describing themselves as 'Blindies' and 'Sighties'. Blind Pride, part of the disability pride movement, celebrates the abilities, strength, and resilience of sight-impaired people and promotes rejection of the idea that blindness is a tragedy or something to be pitied. Understanding the Social Model of Disability and witnessing the shift in emphasis from deficit-based to experience-based constructions of disability has had a fundamental impact on my relationship with disablement and with my own identity. I now feel able to refer to myself as 'disabled'. Not because I am invisible, invalid, or don't function, but because I am 'a person with a visual impairment' AND I am 'disabled' by social and environmental barriers. As a disabled Clinical Psychologist, I have learned to use Social Constructionist thinking to resist internalised ableism, combat shame, and advocate for more inclusive practices within the fields of psychology and healthcare. I can use my perspective to help shift the focus from the individual 'adjustment' I was expected to embrace growing up to the systemic reform I so desperately craved.

Making it work: navigating clinical practice

Individuals with disabilities are often subject to stereotypes that can impact how we are perceived in professional settings. In recent years, there has been increasing attention on the representation of diverse groups within healthcare professions, including disabled people (Thomas et al., 2024). A key impact of social constructionism is the validation of disabled therapists lived experiences as central to their professional identity. In contrast to traditional models that pathologise disability, Social Constructionist frameworks allow disabled professionals to challenge deficit-based societal narratives and assert alternative, empowering identities and language (King et al., 2024). Disabled therapists can thus engage in critical reflexivity, exploring how societal discourses of 'normality' and 'competence' impact their practice and sense of legitimacy within the profession. Despite this recent shift towards increased visibility and validation, clients may still have preconceived notions about the capabilities of visually impaired professionals. Research has shown that the visibility of disability among therapists can disrupt client expectations, particularly when clients hold ableist assumptions about who is qualified to help them (Shakespeare et al., 2009).

The social construction of a psychologist embodies certain key assumptions, including the expectation that psychologists can 'read between the lines' by picking up on unspoken emotions and underlying issues through observing subtle, non-verbal communications, such as body language and facial expressions. Clients might question whether the psychologist can effectively read non-verbal cues or navigate the practical aspects of therapy, such as taking notes or managing paperwork (Pledger, 2010). Because of these socially constructed expectations, visually impaired psychological therapists face unique challenges in the therapeutic relationship, which we overcome with strong communication skills, using alternative strategies to build rapport and mastery of assistive technology (Wagner, 2016, Rushton & Graham, 2020). Over time, visually impaired psychologists can become highly attuned to alternative cues, such as tone of voice and adept at asking people to describe their emotional state or provide feedback on their posture and facial expressions. Disclosure and education become important as a means of fostering openness and trust in the therapeutic relationship, and these conversations can often open up dialogues about the client's own challenges that can contribute to successful therapy outcomes. Clients typically seek competence and empathy in their therapists, regardless of the therapist's physical abilities (Norcross, 2011). Research suggests that once clients experience the therapeutic relationship with a visually impaired psychologist, their attitudes tend to become more positive (Pledger, 2010). This shift is often due to the development of trust, the demonstration of skill, and the establishment of a strong therapeutic alliance.

Visually impaired clinical psychologists often develop a mastery of available tools, such as screen readers, note-taking software, and 'seeing' Apps, to support our practice. We also tend to make increased use of tactile objects, our verbal skills, and the client's imagination in a way that enables us to represent or describe things a therapist might ordinarily draw out with pen and paper. The adjustments most psychological therapists were forced to make during the 'lockdown' periods of the COVID-19 pandemic have only served to enhance the number and usefulness of the alternative strategies available for delivering therapy in different ways. We have become more accustomed to conducting therapy sessions in environments where we can't see one another in the traditional way, such as by telephone or on-line, and technology has developed to support this, with additional aids such as drawing and transcription tools made freely available. If you ever find yourself wondering how a visually impaired psychologist might describe a formulation without drawing it, it's not too dissimilar from giving someone directions over the phone.

Disclosure as connection, not just explanation

Disclosure of personal information and experiences by therapists to clients was once regarded as inappropriate or unprofessional. In the psychoanalytic tradition, for example, self-disclosure has been regarded as counterproductive and undermining of the therapist's neutrality (Meissner, 2002). However, with the person-centred approach came the idea that therapist genuineness and transparency could be essential tools in fostering rapport, and therapists began using self-disclosure strategically to model emotional openness (Rogers, 1957). Research into this phenomenon during the late twentieth century, highlighted some concerns around boundary violations, the perception of self-disclosure as self-serving and the risk that self-disclosure could shift the focus of therapy away from the client's issues (Zur, 2007). Contemporary views have become more nuanced, acknowledging the potential benefits of self-disclosure but only in the best interest of the client and when it serves a therapeutic purpose, such as normalising the client's experiences or helping to model coping strategies (Norcross & Goldfried, 2005). So where does that leave physically disabled psychologists; when theory doesn't account for situations where a visible difference is a disclosure in itself?

Unlike some physical differences, sensory disabilities can be invisible in the right environment, meaning that disclosure can sometimes be a choice. When I am working in private practice, I have full control of the environment of my therapy room, which is well-lit and very familiar to me, so easy to navigate. I have an excellent memory for conversation, so do not need to make notes during sessions. I allow time between each scheduled appointment when I can write notes, using assistive technology as necessary, enabling me to keep an accurate clinical record without any noticeable adaptations in session. However, in other clinical environments, the situation can be very different, making disclosure more necessary. When I have been working in a general hospital, the ward environment can be busy and chaotic, with patients, staff, and equipment constantly moving around, I often need to seek support from colleagues to help me locate my patient and navigate the environment. For the visually impaired psychologist, the issues we commonly encounter when visiting clients in their homes come hand in hand with some additional challenges, such as poorly lit environments and unexpected obstacles. Without a visual indicator of disability, such as a white cane, it is in these environments that I most often feel compelled to disclose my visual impairment.

Visually impaired individuals such as myself, who have the ability to pass for sighted in certain conditions, most often make the choice to disclose when the benefits, such as practical assistance and educating others, outweigh the potential risks, like stigma and undesired attention (Romo et al., 2025). In professional healthcare environments, such as a busy ward, these on-the-fly cost-benefit analyses very quickly come into play, but in the privacy of my own therapy room, the motivations for disclosure are very different. During my career, I have worked with many people experiencing debilitating progressive illnesses and lifechanging injuries and have found that self-disclosure employed in a thoughtful, context-specific manner can communicate empathy and understanding of the challenges of disability. Disclosure does not have to be motivated by seeking assistance, explaining or educating others; it can be about supporting clients to challenge their own internal stigma and generate hope for the future. In the privacy of the therapy room, where disclosure is optional, I can recall numerous occasions where open dialogue around the lived experience of visual impairment has helped normalise the process and experience of the physical, psychological and social adjustments my clients were making. In some cases, self-disclosure has played a significant role in the clients' recovery by disrupting their pre-existing assumptions about competence, power and opportunity.

Clients seeking psychological therapy often make requests for a therapist of a particular race, gender, or sexuality, motivated by the desire for cultural understanding, affirmation, and shared lived experience. Research supports the idea that racial, ethnic and gender matching between clients and therapists can positively impact therapeutic alliance, client satisfaction and outcomes in certain circumstances (Cabral & Smith, 2011, Sue et al., 2012, Mondave et al., 2025). Therapists with disabilities can incorporate their experiences into practice in ways that validate clients' diversity and challenge normative assumptions about health, functioning and success. Although at the time of writing, there have been no published papers examining the impact of therapist matching in the domain of disability, there is some evidence that clients can appreciate and benefit from the unique perspective that a visually impaired therapist can bring. We have already seen clients making requests for therapists with other types of shared characteristics, and I feel hopeful that, in the future, we could begin to see clients asking to be matched with psychological therapists who have lived experience of the societal and environmental limitations that disable us.

References

Barnes, C., & Mercer, G. (2010). *Exploring disability* (2nd ed.). Polity Press.

Berger, P. L., & Luckmann, T. (1966). *The social construction of reality: A treatise in the sociology of knowledge*. Anchor Books.

Burr, V. (2015). *Social constructionism* (3rd ed.). Routledge.

Cabral, R. R., & Smith, T. B. (2011). Racial/ethnic matching of clients and therapists in mental health services: A meta-analytic review of preferences, perceptions, and outcomes. *Journal of Counseling Psychology*, 58(4), 537–554. https://doi.org/10.1037/a0025266

Campbell, F. K. (2009). *Contours of ableism: The production of disability and abledness*. Palgrave Macmillan.

DeJong, G. (1983). *The road to independent living in the U.S.: An historical perspective and contemporary challenges*. Independent Living Institute.

Elbert, T., Sterr, A., Rockstroh, B., Pantev, C., Müller, M. M., & Taub, E. (2002). Expansion of the auditory cortex in early blind humans. *Nature Neuroscience*, 5(1), 90–91.

Erasmus, D. (1500) Adagia (III, IV, 96). Retrieved from: The Quotations Page Classic Quotes. https://www.quotationspage.com/quotes/Desiderius_Erasmus/

Goffman, E. (1963). *Stigma: Notes on the management of spoiled identity*. Prentice-Hall.

Haslanger, S. (2000). Gender and race: (What) are they? (What) do we want them to be? *Noûs*, 34(1), 31–55.

King, G. A., King, J., & Meagher, C. (2024). Belonging in dual roles: Exploring professional identity formation among disabled healthcare students and clinicians. *Advances in Health Sciences Education*. Advance Online Publication. https://doi.org/10.1007/s10459-024-10386-4

Loewenstein, S. (1994). The social construction of gender. *Journal of Adult Development*, 1(1), 37–45.

Mastrella, S.J., Powell, D.M., Bonaccio, S., et al. (2026). Not an ideal worker, not a disabled worker: The experience of disclosing invisible disabilities at work. *Journal of Business and Psychology*. https://doi.org/10.1007/s10869-026-10104-4

Meissner, W. W. (2002). The problem of self-disclosure in psychoanalysis. *Psychoanalytic Psychology*, 19(2), 185–203. https://journals.sagepub.com/doi/10.1177/000306510205000315 01

Mondave, M., Saleska, J., Wang, J.J., Bluma, E., Jackson, D., Tapia, Y., Yashar, L., Zima, B.T. and Choi, K.R. (2025). Feeling like you matter: LGBTQ+ young adult perspectives on affirmative mental healthcare. *Journal of Behavioral Health Services & Research*, 52(1), 155–167. https://doi.org/10.1007/s11414-024-09919-x

Nind, M., & Wearmouth, J. (2006). Including children with special educational needs in mainstream classrooms: Implications for pedagogy from a systematic review. *Journal of Research in Special Educational Needs*, 6(3), 116–124.

Norcross, J. C., & Goldfried, M. R. (2005). *Handbook of psychotherapy integration*. Oxford University Press.

Norcross, J. C. (Ed.). (2011). *Psychotherapy relationships that work: Evidence-based responsiveness* (2nd ed.). Oxford University Press.

Oliveira, O. de F., Gonçalves, M. C., Winckler de Bettio, R., & Freire, A. P. (2022). A qualitative study on the needs of visually impaired users in Brazil for smart home interactive technologies. *Behaviour & Information Technology*, 42(10), 1496–1524. https://doi.org/10.1080/0144929X.2022.2084455

Oliver, M. (1990a). The individual and social models of disability. Paper Presented at Joint Workshop of the Living Options Group and the Research Unit of the Royal College of Physicians. Basingstoke. Retrieved from https://disability-studies.leeds.ac.uk/wp-content/uploads/sites/40/library/Oliver-in-soc-dis.pdf

Oliver, M. (1990b). *The politics of disablement*. Macmillan.

Oliver, M. (1996). *Understanding disability: From theory to practice*. Macmillan.

Pledger, M. (2010). Attitudes of psychology students and professors toward blind and visually impaired psychologists. *Psychology Journal*, 20(2), 45–61.

Pugh, M., & Vetere, A. (2009). Exploring the role of shame and guilt in the development of psychopathic and other antisocial behaviors. *Clinical Psychology & Psychotherapy*, 16(5), 403–414. https://doi.org/10.1002/cpp.612

Rauschecker, J. P. (1995). Cortical reorganization in sensory deprivation. *Progress in Brain Research*, 104, 293–305.

Rogers, C. R. (1957). The necessary and sufficient conditions of therapeutic personality change. *Journal of Consulting Psychology*, 21(2), 95–103.

Romo, L. K., Hooper, M., & Taussig, M. J. (2025). How visually impaired individuals manage disclosure of their visual impairment. *British Journal of Visual Impairment*, 0(0). https://doi.org/10.1177/02646196251331801

Roth, W. D., van Stee, E. G., & Regla-Vargas, A. (2023). Conceptualizations of race: Essentialism and constructivism. *Annual Review of Sociology*, 49, 39–58.

Roulstone, A. (2009). The politics of disability and employment in the UK: A study of stigma, workplace attitudes, and equality. *Journal of Social Policy*, 38(3), 333–345.

Royal National Institute of Blind People (RNIB). (2024). Registered blind and partially sighted people and CVI England 22–23. Retrieved May 15, 2025, from https://www.rnib.org.uk/professionals/health-social-care-education-professionals/knowledge-and-research-hub/reports-and-insight/registered-blind-and-partially-sighted-people-and-cvi-england-22-23/

Rushton, J., & Graham, P. (2020). Non-verbal communication in the therapeutic setting. *Journal of Therapeutic Communication*, 45(2), 123–138.
Shakespeare, T., Iezzoni, L. I., & Groce, N. E. (2009). Disability and the training of health professionals. *The Lancet, 374*(9704), 1815–1816.
Shakespeare, T. (2014). *Disability rights and wrongs revisited* (2nd ed.). Routledge.
Siebers, T. (2001). Disability in theory: From social constructionism to the new realism of the body. *American Literary History*, 13(4), 737–754.
Snow, K. (2007). *People first language*. Disability Is Natural. https://doi.org/10.1177/0003065102050003 1501
Spivak, G. C. (1988). Can the subaltern speak? In C. Nelson & L. Grossberg (Eds.), *Marxism and the interpretation of culture* (pp. 271–313). University of Illinois Press.
Stone, S. D. (2013). The situated nature of disability. In M. P. Cutchin & V. A. Dickie (Eds.), *Transactional perspectives on occupation* (pp. 95–106). Springer.
Sue, S., Cheng, J. K. Y., Saad, C. S., & Chu, J. P. (2012). Asian American mental health: A call to action. *American Psychologist*, 67(7), 532–544. https://doi.org/10.1037/a0028900
Thaler, L., Arnott, S. R., & Goodale, M. A. (2011). Neural correlates of natural human echolocation in early and late blind echolocation experts. *PLoS One*, 6(5), e20162. https://doi.org/10.1371/journal.pone.0020162
Thomas, C. M., Bazzell, M. W., Lee, J. G., & Lovett, S. B. (2024). Increasing diversity, equity, and inclusion in the health and health services research workforce: A systematic scoping review. *Journal of General Internal Medicine*, 40(5), 1487–1497. https://doi.org/10.1007/s11606-024-09041-w
Union of the Physically Impaired Against Segregation (UPIAS) and Disability Alliance (1976). *Fundamental Principles of Disability: Being a Summary of the Discussion Held on 22nd November, 1975 and Containing Commentaries from Each Organisation*. Union of the Physically Impaired Against Segregation and Disability Alliance. https://disability-studies.leeds.ac.uk/wp-content/uploads/sites/40/library/UPIAS-fundamental-principles.pdf
Wagner, K. I. (2016). *Disabling psychology: A crip analysis of deaf and blind psychotherapists in practice* (Doctoral dissertation). Duquesne University. https://dsc.duq.edu/etd/110/
Wells, H. G. (1904). Country of the blind. https://en.wikisource.org/wiki/The_Country_of_the_Blind
World Health Organization (WHO). (2023). Blindness and vision impairment. Retrieved May 15, 2025, from https://www.who.int/en/news-room/fact-sheets/detail/blindness-and-visual-impairment
Young, J. E., Klosko, J. S., & Weishaar, M. E. (2003). *Schema therapy: A practitioner's guide*. Guilford Press.
Zur, O. (2007). *Therapist self-disclosure: The 'double-edged sword' of disclosure in therapy. Psychotherapy*, 44(2), 191–203.

Chapter 12

Working with a tricky brain

A compassion-focussed exploration of disability in occupational health

Amy Millar

An introduction to a compassion focussed approach

Compassion-focused therapy (CFT), developed by Paul Gilbert, uses a biopsychosocial frame, drawing on existing knowledge from evolutionary science, neuroscience, developmental research, and social mentality theory to form an integrative therapeutic approach to managing the functions and challenges of the human mind. Here, I provide an overview of the theory to orient you as the reader to the underpinnings of the chapter.

CFT is grounded in a few fundamental concepts: as humans we have complex 'tricky brains', which were shaped by evolution for survival but which are imperfectly designed for navigating modern life (Gilbert, 2014); our minds are further shaped by our early developmental experiences and social circumstances, contexts which we did not choose; that, in attempts to manage perceived threats, we develop protective safety strategies which can inadvertently lead to suffering and symptoms; and that all of this is not our fault, yet we must take responsibility for learning how to work with our minds and emotions (Gilbert, 2009a).

To elaborate further, because of our evolutionary context, our brain's structure and mechanisms are orientated towards motivations for survival and reproduction. Any threats to our survival, to our attachments, or to our social rank can activate 'brain states' that have a powerful, often unconscious, organising effect on our neurochemistry, physiology, attention, and cognition (Gilbert, 1984). These underlying motives, common across species, and their organisation of our brain state and emotions are referred to as 'old brain' functions (Gilbert & Choden, 2013). However, human brains have also evolved 'new brain' advanced cognitive abilities of thinking, predicting, analysing, reflecting, imagining, and meaning-making. These thinking capacities, although helpful in many ways, can create imagined future threats or become stuck going over events from the past or criticising ourselves, repeatedly switching on our 'old brain' motives and threat-based emotions when they aren't needed, creating problematic circular feedback 'loops' between thinking and feeling (Gilbert, 2010).

While these basic functions of the brain can lead to suffering and distress, we can also make use of them to find a path towards wellbeing. Our 'new brain' is

DOI: 10.4324/9781003636014-13

capable of bringing mindful awareness to these patterns and choosing how to focus our attention and intention, and we can learn to activate our 'old brain' motivation towards affiliative relationships to soothe ourselves (Gilbert & Choden, 2013). These are the building blocks of CFT: we learn to deliberately choose a compassionate motivation because it stimulates brain states which coordinate our attention, thinking, behaviour, and emotions in ways that are helpful to our well-being. What exactly is a compassionate motivation? Gilbert draws on Buddhist Psychology to define compassion as a sensitivity to the suffering in self and others, with a commitment to try to alleviate and prevent it (Gilbert, 2014). His definition emphasises several qualities of true compassion, which include not only the open, nurturing, non-judgemental, empathetic qualities which help us turn towards suffering, but importantly the wisdom and courage to do the right things towards relieving suffering.

CFT outlines three main emotion regulation systems which are stimulated in response to our success or failure in our motives. These three systems – a protective (threat) system, resource-seeking system (drive), and affiliative system (soothe) – utilise our autonomic nervous system and hormonal pathways in different ways. Most people are familiar with the concept of an internal threat detection system and can identify with the intense surges of anxiety and other emotions it can produce (Gilbert, 2009a). Our 'threat' system is highly sensitive, tending to over-estimate threat in a 'better safe than sorry' manner and using fast-acting pathways in our brain that bypass thinking (Gilbert & Choden, 2013). The threat system is flawed in that it struggles to separate real threats (e.g. needing to defend ourselves from attack) from imagined ones (e.g. worry about failing an exam), which can lead to us experiencing rather extreme fight/flight/fawn and demobilising states (Gilbert, 2001) when there is no real threat in the present moment – a perpetuating factor in many mental health problems.

Our other affect systems can assist with regulating this threat, and so there is a focus in CFT on promoting balance between the systems. Our 'drive' system is oriented towards resource-seeking and helps activate the body towards pursuing goals and achievement, with accompanying dopamine release and positive emotions. Whilst this is helpful, there is potential for us to develop an over-competitive mindset or get caught up in pursuit of success, and so our 'drive' system benefits from being balanced by the affiliative 'soothe' system (Gilbert & Choden, 2013). This caregiving and care-receiving (attachment) system responds to cues of care and connection with others, using vagal nerve pathways combined with oxytocin to down-regulate both threat and drive pathways, putting us into a state of 'rest and digest' (Porges, 2007). This state naturally allows us to experience feelings of calm, contentment, and openness.

CFT provides a method to cultivate and 'switch' into our prosocial or cooperative mentality, our so-called 'compassionate mind' from our competitive, comparison-based motives (which drive feelings of shame and guilt). Switching motive assists the three emotional systems to come into balance – for development of our soothing system, regulation of the threat system, and maintaining equilibrium in our drive system. There are a number of therapeutic mechanisms that can be incorporated to build up a compassionate identity, cultivate positive emotions and encourage courageous new behaviours, including rich imagery practices, exercises to balance the autonomic nervous system, a focus on overcoming fears, blocks and resistances to compassion, use of chairwork and other perspective-taking or mentalising exercises, behavioural experiments and exploration of multiple emotional selves to bring insight and compassionate motivation towards the conflicting influences on our behaviour.

CFT has been shown to assist people with long-term conditions with improved quality of life and resilience (Fatollahzadeh et al., 2023) as well as greater acceptance and reduced feelings of isolation (Austin et al., 2021). In the following sections, I share the personal ways that I have made use of CFT concepts and techniques to help me adjust to and cope with the onset of ill health.

Suffering change to my own health

My professional experience working in Occupational Health (OH) and helping others navigate the delicate balance between work and wellbeing, together with the skills and techniques acquired through clinical training, has been a helpful scaffold as my health has declined and I have had to renegotiate my own capacities. For the majority of my working life, my health was unremarkable, and I was limited only by my own procrastinations. That changed suddenly when I developed debilitating symptoms and was diagnosed with an advanced chronic condition that I was not particularly familiar with – endometriosis. Unfortunately, it soon became apparent that awareness of the nature and impact of endometriosis is limited, even among medical professionals (As-Sanie et al., 2019). Many sufferers will recognise how invalidating the common mischaracterisation of the condition as ‘painful periods’ feels. Endometriosis is a chronic inflammatory disease involving tissue similar to the lining of the womb growing in sites outside the uterus, which can lead to the development of painful scar tissue and internal adhesions (National Institute for Health and Care Excellence [NICE], 2024). In advanced stages, this can impact the functioning of organs and nerves, requiring surgical intervention. The condition has a reasonably high prevalence rate of around 10% in those assigned female at birth (World Health Organization [WHO], 2023), but the causal mechanisms remain unclear, and there is no cure. There are limited pharmacological and surgical treatment options which can alleviate symptoms, and persistence or recurrence of symptoms after treatment is common (Horne & Missmer, 2022). The degree and impact of symptoms vary widely between patients and can fluctuate significantly over time, with a more disabling impact on functioning and quality of life during ‘flare-ups’. Symptoms commonly include chronic or cyclical pelvic or multi-site pain, gastrointestinal or urinary symptoms, issues with fertility, and heavy menstrual bleeding (NICE, 2024). There is an increased risk of developing fatigue, mood difficulties, and a number of health comorbidities (Horne & Missmer, 2022). The impact of the disease on work life is substantial, with reports of lost productivity and higher absenteeism at work (Nnoaham et al., 2011), and sufferers more likely to earn a lower average salary and have a significantly greater chance of leaving the workforce than matched controls (Estes, Soliman, Yang, Wang & Freimark, 2020).

My own symptoms began abruptly with an agitating pain in my back when lying down. Over only a few short months, my health deteriorated rapidly. I developed a chronic stitch-like pain in my abdomen that escalated unpredictably into a stabbing, twisting sensation. I struggled to sleep lying down at night due to burning pelvic pain that standard painkillers could not relieve. Over the course of only a few months, internal adhesions began to affect my mobility, making it increasingly difficult to lift my legs to walk uphill or climb stairs, which I found both embarrassing and deeply upsetting. These rapid changes to my health and their unknown trajectory naturally frightened me. I must admit that at this acute stage of adjustment to my health changing I found many, if not all theoretical models difficult to make use of. At this point, without the facts or understanding of my condition, my soothing system was difficult to access, and I struggled to cultivate the necessary attributes of compassion like non-judgement and distress tolerance (Gilbert & Choden, 2013). Instead, the most effective measure for me was finding a consultant physician whom I trusted, and who could provide containment and clear guidance around the next steps to be taken. This co-regulating presence or direct proximity to 'social safeness' (Gilbert, 2009a, 2009b) was the main route back to activation of my soothing system during those early uncertain times.

As time progressed, I underwent surgical intervention and had my first substantial absence from work; issues with shame, self-criticism, and unhelpful safety strategies began to play out. It is in this arena that I have really drawn on CFT principles to support myself. Whilst other theorists and philosophical approaches to compassion posit a very similar construct to Gilbert – for example, Neff's (2023) conceptualisation of self-compassion as comprising of self-kindness, common humanity, mindfulness towards suffering, and self-protective elements – I have found Gilbert's model most applicable to my understanding of my chronic pain. This is because the model emphasises the physiological impact of the activation of our motivational and emotional systems, helping to conceptualise how reciprocal relationships can emerge between pain and activation of the threat system due to changes in hormones and the vagus nerve (Gilbert, 2020). Furthermore, accessing our body's soothing system state releases endorphins which can tone down feelings of pain (Gilbert & Choden, 2013). Compassion, then, goes beyond being a mindset or philosophy to become an important medicinal tool for managing my illness.

Emotional hurdles: managing looming threat

Living with a chronic disease that flares and could progress at any time can easily lead to a state of hypervigilance. When pain and other symptoms recur, my threat-detection naturally kicks in and pulls my focus unhelpfully onto monitoring of the symptoms themselves. I feel anxious and angry about these uncontrollable changes in my body and the dissonance between what I expect of my body versus the reality of its capabilities (Sayer-Jones & Sherman, 2023). Nearly all of the 'old brain' motives – the desire to avoid harm, to acquire sufficient resources, to maintain steady relationships, and to maintain social status (Gilbert, 2014) – feel under threat. My 'new brain' capacities try to predict any potential future threats to my identity, leading to catastrophic future fears of increasing disability and more extreme and invasive treatments. My 'threat' system is intensely activated and so kick in several automatic or conditioned safety strategies which have been shaped by my early experiences (Gilbert, 2009a, 2009b). I am predisposed to a 'fight' response – a kind of aggressive approach to my illness – involving trying to push through, deny, overcome, and control. Behaviourally, this can mean researching and constantly seeking information, becoming hyper-independent and concealing my symptoms, or over-stretching myself with exercise and activity. As these inevitably don't work, my next conditioned response tends towards one of submission – feeling resigned and defeated, self-blaming, and in a 'collapsed' state. When using CFT, we might complete a compassionate functional analysis of these safety strategies, which can help increase awareness of the historical contributors to and various unintended consequences of our responses (Kolts, Bell, Bennett-Levy & Irons, 2018). For example, searching for information and solutions online and in forums can lead to a bombardment of unhelpful news about others' debilitating symptoms and lack of treatment options. This only serves to further activate fears about my future bodily integrity, perpetuate my distress, increase muscular tension that aggravates pain, and maintain a state of hyperarousal that worsens my fatigue.

Placing these ideas into a work context, there are many underlying motives threatened by illness which can lead to chronic activation of the 'threat' system. Work-related motivations include pro-social elements such as giving care to others, cooperating with others towards a shared goal, and experience of a sense of belonging and closeness. There are also inherent competitive motivations that are activated when considering work, such as maintaining or improving social rank, as well as non-social motives to acquire and preserve sufficient resources for the future (Gilbert, 2014). In my case, future scenarios offered by my 'new brain' have posed threat to many of these. I have imagined that I should not go for any promotions because I would be unable to give the dedication and focus needed to work; I have worried about becoming increasingly disabled by my condition and having to leave employment and experience significant loss of income; and worried that I may not be able to maintain my performance or reliable attendance, risking job plan changes, attendance reviews or feeling socially devalued. Concerns about being inadequate or becoming a burden in the workplace are common in those with health conditions and can lead to a de-prioritising of personal needs and self-care (Mazalin, Evans & Van Niekerk, 2025). Unchallenged or left unattended to, such self-concepts devalue our worth and risk creating strong feelings of shame and disconnection from others. They therefore require deliberate intervention from our compassionate mind (Gilbert, 2009b), a process which I will later return to.

In order to prevent or protect myself from these threats in the workplace, a safety strategy that I get drawn into is proving myself and over-compensating through striving. Overworking, over-activity, taking on more responsibilities, criticising myself when I can't do it all, or criticising myself because I keep getting drawn into such unhelpful patterns. This is unhelpful activation of the 'drive' system as, inadvertently, these over-compensating behaviours leave me stressed and frustrated, with less time to look after my health, worsening the impact of symptoms, ultimately feeding back into my fears and perpetuating 'threat' activation. What I know is that going through this off-kilter process is OK and is very human – and so I know that you will have gone through similar things, too. We do not receive a handbook for dealing with a health condition. Whether your protective mechanisms are similar or different to mine, you'll likely make some missteps along the way and need to adjust as you go. No amount of training, analysis, or reflective practice can take away the pitfalls of our human brain. We might get more adept at switching out of threat states, but the threat system will always be there, like an old companion that every so often screams abruptly in your ear! Can we learn to appreciate it for what it tries to do for us and offer it our steady reassurance? Compassionately responding to illness requires empathy for all of these tricky conflicting feelings while learning to respond to our limitations with self-kindness and self-care (Austin et al., 2021). The next section gives some practical ideas on what this could look like in the workplace.

Drawing on experience in Occupational Health

A main component of my role in OH is completing 'fitness for work' assessments, which provide advice to organisations on supporting employees with their psychological health. Many people who come for assessment are unsure of the exact nature of the role of OH. OH consists of a multidisciplinary team of clinicians whose aim is to protect and promote health at work and to provide confidential, impartial advice on health and fitness for work to the employee and, with the employee's consent, their employer. OH can assess and advise upon whether health-related symptoms might permanently or temporarily impact your ability to carry out your normal duties or, conversely, if work-related factors could potentially impact your health. Some people are anxious that OH is an attendance management mechanism, but OH has several functions that serve to support employees, particularly those with a disability. This includes providing consultation to address work-related health concerns; to make recommendations around workplace adjustments that would help safely support your health symptoms at work or remove obstacles to sustaining attendance; to form a rehabilitative phased return to work plan following absence with input from your healthcare team; and to provide advice on additional services or methods to support your health issues (Nicholson, 2022).

It is worth noting that implementation of OH recommendations in the workplace is at the discretion of management. Managers must balance the impact of the adjustments with service needs, and so they determine what is 'reasonable' to accommodate in terms of the practicability, resources, and feasibility for the service. However, where an employee has a disability, this introduces additional legal protections under the *Equality Act 2010* or *Disability Discrimination Act 1995*. This means that an employer must demonstrate that they have not treated the employee less favourably as a result of their disability and that they have given due consideration to any adjustments that might be effective, implementing those that may be viewed as reasonably within the scope of the organisation to facilitate. It is for this reason that OH will typically provide your employer with an opinion on whether you have a disability, unless you would prefer not to disclose this information.

Working in this area has given me an understanding of the types of adjustments that can be useful to an employee struggling with health symptoms and has empowered me in knowing my options around what I could request in the future to support continued attendance at work. A common adjustment would be around physical changes to the environment, for example, a more supportive chair or desk, provision of additional equipment or software, or access to a more private work area or home working if struggling with a shared working space. Another form of adjustment that can be helpful is alterations to shift patterns or working hours, for example, having set working patterns, flexible working to allow for additional breaks, or a variable start time to assist with symptom management. Modifications to how work is done or alterations to duties can also be supportive, for example, a reduced workload, reallocation of certain duties, or another change in job plan. OH might also recommend additional managerial or peer support, coaching, or training. In rarer circumstances, where symptoms are significantly limiting ability to do the job, a transfer of workplace, or medical redeployment to another role may be advised.

Witnessing others benefitting from accommodations at work has reduced my feelings of shame around having specific workplace needs. This sense of connectedness arising from knowing that others are in a similar position helps regulate my threat system, making it easier to take compassionate action like requesting supports or incorporating more self-care into the working day. For example, in terms of coping with long days of office-based work, I requested a standing desk to let me vary my body position so as to prevent a buildup of pain. I have altered my diary to space out tasks in a way that lets me take frequent movement breaks and a short time to reset physically. Where possible, I try to incorporate a gentle walk over my lunchtime to help with alleviation of pain and fatigue. An option of working from home when pain is worse has allowed me to continue to work where I may otherwise have needed time off. Being at home means a physically gentler start to the day, feeling able to do stretches when needed or wear a heat pad for pain, along with more time to ensure I can eat something nutritious and rest in the evenings. I am able to use a degree of flexi-time if things are flaring up to rest and top up my resources. The other thing I have found most beneficial is simply to ask for help. My team know my story, and I draw on them as a resource, for example as a cognitive support when brain fog is making it hard to think about complex matters.

In order to let ourselves accept, seek out, and implement these practical changes, we need to first recognise, name, and tame any shame processes that may interfere with us mobilising social supports (Harris, 2024). This includes both our internalised ideas – our 'shoulds' – creating shame (for example my own rule that I 'should' be able to keep up with every aspect of my job no matter how unwell I feel) and any external stigma or lack of understanding from colleagues or managers, which unfortunately is still an obstacle some face in the workplace. Holding these delicate shame feelings, we can draw on ideas such as that of 'fierce self-compassion' (Neff, 2021) – taking the necessary action to protect ourselves and get our needs met in unhealthy situations. Cultivating self-compassion has been shown to support adaptive coping with illness by encouraging direct actions to address challenges, rather than reliance on escape-avoidant coping styles (Mehr, Nejat, Akbari & Ormoz, 2023). However, many employees struggle to implement self-care, and even the idea of self-compassion itself can feel like a threat to being 'successful' in work.

Work-related fears, blocks, and resistances to compassion

In my role as an OH practitioner, I have met varying types of professionals and people at all stages of their health journeys. A recurring theme I have noted is employees' lack of awareness, recognition, or acceptance of their difficulties as potentially coming under the umbrella of disability. This is concerning, as good knowledge of your rights and limitations is essential to remaining well in any organisation. On one level, this might be linked to stereotypes of disability, the template of which can seem a poor fit for people's own experiences and challenges. An advantage from working in my role has been seeing the many forms that disability can take and the many types of people living with disability, which has altered my internal templates of what this term means. I feel it is a compassionate step for me to claim the word 'disabled', particularly living with a condition that needs explained to others, as it allows me to communicate something of my situation with much more ease.

I have been curious about the fears, blocks, and resistances that can come up in others when it comes to identifying with disability. Where someone has no diagnosis, they might present to OH with burnout symptoms but not recognise the impact of underlying impairments, perhaps because they have been repeatedly (and to a point, successfully) adjusting and adapting to 'fit' their environment and social context. Research into factors that influence whether someone self-identifies as having a disability points both to the severity of their impairments and to stigma – both that enacted by others and stigma internalised as embarrassment (Bogart, Rottenstein, Lund & Bouchard, 2017). Coping with such a social threat – concern perhaps that an employer may not be receptive to your needs or trusting of your genuineness – might understandably lead to protective strategies whereby one may conceal one's experiences or draw on internal defences such as denial or minimising. The concerns are often intensified for people with attachment trauma, who can feel overwhelming emotions of despair, fear, and powerlessness when asking for their needs to be met by authority figures. In these cases, I have noticed the early shaping of the threat system leads to a sense of vulnerability relying on others, with expectations of being let down or abandoned, or deep feelings of shame about having any needs at all.

I see these issues play out in protective strategies such as employees not disclosing their illness, trying to manage symptoms alone, sometimes even avoiding colleagues altogether. The unintended consequences can be that management can have very little information on which to base their decisions. They may feel uneasy asking too much about the employee's health and want to protect their right to privacy and to a work identity separate from illness. However, without the necessary health discussions, the employee can end up feeling further abandoned, believing that there is little understanding and support at work. I make attempts to help employees with mentalising – enhancing awareness that even the most compassionate managers find it hard to keep on top of issues in the workplace and to stay attuned to the needs of all their employees. With this in mind, self-advocacy is probably one of the most important compassionate skills to develop when coping with chronic health difficulties and can prevent unnecessary escalating tensions and even breakdowns of relationships. As previously noted, a compassionate mindset involves not just being open and understanding to our experiences of distress, but requires us to take courageous action towards the alleviation and prevention of suffering (Gilbert, 2014).

Self-advocacy becomes challenging where there is an incomplete foundation of self-compassion. In some professions, for example in the medical profession, where there are such pressures and unrelenting standards throughout training and the career, I have observed that suffering is (sadly) viewed and almost expected as an inevitable component of work. While there is a degree of 'common humanity' sentiment in this 'we're all in it together' perspective (Neff, 2023), there is a resulting sense that 'nothing can be done' to change anything, and so the motivation to turn towards and alleviate the difficulties becomes blocked. It has been suggested that therapists, whose compassion flows easily from self to others, can also find directing compassion towards self or accepting it from others challenging (Kolts, Bell, Bennett-Levy & Irons, 2018). In mental health professionals, including myself, I have noticed blocks towards the sense of 'common humanity' when comparing to colleagues. Instead, there can be shamed-based evaluations akin to, 'everyone else seems to be managing with ease, there is evidently a weakness in me'. This social downward comparison blocks true self-compassion, which can play out in issues such as presenteeism, i.e. continuing to work when unwell, which is linked to exacerbation of health problems and risk of burnout (Kinman & Grant, 2025).

These different dynamics become intensified when adding in a chronic health problem. Prioritising health and recovery can become a complex issue of navigating both external and internal threats. For example, Harris (2024) describes the barriers that wanting to maintain feelings of independence and strength posed to accepting when she was struggling with her chronic illness. Like myself, many people I have worked with respond to these underlying fears by becoming entrenched in an unsustainable level of productivity. The risk is that we keep pushing until something more drastic must kick in and force us to slow down. Or, like many of our psychology colleagues having felt overwhelmed or insufficiently supported, becoming defeated and cutting down hours or leaving the NHS altogether.

Growing into my own ally

I turn now to cultivating a compassionate mind and what has worked for me. Soothing practices and compassionate intention have prompted and supported me to care for my ongoing symptoms, even though my relationship to flare ups remains difficult. I can experience exhaustion which leaves me with little reserve for the things I enjoy after work. I have less emotional capacity when my mind is occupied by sensations of pain. Fatigue and inflammatory processes can take over, leaving me feeling like an understudy who is waiting in the wings to have enough energy to play the part of myself. The change in control over my body and my future repeatedly elicits an anxious mind state. Research exploring the lived experiences of women with a chronic, fluctuating condition has proposed that a linear model of adjustment and post-traumatic growth has less utility in this population; rather, a cyclical model of survival might best apply – a repeated navigation of adapting, accepting, and recovering from the flares and emotions of the 'straightjacket of illness' (Murphy & Harris, 2025). I think of learning to live with my condition as a constant process of evolution and adaptation. This fits well with a CFT approach, where the emphasis is on how to create the conditions that will encourage and support me to compassionately attend to my health on a consistent basis.

When coping with active symptoms, I have been trying to consciously choose tools that I know help expand soothing and vagal parasympathetic activation (Gilbert, 2009a, 2009b). With symptoms of intense pain, it can be overwhelming to try to bring mindful awareness or openness to the discomfort. There are instead certain soothing body-based compassionate mind practices I turn to. Taking a moment to notice the changes that can be brought through establishing a soothing rhythm of breathing, an upright open posture, a relaxed facial expression, nurturing voice tone and comforting use of a hand on the body is important before trying to make any use of thought, in order that the tone and texture of those thoughts can be friendly and supportive (Matos et al., 2017). Expanding awareness beyond my threat-based focus on my symptoms through practice of mindfulness of my senses or breath can also be helpful, but I try to maintain a softness and acceptance towards the existence of those symptoms (Gilbert & Choden, 2013).

When turning to the content of the mind, CFT emphasises the use of imagery, as images can evoke powerful effects on our bodies and minds (Gilbert & Choden, 2013). If I am struggling to stay connected to my own compassionate voice when experiencing symptoms, I find it helpful to tap into a sense of the presence of an ideal, compassionate, and nurturing other (Lee, 2005) who is full of kindness, warmth, and sensitivity and who is able to see the big picture wisdom of the situation. For me, the precise image changes depending on what qualities I most need access to in the moment, but most often this is in the form of a 'most compassionate' version of someone helpful from my past. This compassionate 'other' image will often help me access ideas for a compassionate way forward, perhaps hearing words or ideas about actions needed or how I might see the situation differently. I might then need to draw on courage and work towards behavioural exposure for those actions I may have been finding difficult (Gilbert, 2009a, 2009b). For example, allowing myself to rest when I need to, asking others for support, or adopting more self-accepting standards around the things I am trying to achieve. By enacting compassion through behavioural changes, I am gradually rewiring my threat system to learn that the underlying fears are largely unwarranted, allowing me to slowly negotiate some new rules for what life 'should' look like.

Finding a way to compassionately relate to my symptoms is one thing, but attending to emotional experiences cannot be bypassed. When worn out by physical issues, painful emotions can be hard to make room for. The risk in suppressing these emotions and not checking in is that we perpetuate our problems and can even become internally conflicted. It takes courage to truly be open to emotional experiences rather than simply trying to soothe them away (Gilbert, 2014). In CFT, we encourage clients to attend to multiple emotional selves to help bring openness and awareness to the threat-based emotions. This involves checking in with the angry, anxious, and sad selves one at a time, noticing what they are holding in the body, enquiring about their motives and thoughts, noticing whether they are in conflict with each other, and enquiring about any needs (Gilbert & Choden, 2013). Following this, we ground ourselves in a more supported state in the body and bring in the compassionate self in as an observer of what has happened in the other brain states, in order to guide ways of thinking and behaving. Doing this quickly as a check-in within myself is a lovely way to notice opportunities for self-care: for example, noticing that anxiety held in the body needs attended to and doing some gentle yoga; realising that anger is asking for action and that I need to be more assertive; or that sadness requires comfort and I need to reach out and reconnect to supportive people in my life to reduce feelings of isolation.

Compassion in working with clients

My condition is largely hidden from others, but there are times when its impact is visible in my posture or mobility. This naturally elicits a response from clients, overt and covert. In the healthcare staff group I largely work with, it typically evokes the strong caregiving tendencies within them. Using this observation of their compassionate tendencies provides a wonderful opportunity to begin to integrate a sense of a compassionate self within. This enables us to reflect on the three directional flows of compassion – from ourselves to others, from others towards ourselves, and that directed from and towards ourselves – and how flow in certain directions can become blocked depending on their history and circumstances (Gilbert et al., 2017).

As I have become more accepting of my condition, I have felt more able to make use of it like another 'chair' in the room which can enhance understanding of the client's internal relational world. As I work to reduce feelings of shame associated with my condition, I feel more open and able to receive my clients' compassion. Like in other therapeutic models, it is still necessary to reflect on whether what is being evoked in the client is a healthy, genuine compassion rather than something serving another more submissive purpose, for example potential vigilance to my needs to please me or maintain relationship (Catarino, Gilbert, McEwan & Baião, 2014). All of this is rich material to be worked with within the therapy.

Experiencing ill health has been one of the loneliest experiences I've had. There are many quiet moments of suffering faced by you alone. There is distance created by the awareness that not everybody understands the kind of desperate feeling of a malfunctioning body and the grief of reduced agency to fulfil the roles and activities which construct your identity. When working with clients going through health challenges, I feel much better attuned to aspects of their suffering, which has opened me up to deeper exploration of and curiosity towards their experiences. There are also times when my experiences mirror that of my client, for example if we are both experiencing periods of uncertainty and worry about our health. This can be harder to sit with but is an opportunity to reconnect with a sense of common humanity – seeing these experiences as part of the shared human condition, rather than an isolating individual experience, which can help to bring acceptance and reduced self-blame to the situation (Gilbert, 2009a, 2009b).

Where I feel my own material strongly with clients, perhaps knocking me into a threat state, I find it is important to address this through inner work in supervision or personal therapy so that I can remain really open to what's actually within the client. However, I balance this with something I took from Paul Gilbert's wisdom during training, when as I understood he described the importance as a therapist of taking in that it's OK to have limitations, not to be drawn into narcissistic preoccupation about being a 'saviour' to the client – as it is this very concern that will switch us out of being a safe base and compassionate presence. Rather, the stance I aim to keep returning to is, 'I don't have all the answers about emotionally coping with an illness, I think this is really tricky stuff, but I'm right here with you and believe your compassionate self knows what could be helpful to you'. And when I'm not going to be with them, for example during absences for treatment leading to a gap in therapy, I give consideration to the potential therapeutic use of transitional objects, giving clients little placeholders like shells I have collected that might prompt a little compassionate wave within.

A scaffold to maintain commitment to compassion

I have written this chapter when I am relatively symptom free, in a period of relief from my condition. When things recur and the going gets tough again, some of this compassionate stance will almost certainly collapse. Worry will return, and the initial dominance of the threat and drive systems will return. As such, I need to set up my life in such a way that there are prompts and reminders in place to help regularly mobilise compassion, reignite those care-giving and care-receiving mentalities, and to encourage a recommitment to restoring balance.

I was introduced to wonderful creative ideas about the use of multisensory stimuli to access the compassionate mind during Kate Lucre's training. She describes gathering together a 'Compassionate Kitbag' (Lucre & Clapton, 2020) – a collection of objects that have a strong personal association with compassion and which help provide direct access to the flows of compassion and to embodiment of compassion. She suggests gathering a collection of multisensory items, like calming smells, grounding items, art or images that soothe or which help connect to qualities like strength or courage, items with personal meaning that represent the compassionate self or compassionate others or concrete reminders of one's own resilience. These objects can help provide direct access to our soothe and drive systems or reignite compassionate intention. I like to keep my office space set up in this way, where there are many items of significance, such as an encouraging letter from a wise figure; objects given to me by compassionate others, by clients, or items associated with impactful trainings; poems or mantras; and pictures that represent important compassionate qualities.

Imagery exercises can also be highly motivating, and one I use when I feel worn out is to imagine a flow of gentle compassionate light coming from all those people who passed their skills and qualities to my trainers, supervisors, and therapists, through me, through my clients, and through to those impacted in their lives. Other helpful ways to keep self-resourced with compassionate motivation are through music (Gilbert, Basran, Plowright & Gilbert, 2023), listening to audio of individuals who inspire the compassionate qualities, and through maintaining contact with a compassionate community – whether team members, peer support options, supervision, or maybe even your own medical team. I return here to a key tenet of CFT: we are fundamentally social beings, not meant to cope entirely on our own (Gilbert, 2014). All of these reminders and social top-ups help to renew the ability and dedication required to return to a compassionate stance. Whilst all of the theory and these actions are useful to me, there is a reasonably simple underlying idea. Close your eyes, picture yourself when you are struggling or feeling vulnerable. Notice your struggling self's posture and facial expression and really notice the pain they are carrying. If you can, send them your understanding, warmth, or a gentle light. Let them know that you will not turn away from their suffering and commit to them that you are there to do what it takes to look after them, even if it will take all your courage. This is the work.

References

As-Sanie, S., Black, R., Giudice, L.C., Gray Valbrun, T., Gupta, J., Jones, B., Laufer, M.R., Milspaw, A.T., Missmer, S.A., Norman, A., Taylor, R.N., Wallace, K., Williams, Z., Yong, P.J., & Nebel, R.A. (2019). Assessing research gaps and unmet needs in endometriosis. *American Journal of Obstetrics and Gynecology, 221*(2), 86–94.

Austin, J., Drossaert, C.H.C., Schroevers, M.J., Sanderman, R., Kirby, J.N., & Bohlmeijer, E.T. (2021). Compassion-based interventions for people with long-term physical conditions: A mixed methods systematic review. *Psychology & Health, 36*(1), 16–42.

Bogart, K.R., Rottenstein, A., Lund, E.M., & Bouchard, L. (2017) Who self-identifies as disabled? An examination of impairment and contextual predictors. *Rehabilitation Psychology, 62*(4), 553–562.

Catarino, F., Gilbert, P., McEwan, K., & Baião, R. (2014). Compassion motivations: Distinguishing submissive compassion from genuine compassion and its association with shame, submissive behavior, depression, anxiety, and stress. *Journal of Social and Clinical Psychology, 33*(5), 399–412.

Estes, S.J., Soliman, A.M., Yang, H., Wang, J., & Freimark, J. (2020). A longitudinal assessment of the impact of endometriosis on patients' salary growth and risk of leaving the workforce. *Advances in Therapy, 37*(5), 2144–2158.

Fatollahzadeh, S., Kianimoghadam, A.S., Bahri, R., Khesali, M., Pour Seyyed Aghaei, Z., & Arani, A.M. (2023). The effectiveness of compassion-focused therapy on resilience, shame, internal self-criticism, and quality of life of patients with vitiligo. *Iranian Journal of Psychiatry and Behavioral Sciences, 17*(4), Article e137483.

Gilbert, P. (1984). *Depression: From Psychology to Brain State.* Lawrence Erlbaum Associates, Ltd.

Gilbert, P. (2001). Evolutionary approaches to psychopathology: The role of natural defences. *Australian and New Zealand Journal of Psychiatry, 35,* 17–27.

Gilbert, P. (2009a). Introducing compassion-focused therapy. *Advances in Psychiatric Treatment, 15*, 199–208.

Gilbert, P. (2009b). *Overcoming Depression. A Self-Help Guide Using Cognitive Behavioural Techniques* (3rd ed.). Constable & Robinson Ltd.

Gilbert, P. (2010). *Compassion Focused Therapy: Distinctive Features.* Routledge.

Gilbert, P. (2014). The origins and nature of compassion focused therapy. *British Journal of Clinical Psychology, 53*(1), 6–41.

Gilbert, P., Catarino, F., Duarte, C., Matos, M., Kolts, R., Stubbs, J., Ceresatto, L., de Matos Duarte, J., & Pinto-Gouveia, J. (2017). The development of compassionate engagement and action scales or self and others. *Journal of Compassionate Health Care, 4,* 1–24.

Gilbert P. (2020). Compassion: From its evolution to a psychotherapy. *Frontiers in Psychology, 11*, 586161.

Gilbert, P., Basran, J.K., Plowright, P., & Gilbert, H. (2023). Energizing compassion: Using music and community focus to stimulate compassion drive and sense of connectedness. *Frontiers in Psychology*, *14*, 1150592.

Gilbert, P., & Choden (2013). *Mindful Compassion.* Constable & Robinson Ltd.

Harris, K. (2024). *Coping with Endometriosis: Bringing Compassion to Pain, Shame & Uncertainty.* Sequoia Books.

Horne, A.W., & Missmer, S.A. (2022). Pathophysiology, diagnosis, and management of endometriosis. *BMJ, 379*, e070750.

Kinman, G., & Grant, C. (2025). *Understanding Sickness Presenteeism: Causes, Risks and Solutions: Guidelines Series.* Society of Occupational Medicine. https://www.som.org.uk/sickness-presenteeism-guide

Kolts, R., Bell, T., Bennett-Levy, J., & Irons, C. (2018). *Experiencing Compassion Focused Therapy from the Inside Out: A Self-Practice/Self-Reflection Workbook for Therapists.* The Guilford Press.

Lee, D.A. (2005). The perfect nurturer: A model to develop a compassionate mind within the context of cognitive therapy. In P. Gilbert (Ed.), *Compassion: Conceptualisations, Research and Use in Psychotherapy* (pp. 326–351). Routledge.

Lucre, K.M., & Clapton, N.E. (2020). The Compassionate Kitbag: A creative and integrative approach to compassion-focused therapy. *Psychology and Psychotherapy: Theory, Research and Practice, 94*(S2), 497–516.

Matos, M., Duarte, C., Duarte, J., Pinto-Gouveia, J., Petrocchi, N., Basran, J., & Gilbert, P. (2017). Psychological and physiological effects of compassionate mind training: A pilot randomised controlled study. *Mindfulness, 8*(6), 1699–1712.

Mazalin, K., Evans, S., & Van Niekerk, L. (2025). A template thematic analysis of self-concept and self-compassion in people living with endometriosis: Analysis of qualitative survey responses. *Journal of Advanced Nursing, 81*(7), 4216–4227.

Mehr, S.E., Nejat, H., Akbari, H., & Ormoz, E. (2023). Comparing the efficacy of mindfulness-based stress reduction training and compassion-focused training on stress coping styles in patients with coronary heart disease. *Journal of Fundamentals of Mental Health, 25*(3), 169–178.

Murphy, R., & Harris, B. (2025). Can current post-traumatic growth models capture the lived experience of life with a fluctuating chronic illness? Towards a new model. *British Journal of Health Psychology, 30*(3), e70003.

National Institute for Health and Care Excellence (NICE). (2024). *Endometriosis: Diagnosis and Management* [NICE Guideline NG73]. https://www.nice.org.uk/guidance/ng73

Neff, K. (2021). *Fierce Self-Compassion: How Women Can Harness Kindness to Speak Up, Claim Their Power, and Thrive*. HarperCollins Publishers.

Neff, K.D. (2023). Self-compassion: Theory, method, research, and intervention. *Annual Review of Psychology, 74*, 193–218.

Nicholson, P.J. (2022). *Occupational Health: The Value Proposition.* Society of Occupational Medicine. https://www.som.org.uk/sites/som.org.uk/files/Occupational_Health_The_Value_Proposition_March_2022.pdf

Nnoaham, K.E., Hummelshøj, L., Webster, P., D'Hooghe, T., De Cicco Nardone, F., De Cicco Nardone, C., Jenkinson, C., Kennedy, S.H., & Zondervan, K.T. (2011). Impact of endometriosis on quality of life and work productivity: A multicenter study across ten countries. *Fertility and Sterility, 96*(2), 366–373.

Porges, S.W. (2007). The polyvagal perspective. *Biological Psychology, 74,* 116–143.

Sayer-Jones, K., & Sherman, K.A. (2023). "My body…tends to betray me sometimes": A qualitative analysis of affective and perceptual body image in individuals living with endometriosis. *International Journal of Behavioral Medicine, 30*(4), 543–554.

World Health Organization (WHO). (2023, March 24). *Endometriosis* [Fact sheet]. https://www.who.int/news-room/fact-sheets/detail/endometriosis%E2%81%A0

Index

Note: *Italic* page numbers refer to figures and page numbers followed by "n" denote endnotes.

For Product Safety Concerns and Information please contact our EU representative GPSR@taylorandfrancis.com Taylor & Francis Verlag GmbH, Kaufingerstraße 24, 80331 München, Germany